HOW CUSTOMERS BUY . . .
& WHY THEY DON'T

HOW CUSTOMERS BUY ...
& WHY THEY DON'T

MAPPING AND MANAGING
THE BUYING JOURNEY DNA

MARTYN R. LEWIS

RADIUS BOOK GROUP
NEW YORK

Distributed by Radius Book Group
A Division of Diversion Publishing Corp.
443 Park Avenue South, Suite 1004
New York, NY 10016
www.RadiusBookGroup.com

First edition: August 2018
Hardcover ISBN: 978-1-63576-514-4
Trade Paperback ISBN: 978-1-63576-522-9
eBook ISBN: 978-1-63576-523-6

Cover design by Nicole Hayward
Interior design by Scribe Inc.

This book is dedicated to all those who depend
on someone, somewhere buying something that
they invent, create, design, develop, manufacture,
distribute, finance, market, support, or sell.

Contents

ACKNOWLEDGMENTS   ix

PROLOGUE   A Revelation   1

CHAPTER 1   From the Outside-In   5

CHAPTER 2   Three Generations of Customer Creation   11

PART 1: MAPPING THE CUSTOMER BUYING JOURNEY

CHAPTER 3   The DNA of the Customer Buying Journey   23

CHAPTER 4   Strand 1: Triggers   27

CHAPTER 5   Strand 2: Steps   32

CHAPTER 6   Strand 3: Key Players   43

CHAPTER 7   Strand 4: Buying Style   47

CHAPTER 8   Strand 5: Value Drivers   64

CHAPTER 9   Strand 6: Buying Concerns   69

CHAPTER 10   Case Study 1: DiaNascent: A Buyer's Tale   86

CHAPTER 11   DiaNascent Case Study Analysis: Mapping the Customer Buying Journey of DiaNascent   104

CHAPTER 12   Case Study 2: CCHN: Does the Glove Fit?   113

CHAPTER 13   CCHN Case Study Analysis   133

PART 2: DEVELOPING THE MARKET ENGAGEMENT STRATEGY

CHAPTER 14   What to Do about It   151

CHAPTER 15   Crafting the Market Engagement Strategy   159

CHAPTER 16   Goal 1: Harmonizing to the Buying Style   166

CHAPTER 17   Goal 2: Into the Customer Buying Journey: Trigger or Engage?   189

CHAPTER 18   Goal 3: Ensuring Adequate Motivation   203

CHAPTER 19 Goal 4: Staying Engaged and Ensuring
Positive Progress   212
CHAPTER 20 Goal 5: Overcoming Friction in the Customer
Buying Journey   225
CHAPTER 21 Engaging the Market with Orion Technologies   242

PART 3: MANAGING THE CUSTOMER BUYING JOURNEY

CHAPTER 22 Translating Strategy into Application   251
CHAPTER 23 Outside-In Marketing   260
CHAPTER 24 Outside-In Selling   281
CHAPTER 25 The Outside-In Revenue Generation System   315
EPILOGUE How Customers Buy . . . and Why They Don't   332

RESOURCES   337
NOTES   339

Acknowledgments

THOSE WHO HAVE written a book know what a challenge it is to go from an idea to a typeset manuscript. Those who have not are perhaps better off not knowing the mountain it is to climb and thus like me may one day set about writing a book in a blissful combination of passion and naïveté. Along the way, they would discover, as I have, that you can't go it alone, so I would like to acknowledge and thank everyone who has contributed to my journey and helped along the way. The list is long, including many who may have no idea how much they helped, challenged, and shaped my thinking. I couldn't possibly list them all, but for everyone who has at any time engaged with me in discussion about business, its strategy and tactics, marketing, and sales—many thanks.

In particular, let me thank the following:

Tom Percy. After we worked together in corporate sales in the early 1990s, Tom joined Market-Partners as its second employee in 1997. Since then he has challenged my thoughts and provided much sage advice along the way. He is the talented individual who takes my notes and translates them into the pages you read. This book would never have happened without his help, support, and guidance.

My clients. I owe you a sincere thank-you not only for the business you have trusted us with but for the laboratory you have provided for our research and development.

My clients' customers—the buyers. I thank all the individuals whom we have interviewed for their time and their candor in sharing their observations and experiences.

My publishing team. It comes toward the end of the journey when the book is drafted, but there remains a significant divide between a Word document, albeit a very large one, and a published book. We went looking for help as a customer buying in the top-left quadrant (for those who haven't read the book yet, that indicates our perception was that we had plenty of choice of publishers, but we knew we needed a lot of help to know what it was we were buying). We found Mark Fretz at Radius Book Group, and he quickly moved us to the top-right quadrant by demonstrating his expertise and the partnership we could gain with him in successfully launching a book. So my thanks to Mark and his team at Radius; my editor, Jennifer Boeree at Scribe, for her elegant command of the language and her steady patience in working out all the details with us; and our illustrator, Angie Lagle, right here in Napa County, for her work in turning the various diagrams and doodles into what you now see in the book.

How Customers Buy . . . and Why They Don't represents a milestone on my personal journey of learning—learning about business, strategy, marketing, and sales. My thanks to my family, friends, and colleagues for the role they have played along the way. I look forward to the continuing journey with all of you.

Martyn R. Lewis
Calistoga, California
August 2018

PROLOGUE

A REVELATION

WHY DID IT take me so long? Why didn't I figure it out sooner? Perhaps I needed to look at it, yet not see it, many thousands of times. Perhaps I needed to fail or be part of failure many times. Perhaps it hadn't always been this way. Or maybe I was simply accepting a common belief by going down the same well-worn path as so many had before me.

In the beginning, I believed that if a business had a superior product offering that provided a clear value to a prospective customer, then that customer would likely buy. I believed it was the role of sales and marketing to position such an offering in the marketplace so that customers would be convinced of the value and—given time and perhaps a nudge or two—would be motivated to buy. I also believed that if a customer failed to buy yet clearly had the means to do so, then it was *a failure on the part of sales and marketing* to correctly position the value and convince the customer of the inherent merits of the offering. And I was not alone.

While strength in numbers may not be the most responsible defense, I suggest that the clear majority of entrepreneurs, investors, business executives, and sales and marketing professionals share this worldview. Simply put, the success formula is to come up with a great new mousetrap and then tell the world about it. And in the always-misquoted words of Ralph Waldo Emerson, "the world will beat a path to your door."[1]

My beliefs had been shaped and honed over two decades of immersion in sales and marketing, starting as a frontline salesperson. I had been steeped in the gospel and logic of the return on investment (ROI) analysis showing the customer what they would *undoubtedly gain* by acquiring the various offerings I was responsible for taking to market. As I became more familiar with consultative selling methodologies and value selling techniques, they all reinforced this same theme. There were tweaks and twists, adding techniques such as finding the decision maker, calling high, linking the value of your offering to the things that mattered most to your prospect. Everything I saw, everything I did—indeed, everything I believed—was based on this same theme of *positioning the offering so that the value was clear to the buyer.*

Along the way, my career advanced from sales to unit manager and regional sales manager, to VP of marketing for one of the largest computer technology companies in the world, and then to CEO of a multinational that included several hundred salespeople. During this time, I participated in countless sales training programs; my proficiency rose to the point that I became certified to deliver one of the leading sales methodologies. I attended peer-level executive retreats, where I met and worked with the key opinion leaders and authors on the topics of business, sales, and marketing. All these interactions reinforced my belief that if you have an offering that will deliver value to a particular market, then the salesperson's job is to convince that market of the inherent value they will gain and then take the order. If they don't buy, then you have obviously failed to convince them of the value.

In the mid-1990s, I left corporate life and the position of CEO to start my own consulting company, Market-Partners Inc. It would be easy to say that I did so to escape the clichéd "corporate grind," but the reasons were much more complex. Because as successful as I had become, I was not what most would define as a "natural salesperson." I began life as a programmer. My interests ran to engineering, taking apart and rebuilding the engine of my Lotus, designing and handcrafting high-end speaker systems—science, methodology, planning, and results. Yet throughout my sales career, I continually ran into the myths and legends of the "art" and "black magic" supposedly utilized by top-drawer sales wizards. And perhaps for a tiny minority of overachievers, those particular shoes might fit. But my concern had always been for the majority—the whole sales force—to succeed, and perhaps not spectacularly, but certainly consistently and profitably. I wanted to apply the elements and rules of science to sales, to prescribe method where madness often prevailed. And I wasn't going to be shy about it, as my company's original tagline was "The Science of Sales and Marketing." Of course, with science comes research, and research we did. I also knew that if we were to bring true scientific discipline to the needs of our clients, we had to exercise that same discipline in our own efforts of observing, recording, and analyzing what we found.

Working now at arm's length with our clients' sales forces brought a much wider view of all the inherent issues that affect sales success. And I started to see a repeating pattern. These organizations all had offerings that delivered value to a particular market yet too often were falling short of hoped-for results. Sure, some of those organizations were clearly targeting the wrong markets, some perhaps the wrong players. Some really needed help in focusing their value propositions, and others just needed work on basic sales skills. But generally speaking, most were doing a good job, but their results suggested otherwise. After seeing this phenomenon so many times, it was obvious to me that something was missing; there was something more at play, and I needed to find out what that was.

Fortunately, I have always believed in the value of talking to actual customers. So I started by putting in place a systematic format in which to talk to our own client's customers and prospects. We talked to them about what they were doing and how motivated they were (or weren't) about buying our clients' offerings, and we started to build up a behind-the-scenes view of their buying activities. The more organizations and individuals we talked to, the clearer the picture became. Our research team was finding repeating patterns—patterns we were not expecting. To our surprise, we were finding time and time again that the prospective buyer totally understood the offering and indeed the value it would deliver to them or their organization. They truly believed in the ROI equation and needed no persuasion that their investment of $12 today would yield $20 in the very near future. However—and here was the real surprise—despite their belief in the offering, they were hesitating or failing to buy. As this simple observation repeated itself, the foundation for my epiphany was laid.

I was a puzzled man. Why does the world no longer beat a path to the door of organizations offering a better mousetrap? Why don't customers buy products that provide them a clear return on their investment? Why do customers hesitate to invest in new alternatives that offer a superior and/or less expensive approach to what they may be doing today?

Well, I have to admit that all those years of ingrained training still led me to initially believe that it was a simple failure to position the offering appropriately, a failure of a salesperson to correctly articulate the value of an offering, a failure to use the right words in the marketing message, a failure to talk to the right person, the decision maker. But deep down I knew that was wrong, because for the most part, these were good salespeople from good organizations marketing good products. People were selling and selling hard; the problem was that nobody was buying.

Then I got it—not suddenly, not like in a dream or a Eureka moment. It crept up on me, tapped me on the shoulder, and quietly opened my eyes. I stopped looking at *how things are sold* and started looking at *how things are bought.*

It took talking to thousands of would-be customers about how they buy. It took combing through hundreds of organizations to delve deeply into their buying processes. It took years of analysis, of talking to sellers and buyers, to finally realize that in today's world, it takes more than simply convincing a customer of the value of the offering to get them to make a purchase decision. To gain a customer's interest and belief in the offering is one thing, but gaining their commitment to acquire and adopt a new offering is quite another.

That was when I started to map out all the factors that impact buying. And that was when I let go of my attention to the selling process and placed it on the buying process, what we now call the Customer Buying Journey. That was when we started to decode and derive the DNA behind each and every Customer Buying Journey. That was when I started to understand *how customers buy . . . and why they don't.*

CHAPTER 1

FROM THE OUTSIDE-IN

I CAN ASSURE YOU that this is not another sales process book. It is a book of discovery, of uncovering and decoding an enigma that plagues too many commercial organizations. It introduces a concept I have developed and named Outside-In Revenue Generation. This concept posits that the key to successful revenue generation in today's business environment is to *look beyond the internal view of how something is sold to the external reality of how customers actually buy.*

It is important to realize, and this is what is in fact the underlying foundation of this book, how Outside-In Revenue Generation differs from the much-used (to the point of clichéd) notion of "customer-centric" marketing techniques. For decades, it has been touted that commercial enterprises can gain the world by being customer oriented. This probably started with the wise idea that customer satisfaction differentiates one provider from another. From that starting point, few functions of organizations have been left untouched by the movement to consider the customer. From R&D to after-sales service, organizations have adopted more customer-oriented approaches and processes, and no doubt this represents sound thinking. And I'm not suggesting that business initiatives that put a priority on the customer don't yield results. They should and they do, but they could be doing so much more.

I must say that more recently I have heard people starting to talk about the buying process and buying journey. However, when I dig a little deeper, what I really see and hear are the selling organizations' thoughts (and hopes and prayers) of what the customer is doing, or more precisely, what the seller would like them to be doing—a vendor-centric buying process, if you will. In some cases, I have even seen organizations take their own sales processes and graft on what they imagine or wish their customers would do at each step.

Although somewhat laudable, these attempts to define the Customer Buying Journey from the selling point of view have proven to be myopic. They look no further into the customer's world than laying out the hoped-for reactions that result from their own sales and marketing actions. I call this an inside-out approach because it centers internally on the selling company, their offering, and their sales and marketing initiatives.

At one time, this all seemed okay to me—until we talked to hundreds of customers about how they buy. It was only by going behind the scenes of the buying process that I found the truth. Outside-In Revenue Generation has nothing to do with imagining what a customer *should* do when you sell to them; it defines precisely what a customer *will* do when they are engaged in a buying journey. Our research has proven again and again that a clear and perilous dichotomy exists between these two ways of thinking about how customers actually buy.

We need a new approach to address the primary purpose of business: *to determine how to consistently and predictably create customers*. This book introduces this new approach and addresses revenue generation in a way not only much deeper than before but also diametrically different from what has previously been available.

Outside-In Revenue Generation uncovers and decodes the "DNA" of the target market's buying process, allowing us to ultimately map the entire Customer Buying Journey. It lays out exactly how the supplier can apply that DNA mapping to understand how customers will buy a specific offering and what may cause them to hesitate or stop in their overall buying journey. This book, perhaps for the first time, will fully reveal and discuss how and why customers don't buy in the manner sales organizations would like them to. They certainly don't follow a buying journey that echoes any sales process I have ever seen. Outside-In Revenue Generation focuses totally on the customer and all that they will do and consider throughout their buying journey from start to finish.

How Customers Buy . . . and Why They Don't is not simply about sales and marketing or written only for sales and marketing professionals; it is about business. As Peter Drucker has so notably stated, "The purpose of business is to create and keep a customer." Drucker went on to tackle the notion that to provide a return to shareholders is akin to breathing for the human body. Just as you must breathe to live, so must a business make a profit and a return to its shareholders. But just as the purpose of life is not to breathe, the purpose of business, he argues, is more than making money. The purpose is to create a customer, because what do you have without a customer? You might have a fine research center or a noble philanthropic organization, but you don't have a business. Thus the very purpose of business is to focus on how to create a customer.

It would therefore follow that any business should invest a lot of time and attention in exactly how they are going to do that. Traditional ways in which to look at the equation of creating customers have simply been too superficial. They may have worked in the past, but in today's world where customers have unprecedented access to information, where customers are faced with an endless spectrum of offerings that will all benefit them, where decisions are no longer made by a single decision maker but by a dynamic network of decision influencers, traditional approaches fall very short of the mark.

Arthur "Red" Motley famously said, "Nothing happens until somebody sells something."[1] Many, including myself, have embraced this as a business mantra. But I suggest that we tip this on its head and change it to "Nothing happens until somebody buys something." Perhaps that sounds a bit chicken-and-eggish, but I would maintain that the implications of this mirror inversion of thinking are far from simple and do merit attention. Organization after organization believes the path to sales excellence is to design, implement, and manage a great sales process. However, I now realize that no one buys anything because of a sales process. Customers only buy because of their own buying journey.

I must make one thing very clear. In flipping Motley's comment, I do not for one moment want to leave any impression that sales and marketing, and indeed salespeople themselves, have any less of a role. In any situation other than selling truly commoditized offerings, the salesperson plays as important a role as ever. What I am suggesting, though, is that you start by understanding the Customer Buying Journey and determining an overall Market Engagement Strategy before simply turning a sales force loose armed with little more than product information, value propositions, and "a smile and a shoeshine."[2]

By understanding the Customer Buying Journey and what is really going on behind the scenes of the buying process, you will see how many organizations are woefully unprepared to engage in the process of creating a customer. In some cases, they would be better off taking their money to a casino; at least they would know the odds.

It is also maddeningly ironic to see many organizations so diligently operating and investing in all their other business functions. The vast majority of businesses invariably show constant and careful attentiveness in their manufacturing, operations, finance, distribution, and research activities. But when it comes to creating a customer—that is, sales and marketing—they are anything but deliberate and mindful. Perhaps it is because sales functions are often viewed more as an art—often a black art by nonsales folks—than a science.

The underlying malaise, however, is the mistaken logic that the customer will buy the offering based on the seller's belief in its inherent value while paying scant attention to the buyer's wants, needs, and the world in which they operate. Throughout the course of this book, I will show how faulty this logic is and consequently how incomplete and wasteful most sales and marketing investments have become. To illustrate this elemental principle, let's look at an actual better mousetrap.

Someone invented a new mousetrap that was indeed superior to previous iterations, and those supposedly in the know reviewed it. They extolled the mousetrap's technological superiority, which justified the slightly higher price by observing that its more robust construction would allow for multiple usages, thereby lowering the cost per dead mouse accordingly. But the market did not beat a path to the door of the provider of these new-and-improved traps. Why?

Well, the answer lies in understanding buyers and their buying process. Simply put, buyers preferred to use the old cheaper traps, as they could be thrown away complete with the offending rodent and so spare them the unpleasant task of cleaning and resetting the trap. The introduction of the "better mousetrap" actually generated more sales of the old commodity trap, which was now advertised as the handy disposable trap rather than the messy reusable variety.

In this case, the buying journey, though relatively simple to map in hindsight, was obviously misunderstood and seemingly not even considered at the time. As you will see, the secret to understanding business success in any market lies in closely mapping the target market's end-to-end Customer Buying Journey. Anyone charged with conducting business must fully understand what it takes to create a customer, and in today's world, that means far more than providing a superior offering.

How Customers Buy . . . and Why They Don't is based on many years of research and analysis into how customers really buy. I wrote it to help those concerned with revenue generation to uncover what they need to move a customer into a buying journey and then through all the steps to the acquisition and successful adoption of a particular offering. With this book, organizations, probably for the first time, can have a navigation system by which to design and implement truly effective sales and marketing endeavors that will lead to a predictable, scalable, and consistent approach to creating customers. This is in no small part due to one of the most enlightening results that our research turned up. We found that buyers within a target market for a specific offering will behave in remarkably similar ways. This meant that we could decode the DNA of that specific journey and then map the complete Customer Buying Journey for that target market.

In part 1, I will define and examine the six DNA strands of the Customer Buying Journey (CBJ). I will introduce the 4Q Buying Style quadrant, which unerringly reveals how customers are motivated in their buying activities. In part 2, I will share how to develop a Market Engagement Strategy based on what has gone before. In part 3, I will then translate that Market Engagement Strategy into real-world sales and marketing activities. In so doing, I will define the four Sales and Marketing Imperatives and introduce the CBJ Navigator™ and its inherent power and efficacy.

And throughout everything will be the all-encompassing principles and practices of Outside-In Revenue Generation. I will use many examples to illustrate various points. Some of these will be real-life examples; others are more generic. In some cases, I will use very simple everyday examples that could be construed as trivial, but I trust that they will serve to make the point—and perhaps add a little fun along the way. I have also included two highly detailed and realistic case studies with full analysis to further illuminate our concepts.

So we have lots to cover. Next up is a brief history of buying and selling. I'll look at the constants that have always endured as things are bought and sold. And as much as the world has changed—especially since the turn of the millennium—there are really only two major changes in the commercial exchange of goods. The first is communication technology and its impact, which has led to the second major change: that the buyer now has dominance in the parallel processes of buying and selling. Away we go.

CHAPTER 2

THREE GENERATIONS OF CUSTOMER CREATION

LET'S LOOK AT the history of how things are sold and focus on not just how suppliers sell but also how customers buy. I believe a sale is made not when someone *sells* something but when someone *buys* something. And although it may sound counterintuitive, I think of it as an equation. If I express this equation algebraically (with apologies to all real mathematicians), the constants would be A (Selling), B (Buying), and the problem is to come up with the solution $A = B$. As much as I like Red Motley's concise zingers and other pithy epigrams from the likes of Zig Ziglar and Bob Hooey, here's what I really believe: the sales professional's role is to positively influence the equation that results in somebody buying something.

But here's the thing: a lot of selling is going on out there with no one buying, and a surprising amount of buying is going on with no one selling. Again, algebraically, this might be expressed as $A = y$ and $B = x$, where $y = 0$ and $x = \$\$\$$. How can you decipher these new equations and identify the x factor? I maintain that it is only by synchronizing the procedures of selling with the reality of buying that you can really be successful. With that in mind, let's look at the three generations of the selling/buying equation.

G1: THE FIRST GENERATION OF CUSTOMER CREATION

To understand the origins of the seller/buyer relationship, you need to go back to the earliest days of commerce. Even before the emergence of money around 9000 BCE, people bartered. With bartering, an individual possessing something of value could directly exchange it for something they believed to have similar or greater value or use. However, bartering use is limited because it depends on a concurrence of complementary needs.

You can still see bartering today in Southeast Asian street markets, where people essentially buy and sell everything. It is not unusual for the suppliers, mostly women, to go to the market a couple times a day, occupy their regular spot, and display their wares. These purveyors of goods tend to have a very specific inventory. For example, if you are the supplier, you might focus on a particular vegetable, herb, or fish. If people want fish for dinner, they either barter for that fish with what they have or agree to a fair price and pay with money. They get their fish for dinner, and you get what you need—in kind or in cash.

Money (e.g., small bits of obsidian, seashells, metal) was first seen in the ninth millennium BCE in the Mediterranean region. The new relative ease of payment expanded both the buyers' and the suppliers' ranges considerably, but it didn't really change the sales method. A cow was still a cow, and if its value—and therefore its price—was three goats, it was easier to go shopping with a bag of shells than drag three goats around. Conversely, the supplier could place herself in a static spot with a few cows and not have to deal later with several goats, dozens of loaves of bread, several sacks of barley, and so on—she could just stroll home with a fat purse.

Whatever the method of payment, this style of selling and buying is highly transactional. A buyer sees what he wants, agrees on the price, and the deal is done. Buyers might look around at a few other suppliers offering what they needed, but this simple, well-defined, finite buying process would still take only minutes. Usually, only one other person is involved, and the search for the required goods is short and simple. Buyers can easily discover (although they probably already know) who is selling what they need, and they can quickly assess the offerings.

Let's consider the sales skills and process required here. The secrets of success are the basic sales skills of connecting, discovering, presenting, negotiating, and closing. It all starts with connecting with a prospect, so as a supplier, it would be helpful for you to physically be in a good location and occupy it regularly to attract and retain customers with good offerings. Assuming you have a good spot and the seller is regularly there, this sale is easily made. Then one of four things usually happens.

By far the most common customer is the repeat customer: someone you know with a need you've dealt with before comes by just as he always does. Provided your goods and service are still as expected, the repeat sale always was and still is the easiest sale going.

Less common, though just as effective and still an industry winner today, is word of mouth. One of your customers recommends you to someone else, and she drops by, sees the goods, and knows from her friend that you are trustworthy. This is another easy sale, and it often results in another repeat customer.

Then there are the casual shoppers or first-timers who pass by and love the look of your fish. If they don't buy right away, they might circle the block to see if anyone else has anything better or give themselves some time to browse. But once they have decided, they are usually confirmed and happy buyers, though they are not really a customer base you can depend on.

Finally, you can shout at or otherwise draw the attention of potential customers as they walk by. Note that this style of attracting new customers is seldom used in these situations, as customers with a need usually know where to find what they want, and there are few impulse purchases. In any event, you physically connect and talk with your buyer. It is essentially a "live" commercial.

Once you connect with a potential buyer, the key is discovering what she is looking for and what she has to barter or pay with. Strong discovery skills can help you discern exactly what the prospect is looking for, and based on that discovery, you can position and present your offering in its best possible light, emphasizing the characteristics that match what your prospect desires. With the prospect now more than interested, the negotiation can start, and hopefully end, with you closing the deal—simple and straightforward. All this is done face to face, often with someone you know, in minutes in a single conversation. The entire process is very stable, and you usually sell the same thing to the same people over and over again.

G2: SECOND GENERATION

Up until the early twentieth century, selling and buying continued in very much the same way. Buyers generally knew exactly what they wanted and where to get it, and the buying and selling process was very straightforward and conducted in person in one short conversation. But things changed in the early twentieth century.

Buyers now had a choice. Thanks to the telegraph, telephone, fax, advertising, mail-order catalogs, radio, and television, they were exposed to new suppliers and could communicate in ways other than physically being there—either by reaching out to suppliers or by connecting with a traveling salesman. These became the glory days of the yellow pages and the 1-800 number. Companies invested in mail-order catalogs and radio and television advertising. Buyers spent more time exploring their options, because they could. No longer was a deal transacted in a single discussion, and often more than one person was involved in the overall buying process.

In the late 1940s and early '50s, it became clear that great sales skills were no longer enough. IBM, Burroughs, and NCR—all selling complex accounting equipment—took note of the change. These companies led the way into a new era of sales, reflecting the new era of buying. Thus the notion of the sales process was born.

Their sales processes reflected the growing complexity of buying. The process is still founded on basic sales skills, but they are now formally documented into a sequence of activities, such as identifying a prospect, qualifying, presenting, negotiating, and closing. The sales process usually emphasized qualification and played out over a series of conversations within the different stages of the buying process and with its *key players*. This process was further refined over the decades by countless sales training companies. Even today, new selling systems and methodologies are all essentially based on this same sales approach.

The second generation of buying and selling is typified by three distinctions: a higher level of choice available to the buyer, the ability to transact remotely, and the overall transaction usually taking place in a series of discussions over time.

Then came the World Wide Web.

G3: THIRD GENERATION

The internet and how people use that technology to communicate has changed the game and given rise to the third generation of selling and buying. As a result of the internet, the dynamics of the buying process have significantly changed. I imagine you have already predicted the trend here: greater choice, greater complexity, and a greater number of people involved in the buying process. Let's look more closely at today's reality of buying and selling.

Buyers are now overwhelmed by the information they have at their fingertips and the choices they have in today's market. However, along with a greater choice of options comes a greater number of issues that can hinder, delay, or downright nullify the most persistent of sales efforts. Note that these five root issues rarely have anything to do with the quality or value of what's on offer.

1. *There's no shortage of things to do.* In today's world, few business professionals are short on things to do. Their days are full, as are the days of their team members. They simply do not have the time to evaluate new ideas and approaches. They are so saturated with marketing messages, sales calls, and other great stuff coming at them that they have learned that they can, and indeed must, switch off, no matter how enticing things may sound. They're just too busy.

2. *Resources are fully deployed.* Similarly, they have no additional funds or other resources. Rarely is any spare cash sitting around waiting for some new idea, however compelling that idea may be.

3. *The bets are already placed.* Sit at the roulette wheel in any casino and you will see the dealer wave his hands across the table to signal that the bets are placed and closed prior to the wheel slowing down and the winning number becoming more apparent to the keen observer. Approaching a company with a new product offering and asking them to invest is like trying to place a bet after the betting has closed. Imagine a CFO who goes back to her board and proclaims that she's found another way to save money. You might

think they would meet such an initiative with applause, but the opposite is usually true. The board might wonder how many other ways to save money that the CFO overlooked. The simple truth is that—as at the roulette table—people have already placed their bets, and the organization has committed to certain directions, investments, and initiatives. Trying to change those bets, no matter how rewarding, is tremendously difficult once those hands are waved.

4. *Organizations avoid change.* It's no secret that change is hard, but people often trivialize it in the traditional selling approach. There is a belief that if the benefits of adopting a new product are clear and distinct, then surely the customer will buy. This is simply not the case. Our research has shown that time and time again, even when faced with a credible business case, individuals don't buy. The change this purchase represents, no matter how trivial it may seem, is simply too great for the customer.

5. *The single decision maker is a myth.* Many second-generation selling approaches are based on a belief that a decision maker, usually in a senior position, will make the purchase decision. Salespeople then seek out this individual with all manner of approaches to sell high and close. This may have been the case previously, but in today's empowered and connected world, decisions are made through a dynamic network of influencers rather than by a predetermined senior executive. Selling today is typically more like mounting a political campaign to identify the influencers and understand their motives.

Things have changed, and these five issues underscore the challenges selling organizations now face in their sales and marketing activities. Company after company is still mired in G2 thinking, trying to overcome these challenges by honing their messaging with even more assertive persuasion about how great their products are. And here's the kicker: it's not that these prospects aren't interested, don't believe, or need more information—it's that they haven't committed to a buying journey.

DISCONTINUOUS CHANGE

The difference between the second generation and the third, like the difference between the first and the second, is not a gradual evolution but a revolution. It is not a trend line that slopes gently up but a step function showing a discontinuous change between these generations of buying and selling. The root cause of this is simply the technology that the buyer can utilize and how the buyer uses that technology to communicate.

SELLING IN TODAY'S WORLD

Customers' new buying methods have completely changed the buying/selling equation. Through the first and second generations of buying and selling, the salespeople held the keys. The buyer had to come to them to gain information, understand the product, and determine if the offering matched what was required.

In my days of selling in the 1980s, we had the "sales desk." Every call into the company on the 1-800 number was answered by a live salesperson. Imagine that in today's world! We took turns sitting at the sales desk, and the incoming calls covered an amazing array of questions: people looking for our fax number, technical inquiries, support—you name it. In most cases, we would simply reroute the messages to the appropriate resources. But every so often, a call would come in from somebody looking for help understanding our products, our services, and of course our pricing. These were the calls we lived for. We would offer to drop by and meet them. Such

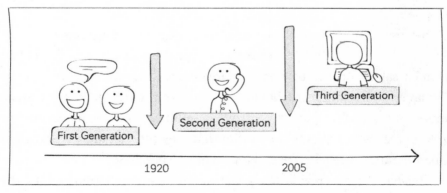

ILLUSTRATION 2.1. Discontinuous generational change

offers would usually be met with a response such as "It's okay, thanks, I just want this information," as the last thing they actually wanted was a salesperson landing on their doorstep. But we would laugh at the newbies who would dutifully package up the information and send it out.

There was a famous expression back in those days: "The selling stops when the brochure is delivered," and that is exactly what usually happened. When the brochure was delivered, the salesperson lost control. The prospective customer then had no reason to work with a salesperson. They had the brochure, so they could figure it out themselves.

Life was great back then—when we received those phone calls, they were often from prospective customers at the start of their buying journey. And we didn't send out brochures; we sent out ourselves. We met with the prospects and discovered what they were doing, and then helped them determine the best possible solutions. Buyers had to wait for salespeople to send or bring information, and then they had to wait for salespeople to deliver quotes. Salespeople were equipped with the knowledge and the numbers, and with that information, they drove the deal.

This has all changed. Today, those prospects have the biggest and best brochure in the world right on their desks—the internet. This is where today's customers get their information, and perhaps rather ironically, this is where each and every company puts all the details of their offerings. So is the brochure delivered? Has the selling stopped? Well, if that's all salespeople were—walking, talking brochures—then the internet has certainly replaced them. So at the very least, that style of selling has stopped.

But now buyers have all the information they need at their fingertips and can be overwhelmed by choice. Surveys show that buyers don't even contact salespeople until they are already well into the buying process: "Today's buyers control their progress through the buying journey much more than today's suppliers control the selling cycle. In a recent survey, 74% of business buyers told Forrester that they conduct more than half of their research online before making an offline purchase."[1]

This has caused a revolution in the buying/selling equation because the power has shifted from the seller to the buyer. The buyer is no longer at the mercy of the seller to get information and pricing. The buyer now dominates the parallel processes of buying and selling, sets the cadence, and moves the process forward. This is why the very notion of a sales process is outdated. The sales process no longer sets the pace. The sales process no longer dictates what happens next. It is the buying process. G3 is here, and the buyer is driving.

PART 1
MAPPING THE CUSTOMER BUYING JOURNEY

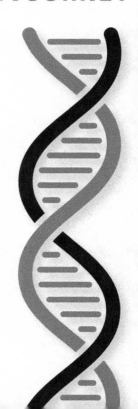

CHAPTER 3

THE DNA OF THE CUSTOMER BUYING JOURNEY

THE MORE CUSTOMERS we talked to about their buying processes, the more information we gained, and discernable patterns began to emerge. Looking back, I realize we had started to look at sales from the outside in. We didn't call it that at the time, and perhaps we didn't even recognize it, but from what followed, it was clear that we were starting to shift our focus from the selling perspective to the buying process. I came to visualize this process as a journey, and these early endeavors confirmed that vision, giving us fledgling ideas of what it looked like, and led us to create some superior selling strategies for our clients. I called this process the Customer Buying Journey.

However, we were continually faced with sorting through a daunting amount of information to determine what was useful and relevant and what was not. We wanted a way to view a particular buying journey—a view that delivered insight without the onerous task of continually reanalyzing relatively similar data. Over time, we developed a model that enabled us to do just that—to effectively decode and, in so doing, create a map for any particular buying journey. This is the DNA of the Customer Buying Journey.

This DNA model has six major strands. The nature of these strands can vary greatly among different markets, but for any particular market, when buying a specific offering, they will share the same code. These strands will allow you to determine the unique elements of any market's buying journey and develop in-depth knowledge of what really happens throughout the end-to-end buying journey.

THE SIX STRANDS OF THE CUSTOMER BUYING JOURNEY DNA

Let's take a look at the six DNA strands of the Customer Buying Journey. The following six chapters will then explore each of these stands in greater detail. Keep in mind that I have chosen to describe all these strands in the context of *how the customer buys*. We do not mix the selling and the buying but start by developing insight into the buying journey strictly from the customer's point of view.

I know anyone involved in the revenue generation side of business—a CEO, a marketer, an entrepreneur, or a salesperson—will be tempted to jump to the other side and look at things from the selling viewpoint. As a supplier reading about how customers buy, it will be only natural to think about how this applies to your own selling situation. By all means, feel free to consider how customers do buy and use them as real-life examples as I discuss the strands of the DNA of the Customer Buying Journey.

However, I encourage you—at least for now—to resist the temptation to consider how this may impact sales and marketing. Rather, first get the full picture of how customers buy before thinking about how to engage their market. You will learn in detail the implications and strategies for

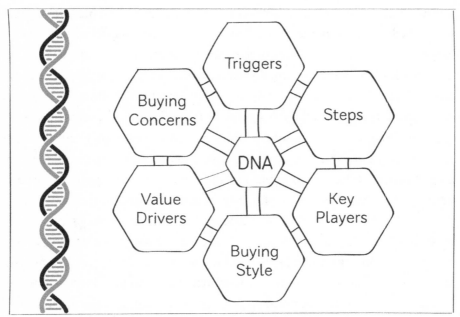

ILLUSTRATION 3.1. Customer Buying Journey DNA

market engagement in part 2 of this book, but for now, I will get into how customers really buy. I am going to decode the DNA and, in doing so, map the Customer Buying Journey (see illustration 3.1).

1. TRIGGERS

Triggers determine what activities, events, or experiences initiate a buying journey. You will also see dependencies added to and included with this strand.

2. STEPS

These are the activities buyers are likely to engage in throughout the buying journey. They are usually grouped and sequenced as a series of sequential steps that comprise the total journey. I will also highlight the activities, or touch points, during which a buyer is likely to reach out and interact with a potential supplier.

3. KEY PLAYERS

Here you want to determine what roles across an organization, or outside of the organization, are likely to be involved in which steps across the buying journey.

4. BUYING STYLE

As we talked to more and more buyers about how they actually approached their buying decisions, we began to notice important patterns. We have captured these in our 4Q Buying Style model, which I will show in detail in chapter 7. The dynamics of the customer's buying style are often ignored, trivialized, or just plain missed, and I cannot overstate their importance. We have seen companies not only change their overall approach to the market but actually change how they are organized and even how they think of their company based on gaining insight into their customers' buying style.

5. VALUE DRIVERS

The *value drivers* provide the motivation for the buyers to move forward into and through their buying journey. They are the rewards the buyers expect to gain—the carrot, so to speak—by the acquisition and adoption of the offering.

6. BUYING CONCERNS

Buying concerns—perhaps the most important facets of the DNA—are widely overlooked and the least understood aspects. These are inhibitors that can slow down or stop a buying journey. They come in all shapes and sizes, yet we found there was great commonality of buying concerns across a particular buying journey for a specific offering in a given market. After much analysis, we were able to define nine categories of buying concerns.

Over the next six chapters, each strand of the Customer Buying Journey DNA will be explored in full detail.

TAKEAWAYS

⇒ Buyers buy in remarkably similar ways. When faced with buying a particular offering within a particular market, buyers will exhibit very similar buying behavior.

⇒ If customers are buying a particular offering in a dissimilar way, this denotes more than one market. *Indeed, the true definition of a market is one in which buyers behave in a similar manner.*

⇒ A buying journey can be decoded and mapped. There is a method for decoding the "DNA" of a market's buying approach, which reveals six specific strands. These strands can then be compiled into a complete map of the Customer Buying Journey.

⇒ Buyers across a market may proceed through the buying journey at different rates but they follow the same buying journey with a common DNA.

⇒ Key players, buying style, value drivers, and buying concerns will likely change across the buying journey, but in a predictable fashion.

CHAPTER 4

STRAND 1: TRIGGERS

THE CUSTOMER BUYING Journey *trigger* is an event, experience, or activity that causes a customer to enter into a buying journey. This does not imply that they will conclude that journey or even get very far with it. Neither does it signify any particular rate at which that buying journey may proceed. The events, activities, or experiences that trigger a Customer Buying Journey can be internal or external to the buying organization.

Internal triggers might include dissatisfaction with the current state or the realization that a certain area needs to be changed. Perhaps costs in a certain operational area have continued to climb past what is considered reasonable, so a buying journey is triggered in an effort to explore possible alternatives. However, note that a new need or dissatisfaction with something already in place does not necessarily trigger a buying journey.

External triggers can come from many different sources. Perhaps reading an article, visiting a trade show, or researching online prompts interest in a new or alternative approach. Maybe a salesperson calls on the company and introduces new and relevant insight that triggers a buying journey.

THE SOURCE

In our work, we gave considerable thought to what truly constitutes the start of a Customer Buying Journey. When buyers talked about the start of their buying journeys, they would mention, for example, that they came across a particular offering or supplier, perhaps at a trade show. Does that then suggest that any supplier they came across at such a trade show could start a similar buying journey? Of course not; after all, they may have become aware of dozens of different offerings at that same trade show, the vast majority of which did not trigger a buying process. It would therefore be wrong to conclude that a certain trade show booth triggered that buying process. It may have, but you have to get much more specific about exactly what conditions triggered that decision. Most likely they were already aware that they needed an alternative approach to something they had or were doing. And if this indeed is the case, you have to dig further back to discover the real trigger—what it was that started them on their buying journey.

Let's consider window-shopping. As you walk past a series of shop windows, you might be informed, entertained, amused, or even inspired as you gaze at the merchandise. But none of this—in and of itself—necessarily triggers a buying journey. Many sales and marketing people have been caught out by this simple fact. While you can entertain, inform, or inspire a potential buyer, none of these conditions implies that a buying journey has been or will be triggered.

After considerable research and testing, we discovered that a buying journey starts when someone who is in a position to buy, or has influence on those who could buy, has decided an unsatisfied need should be addressed or a value should be gained through the acquisition of an offering and is willing to take action. The wording is important here; I am saying "should" as opposed to "could" or "would." *Could* implies that he or she is able to address the need or the value, but there is no assumed intent to do anything. *Would* implies a conditional belief in the satisfaction of a need or the value to be gained only if he or she proceeds. *Should* indicates a belief in further action.

Let's go back to our window-shopping—a shoe store, for example, and a very smart pair of walking shoes in particular. I *could* buy those shoes—I have my credit card with me, and I'm pretty sure I don't have any holes in my socks—but I'm in a hurry, so I'll pass. I *would* buy those shoes—they're a very good brand and they look super comfortable—but I have a perfectly good pair at home, so I won't. I *should* buy those shoes—they're a great price, and I have a hiking vacation coming up. As a result, a buying journey is triggered because *should* must lead to further action.

We worked with a company that offered a wonderful 3D display. Their demo was one of the highest-impact presentations I have ever seen. You put on the glasses and then images appear in high-definition 3D right in front of your face. As creatures rush toward you, you duck. As scenes are presented, you are amazed. Never did they fail to entertain, amuse, inform, educate, or impress. However, none of this implies that a buying journey has started. The buying journey only started when someone (a possible buyer or someone who could influence a possible buyer) seeing the demo gains the belief that this technological device is indeed something that should address a specific need or bring certain value in a particular application and is willing to do something about it.

It is obviously very important to understand the real triggers for certain buying journeys—to track back to the real root causes. Likely more than one condition triggers a Customer Buying Journey, and sometimes these conditions depend on each other.

Take, for instance, an organization that continues to deal with an insurance broker who they don't think is providing the best service. No real issues develop to stop them from buying from that broker, so they continue this service for several years. But perhaps they hear about a different broker who is providing outstanding service to a neighboring company, which then triggers a buying journey. In this case, two things had to happen to trigger the journey. First, dissatisfaction with the current provider (internal), and second, the emergence of a viable and proven alternative (external). Both conditions had to exist to trigger the buying journey. If a new broker had been recommended but the organization was not dissatisfied with the service of the current one, nothing was likely to happen. And conversely, despite poor service, nothing would have happened without there being a viable alternative.

THREE MODES OF THE CUSTOMER BUYING JOURNEY

Once triggered, the Customer Buying Journey can be categorized into one of three modes, each of which tends to dictate the nature and complexity of that buying journey

1. SUBSTITUTION

Substitution is when a buying journey is triggered by the customer's need to explore—and potentially acquire and adopt—an alternative offering for or supplier of something that is already part of the standard operating procedures. In other words, the buyer is simply substituting one solution for another. Maybe a cheaper, faster, or higher-quality solution has been discovered. Perhaps a particular supplier has failed to deliver the required quality or service, and this has triggered a Customer Buying Journey to find an alternative provider.

Substitution is the simplest overall buying journey. Usually, buyers know what they require, and their current approach offers a benchmark by which to judge possible alternatives. As you shall see, however, it is risky to assume that this implies the journey will be straightforward and easy, because any change—no matter how small—can present a barrier to the successful completion of the journey.

2. AUGMENTATION

Augmentation is a buying journey in which the buyer explores the potential to acquire and adopt an offering with greater functionality or potential than a current approach. Such a journey may be as straightforward as upgrading a current product or service, or it could involve switching providers to add greater functionality.

For example, in the high-flying world of corporate aviation, if a company is exchanging one turboprop for another, that could be considered substitution. But if they are upgrading to a jet, then that would be augmentation. At a more mundane and earthbound level, switching from Dell/Windows to Lenovo/Windows laptops could be considered substitution if the specs and usage remained largely the same. But upgrading to Cloud computing with iPads could be considered augmentation.

3. DISRUPTION

Disruption is when a buyer considers something totally new, whether that journey is long planned or more spontaneous. The acquisition and, more importantly, the adoption of such an offering will disrupt the current approach in some way. As an example, think of a distribution business moving from old "green screen" monitors in its warehouses to tablets and RFID. Although there may be many benefits associated with such a change, it will require workflow changes, reskilling, redefining job roles, and likely major installation challenges. That would be disruption.

To contrast these three modes, consider the world of health care providers and one aspect of orthopedics. If a hospital is looking at switching from one artificial joint provider to another, that would be substitution. If it is

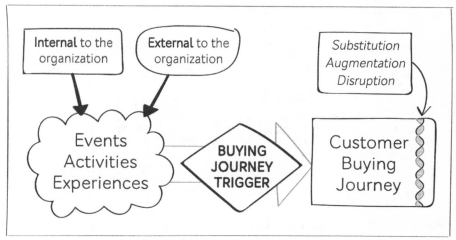

ILLUSTRATION 4.1. Buying triggers flow chart

considering a provider with a new form of infection-preventing joint coating that otherwise requires the same surgical processes, that could be considered augmentation. However, if the hospital is contemplating adopting 3D imaging and the custom design and 3D printing of joints, that would likely be a disruptive buying journey, as their surgical procedures and schedules would need to change to accommodate this new approach to joint replacement.

TAKEAWAYS

⇒ There is a very important distinction between someone with an intent to buy and someone purely educating himself or "window-shopping." One is on a buying journey, and the other is not.

⇒ It's important to know what can trigger a buying journey and the dependencies that enable the successful conclusion of that journey.

⇒ There are three modes of the Customer Buying Journey:

  ○ *Substitution.* The buyer is simply exchanging one supplier or offering for another.

  ○ *Augmentation.* The buyer will continue to buy what they have in the past but do so in a way that adds something more to the equation; this could be with the same supplier or offering or with a different supplier or offering.

  ○ *Disruption.* The buyer is going to buy something that either is new to them or will change something they are already buying.

CHAPTER 5

STRAND 2: STEPS

THE TRADITIONAL SALES and marketing view of a buying journey assumes buyers have little else to occupy their time other than the acquisition of the chosen offering. Sellers often assume that the buyer follows a simplistic path of discovering the offering, evaluating its benefits, and purchasing it. The 1950s and '60s ushered in the alluring logic of the ubiquitous sales process, which assumed that the buyer would obligingly follow that logic. Life would be so easy if that were the case! Nothing shows how myopic, simplistic, and incomplete that logic is than the second strand in the DNA of the Customer Buying Journey, which covers every activity a buyer engages in from start to finish.

When buyers talk about what they do throughout their buying journey, a strange thing happens. They energetically start to describe what they did, thinking this will be a short and simple story. But they rarely get very far before adopting a different tone as they unravel a surprising complex web of activities. Often, they will share their own surprise as they think back to everything that happened—and had to happen—to move through the buying journey. With the exception of impulse buys, the journey is never simple, and perhaps that is why impulse buys are a category unto themselves. However, even impulse buys should be viewed in the wider construct of what led the buyer to be in that place, at that time, and prepared for the impulse buy.

There is no substitute for the information gained by talking directly to customers and potential customers in your target market. They will need careful prompting to recall all the activities involved in their overall buying journey, and then they will need time to think it through, but with the right level of prompting and support, they will unravel all that happens in the real world of buying. When we try to map out the activities without actual customers and simply talk with a sales and marketing team, we find the focus is on a significant but small subset of the actual buying journey. Perhaps counterintuitively—though it doesn't surprise us anymore—when we facilitate the same process with a company's executives or engineers, we get an even more myopic view of the buying journey. Even if the salespeople don't really think of everything that happens throughout the journey, they are usually close enough to their customers to have an approximation. With apologies to those whom I am about to offend (and noting that there are always exceptions), I find that those removed from the front line have a very limited view of what really happens across the Customer Buying Journey.

The first key to mapping buying activities is to ensure you really are considering the complete buying journey; in so doing, you widen the focus considerably from the simple acquisition of the offering. Interestingly enough, often very important activities happen even before the buying journey trigger. Consider the case of changing from one supplier of a commodity offering to another. This buying journey could be classified as a substitution, as I discussed in the previous chapter when looking at triggers. The fact that the buyer was actively engaged in purchasing and using a similar offering from a different supplier could be considered an important activity in the overall buying journey, even though it occurred prior to the trigger.

Consider a hospital buying surgical gloves. They have probably been buying such gloves for a long time, but somewhere along that timeline, they probably evaluated their usage, considered various alternatives, and decided to go with a specific supplier. Perhaps lately they have experienced delivery problems, so their decreased dissatisfaction triggers a buying journey where they will evaluate potential alternative suppliers. Clearly, their previous activities of evaluating alternatives and their experience with delivery issues are going to impact how they proceed with a possible switch of suppliers.

In a totally different style of Customer Buying Journey, let's consider the acquisition of a single high-ticket item by a corporation such as new real estate or a corporate jet. If you think of the buying journey starting when they commence their search, you will miss many steps in the buying journey. This buying journey may have started with long-term planning several years before the actual acquisition. These activities, which might include capacity planning, strategy, and long-term planning, should be considered part of the end-to-end buying journey. Successful salespeople selling high-ticket items, especially to institutions such as federal government bodies, know that the buying activities that will influence the eventual purchase can happen years ahead of the purchase.

In the same way that you must track *back* to all the possible activities that led up to and follow the trigger, you also have to go forward to consider the delivery and adoption of the offering. The buying journey doesn't end at the point of purchase. Ask any buyer, and you will quickly discover that their view of the journey doesn't end with the purchase order. In most cases, their objective throughout the buying journey is placed not on the purchase but on the use and inherent benefit of the offering. In many situations, the business relationship between the supplier and the buyer doesn't end at the point of purchase but continues through service and support and quite possibly the sale and delivery of further products and/or services. In today's world, an increasing number of companies conduct business with their customers on an ongoing basis. The "As a Service" model has been widely adopted across the technology sector, because not surprisingly, a recurring revenue stream is in many ways the Holy Grail for a broad cross section of industries. These trends simply reinforce the need to consider the activities that happen after the point of purchase and indeed throughout the entire life cycle of the offering as components of the overall Customer Buying Journey.

At this stage, then, you have ensured a focus on the total buying journey. For each activity, you need to ask, What led to it? What had to happen for it to occur? Then the answers to those questions will likely lead to adding even more to the list of buying activities. You also need to consider all the people who likely influence the buying journey and once again examine what they did and how they became involved. This all adds to the growing list of activities that will or may occur along the overall buying journey.

SEQUENCING THE BUYING ACTIVITIES

After completing a list of all the possible buying activities in the Customer Buying Journey, the next step in decoding and mapping the DNA is to sequence those activities into a timeline. This can often cause concern, as people tend to think that the buying journey lacks a logical sequence. Some believe the process is far more random or chaotic in today's world. I am certainly not going to say that there cannot be an element of such disorder, and I would totally agree that there is often the appearance of such randomness, but our research has shown that *most significant activities occur predictably and sequentially.*

To illustrate the seemingly opposing points of sequence, consider very simplistically a few activities across the buying journey for a new mobile phone. For the sake of the illustration, assume that the discovery of an enticing new feature associated with a particular new model triggered the buying journey. The following activities give an idea of what may occur:

1. Evaluate the phone
2. Search for alternatives
3. Compare functionality
4. Determine requirements and priorities
5. Select new phone

This example focuses on a very small subset of all the buying activities that are likely to occur in such a transaction, but it serves to make the point of order versus chaos. In this example, the buyer discovered a new function she considered highly desirable, thereby triggering her buying journey. At that point, perhaps the buyer determined she wanted that new feature and thus would purchase that particular phone. However, buyers being who they are and phones being what they are, the buyer considered she should look at other phones in her buying journey. You will see later when I discuss buying styles exactly what is responsible for this buyer behavior, but for now, let's just go with it.

The buyer, in her search across other choices for a phone, will likely come across other new features and functions. Based on that new knowledge, she will then again look at her requirements and priorities. The fact that she looked at other phones likely led to this new knowledge, which in turn led her to examine and possibly modify her perceived requirements. You can look at this in a number of ways. Those who subscribe to the chaos theory can argue that the buyer's requirements and priorities are in a constant state of flux. But I prefer to look more deeply to uncover what causes that apparent state of flux and reveal that as the buyer looks at other phones and becomes more knowledgeable about what is available. In turn, this influences how she sees and values her overall needs and priorities.

What can make the equation even more confusing and lead to apparent randomness in the buying journey is how a buyer may appear to move backward and forward through a possible sequence of activities. A particular buyer could evaluate her needs and priorities before even looking at a new phone. She could then reevaluate those needs after looking at the first phone and then again after looking at the alternatives. You would not consider this the same buying activity being performed many times or being done randomly. In a case like this, you would map each of these likely activities along the sequence. For example, you could then map this out as follows, with the new activities noted in italics:

- *initial thoughts on requirements and priorities*
1. Evaluate the phone
- *formulate a more informed opinion of requirements and priorities*
2. Search for alternatives
- *learn more about possible features and functions*
3. Compare functionality
- *reassess requirements and priorities*
4. Determine requirements and priorities
- *based on new knowledge of possibilities*
5. Select new phone

This adds more work, more analysis, and more buying activities to be sure. However, I believe that only by decoding the DNA to this level of precision does it becomes truly insightful and useful to our needs. To summarize this point, buying behavior can often give an appearance of randomness and chaos, but most buying activities tend to follow a certain sequence.

After completing the list of buying activities, we recommend laying them out along a timeline. We often use yellow sticky notes with each individual buying activity written on its own note, which we then place sequentially on the wall from left to right. If we come across an activity that could occur at any particular time or ones that occur all the time, we simply place these in their own pools. In this way, we invariably discover three things: over 90 percent of all buying activities can indeed be sequenced, we come across additional activities, and we need a longer wall.

One final important point is to underscore that the process of decoding the DNA is like peeling an onion. As we move through the process, it is very likely—in fact, suspicious if not—that we will uncover additional buying activities we should add to the list. And it's not just the buying activities—as we explore the other components of the DNA and continue to ask the leading questions of what, why, how, who, and when, the onion will likely reveal more layers and greater depth. This is perfectly fine. We expect to keep adding and adjusting the code as we delve further into it.

TOUCH POINTS

Once compiled, we can now look across all the buying activities we have identified and highlight those that are touch points, which are buying activities where we would expect the buyer to reach out and interact with a potential supplier or the supplier to interact with the potential buyer. Illustration 5.1 shows examples of these touch points, which include the typical activities and potential ways in which those interactions may occur.

This table offers just some of the examples of common touch points. Note that these are all stated and documented from the buyer's perspective. I should repeat the warning that when we complete this exercise with a client, it is usually extremely difficult for them to put themselves into and stay in the role of the buyer. The result is that the buying journey DNA can too easily become what the supplier would like it to be rather than what it is likely to be. In the case of touch points, we would quickly see this become a list of how and when the supplier would *like* to interact with and influence their prospective customers rather than what a prospective buyer is likely

ILLUSTRATION 5.1. EXAMPLES OF TOUCH POINTS

EXAMPLE ACTIVITIES	VEHICLE TO CONNECT BUYER AND SUPPLIER
Search for information	Website
	Telephone call
	Email
	Online chat
Gain assistance in defining the solution	Website
or configuration	Sales rep
Request for quotation/pricing information	Website
	Sales call (in person or virtual)
	Email
Request technical assistance/support	Website
	Telephone call
	Email
	Online chat
View or participate in a demonstration	Live (in person)
	Live over the web
	Website using prerecorded material
Participate in a presentation of proposal	Sales call (in person or virtual)

to do. This points to the importance of talking with actual customers to discover what they really do. Invariably, buyers do not behave in the perfect way a supplier would like to imagine.

It's also important to look at how potential customers are actually interacting with potential suppliers. This is one of the major impacts of what I earlier described in the third generation of customer creation. In earlier times, touch points would have largely have been live and often between the salesperson and the prospective buyer. But thanks to technology, this is perhaps where we have seen the biggest difference in how buyers behave today. Not only are many more touch points served by the internet without any live communication, but now the touch points themselves are quite different. We know that buyers now can get a lot further into their buying journey without any live interaction with a supplier. Rather than having to talk to a salesperson, they can get the information they need from a website.

When considering the touch points and how they may be realized, you can also drill down further to determine the vehicle that they interact with.

Numerous options are available to our example mobile phone buyer, for example, including the following:

- go online and conduct a general search for new phone
- go online to a particular consumer review site
- go online to a particular forum or social media site
- walk into a store in a mall
- go to a particular store
- text a particular friend
- talk to a particular friend
- talk to several friends
- call or text a particular salesperson

All of the above are viable vehicles for the touch point of gaining a recommendation. The important question here is "What will determine which way the buyer goes?" Exploring this question may once again lead to discovering more buying activities. Perhaps it was the buyer's experience purchasing her previous phone, which then implies that this buying journey may have to go back to include the activities associated with buying that previous phone.

Interestingly, if you assume for a moment that many buyers acquire a new phone every year or so, then you could argue that there is no discrete buying journey for acquiring a phone but rather there is a continuous buying journey that includes the many times a new phone may be acquired in a buyer's lifetime. This leads to the topic of recursive "looping" buying journeys, which I will explore later.

COALESCING BUYING ACTIVITIES INTO STEPS

At this point, you should have a timeline of all the potential buying activities a buyer may undertake throughout their overall buying journey. I can assure you that this will include a multitude—perhaps even an overwhelming number—of activities. We recommend, then, that you review the activities and group them into subsets of overall buying steps. In most cases, it is not difficult to group activities together and then give them a meaningful name that aptly describes the group. In most cases, we find that the buying activities come down to a series of five to twelve buying steps. At this point, it is most important to never lose sight of the detail—the buying activities themselves. Although you might be tempted to disregard some of the activities at this stage and simply consider the steps, always remember that the devil really is in the details. However, the buying steps will give you a very useful way in which to conceptualize and examine the overall Customer Buying Journey without getting lost in the detail.

A BUYER'S PROGRESS ALONG THE CUSTOMER BUYING JOURNEY

Different buyers may go through the steps of the buying journey at a different rate, or they may get stuck at different steps or even jump back to previous steps. Once again, this is not chaos but the result of predictable and observable factors. Let's look at the steps of a hypothetical buying journey for acquiring a server for a small office:

1. Determine requirements
2. Identify potential suppliers and models
3. Create a short list of possible servers
4. Compare functionality and pricing
5. Research recommendations and reviews
6. Make a selection
7. Negotiate and purchase
8. Take delivery and install
9. Launch and utilize

What might happen here? Perhaps someone in the organization has had a previous positive experience with servers from a particular company. The buyer might then appear to move from step 1 straight to step 6, where he favors a particular model with no further research. This may work for him, but perhaps as he further explores his chosen option, he discovers that it no longer comes in the configuration he liked or is incompatible with certain aspects of the operating environment. Such a discovery could then drive the buyer back to step 2 or, in some cases, even step 1, where he realizes he should start with a clean slate and determine the overall requirements for a server in that environment.

To the casual observer, this may look like random buying behavior, but as you can see here, it is simply a case of the buyer navigating the buying journey in a less direct manner. There were logical reasons for both the departure and return to the buying journey. I will further explore the reasons why this is so important as I explain how to develop a Market Engagement Strategy and sales approach for navigating and managing the Customer Buying Journey.

RECURSIVE BUYING JOURNEYS

As I widen the lens to examine the full end-to-end Customer Buying Journey, you will often see how many such buying journeys are recursive and loop back on themselves. The easiest example of this is the acquisition of a continuing commodity item such as insurance. Obviously, most buyers want their insurance coverage to continue year after year, but in most cases, the actual purchase is conducted annually. At a macro level, this particular buying journey may look something like this:

1. Realize need for insurance
2. Contact broker
3. Discuss requirements and explore options
4. Review detailed proposals
5. Select option and commit to purchase
6. Process claims as required
7. Review if coverage is appropriate

In this instance, you can see how steps 6 and 7 are optional, as they may or may not occur. If there are no claims, there is no need to review the coverage, no change in circumstances that impact the coverage required, and so no problems with the broker. The buyer might just loop from step 5 back to step 4 each year. But that statement contains a lot of conditions. Obviously, if any claims become due, then the buying journey must include step 6. Some may argue that the process of claims is not in and of itself a buying activity. However, all you need to do to change that perspective is to talk to any successful insurance broker. They will quickly tell you how good or bad experiences in claims processing will have a very significant impact on what happens when the renewal comes due.

Let's then look at what happens if the buyer's insurance requirements change. Then the buyer moves into step 7 and probably loops back to step 2 to contact their broker, discuss their requirements, and explore their options.

Many buying journeys—unless they are for a discrete, one-time purchase—are recursive. The buyers' experiences in the later stages of the buying journey will often impact how they behave as they loop back into the early stages for a repeat acquisition or to augment with related products or services.

TAKEAWAYS

⇒ Buyers engage in a sequence of activities across their end-to-end buying journey, and these activities can be organized into a rational sequence of events.

⇒ Buyers can take different amounts of time as they go through their buying journeys, and they may also slow down or stop at any time.

⇒ If buyers seem to be jumping around in the buying journey, there is a reason why that needs to be understood, because it's rarely random activity.

⇒ The supplier must be concerned with the entire end-to-end Customer Buying Journey, not just the acquisition and purchase steps.

⇒ Touch points are the buying activities within the Customer Buying Journey when the buyer would expect to connect with a potential supplier in some way.

⇒ Some buying journeys are recursive and loop back on themselves, and some buying journeys never end.

CHAPTER 6

STRAND 3: KEY PLAYERS

COMPANIES AND ORGANIZATIONS, in and of themselves, don't actually start any buying journeys. Nor can they move along through a buying journey or even buy something. The only way these things happen is if *people* get involved. Living, breathing individuals determine if a buying journey is worth starting, and it is they who move that buying journey forward. These *key players* make up the third strand of the Customer Buying Journey DNA and as such need to be fully understood and mapped.

We live in a world that is more connected than ever before in which individuals within organizations are more empowered, better informed, and increasingly involved. Although organizations still make some autocratic decisions in isolation, these are becoming rare. Organizations now work through dynamic networks of individuals. And sometimes it's hard to unravel just how decisions get made and who is involved in what. But unravel we must.

When we conduct our primary research, we invariably get to the point where we have to ask buyers who made the decision to move forward in a particular buying journey or who made the decision to go with product A over product B. Almost always that question is met with a sharp intake of breath. Sometimes we hear "That's a good question" as they think it through for themselves. Ultimately, the most common response is "Well, a lot of people were involved." This speaks to the exact nature of how today's organizations make decisions.

Now, maybe you are thinking that doesn't fit your situation. If that's the case, I'm willing to bet your situation is one where the customer buys from the cheapest supplier. Okay, so that's a simple buying decision that one person can indeed make. But once again, let's track that back in the buying journey. Who decided this would be the appropriate buying style for the company? Who determined which potential suppliers would be on the list?

As an example, here in the United States, many hospitals and hospital networks buy what they consider to be commodity items from the cheapest provider. But who determined which suppliers they would entertain a bid from, or who decided that a particular item would be purchased that way? A network of administrators, clinicians, and materials management people likely made these buying decisions. So when we look at the end-to-end buying journey, we are likely to see that multiple individuals are involved in fulfilling various roles across the buying activities.

Let me now dispel the myth of calling high and finding the decision maker. This is, of course, a well-worn sales approach. Although I am not going to say that high-level executives are not involved in the decision-making process, the days when decisions were made on high and passed down for implementation are long gone. In talking with buyers, we found that senior executives would invariably make decisions with their teams, once again relying on a network of individuals to participate in the process.

Although I am going to resist the temptation to start talking about sales and selling, this singular point of calling on the senior executive or decision maker remains a key tenet of selling. Although I am never going to state that it is not valuable to have such friends in high places, let's make sure we really understand what happens in the buying journey. In order to do so, we have talked to many senior executives to gain insight. The same conclusion can be drawn time and again. It is extremely rare that such senior individuals make decisions in isolation about what to buy and who to buy from. Repeatedly, these senior executives shared with us that they have their teams in place and individuals across their organization who are accountable to make such decisions.

For example, when I was a CEO myself, I would occasionally answer my own phone if I happened to be in the office and free, especially outside of the usual business hours. I well recall picking up the phone one evening and an obviously enterprising sales rep had made that "call high" connection. She explained that she could provide my company with a better deal if we consolidated all our water cooler purchases, across some seventy offices, with her. It seems her company provided about 70 percent of our water cooler services, and she was after the other 30 percent. She shares with me how much she thought we were spending a year and how much she could potentially save us if we gave all our business to her. I thanked her for pointing out how much we were spending on water coolers and that I would immediately look to reduce that expenditure, probably to zero. She quickly responded that she didn't intend for us to stop buying water coolers, just that we should purchase them from her. I thanked her for calling and bringing this expenditure to my attention but pointed out that she was talking to the wrong person. If she wanted to continue the dialogue with me, it would likely result in a radical reduction in the amount of money we were spending with them. She wisely opted to go talk to our facilities manager. Of course, I had a facilities team, a purchasing department, and office managers. I wasn't about to overrule them and make a decision on our water suppliers.

Water coolers are a small expenditure, but the argument holds even truer for more significant expenditures. I wasn't going to start second guessing my staff, overruling their decisions, or telling them what to do. Sure, I would be a key player, but I put these people in place to do the work, evaluate alternatives, and make decisions or recommendations. So, yes, some senior executives are going to be key players at some of the steps of the overall Customer Buying Journey, but to think of them as the sole decision makers in today's world is simply naïve.

In order to decode this component of the Customer Buying Journey DNA, we need to examine each of the key players in the overall journey. We need to consider not only key players inside the organization but also those that may be outside. Examples of outside roles that can impact the buying journey could include consultants and key opinion leaders. We also see many individuals reaching out to their peers in other organizations and to industry associations to gain insight into different approaches that will impact their buying journey. Of course, with the advent of social media and the general increase of connectedness, this has become even more important and has given rise to the third generation of customer creation. So we should consider such groups, associations, and affiliations as potential key players as we decode the buying journey DNA.

ILLUSTRATION 6.1. POSSIBLE ROLES ACROSS THE CUSTOMER BUYING JOURNEY

Approver	Someone who needs to approve something for the buying journey to progress
Resource provider	Someone who owns resources that will be required for the buying journey to progress
End user	Someone who will become a user of the envisioned offering
Expert	Someone with expert knowledge who may be required for the buying journey to progress successfully
Reference	A current user of the offering
Stakeholder	An individual who will be impacted in some way as a result of successfully completing the buying journey
Influencer	Someone who should or would influence the progress of the buying journey
Owner	Someone who is accountable for the completion of a key activity within the buying journey

For each key player across the buying journey, we then document their degree of influence and their most likely roles for each of the stages of the journey. For instance, at what stage might the CFO, a consultant, or an industry association become involved? Their possible roles are given in illustration 6.1.

TAKEAWAYS

⟹ In today's world, the notion of a single decision maker is dangerously outdated.

⟹ In today's organizations, buying decisions are made by a dynamic network of individuals, and it is often hard for buyers to even isolate who made a specific buying decision.

⟹ Individuals at low levels in an organization can have a significant impact on buying decisions.

⟹ Individuals from outside of the organization can play a significant role in the decision-making process. In today's highly connected world, these external influences are not always easily identifiable, such as a consultant may be. Connections made across the virtual world and the impact of social media must be considered in terms of their impact on the Customer Buying Journey.

CHAPTER 7

STRAND 4: BUYING STYLE

T HE FOURTH STRAND of the Customer Buying Journey DNA, and certainly the most underrated and misunderstood, is the *buying style*. Though often guessed at, this component is rarely discussed, and then only anecdotally with little or no sound foundation. This is because, to the best of my knowledge, no one has ever fundamentally investigated, analyzed, and defined buying style. I'm not talking about personal behavior here—for example, someone buying cautiously or flamboyantly. I'm talking about the very specific and invariably consistent manner in which people and their organizations go about their purchasing.

Seemingly never straightforward, the buying style and its importance became more and more apparent to us as we talked with more buyers. We were continually trying to determine what led customers to buy in certain ways, as we were faced with a seemingly insurmountable number of variables. However, through our research and repeated analysis, we eventually compressed the many variables down to just two polarized scales that we now use to determine the buying style: choice versus value and solution versus product.

I can't overemphasize the importance of these two scales, as you will see when I discuss strategy, but for now, let's stick with the question of how customers buy. First, I will explore the two polarized scales. Then I will bring them together to create the Four-Quadrant (4Q) Buying Style model, *what I now know to be arguably the most powerful means of analyzing and thus discovering, how people buy*. Once I have defined the 4Q, I will then come back and see how it explains the buying style for *anyone buying anything*. You must resist the temptation to move across the divide to consider the strategy and approach for sales and marketing—that will come later. For now, let's consider the buying style from the buyer's point of view.

CHOICE VERSUS VALUE

The first of the two polarized scales is choice versus value. We chose these words as we found them the most representative of what customers told us, but they are just labels. More important than these actual words is what's in the customer's mind, and this perception is key *because it is a perception.*

When buying on the *choice* end of the scale, the buyer perceives that they indeed have a choice: they can buy from Company A or Company B, or they can buy Product X or Product Y. At the end of the day, they know they may buy from Company A because the price is lower or Product Y because they can get it delivered in one day instead of three, but they approach their buying journey believing they have a choice.

At the other end of the scale, you have *value*, where the buyer perceives that one particular company or offering provides a unique value to them. In fact, they believe it is so unique and of such value that it will drive them to acquire that offering or buy from that company time and time again. Value can come in many different manifestations, but whatever it may be, the buyer perceives it to be valuable enough to compel them to buy that offering without due consideration for the alternatives. In fact, they rarely perceive any worthy alternatives.

Let's explore this value equation a little deeper. Personally, I bought three BMWs in a row without considering another marque. On the other hand, my wife bought four Hondas the same way. Who was right? We both

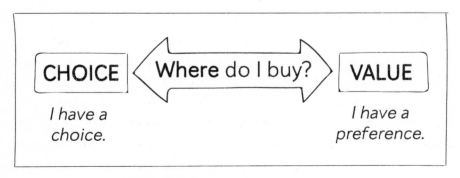

ILLUSTRATION 7.1. Buying style: Where do I buy?

were. I valued the handling and engineering of the BMW, while she valued the low maintenance cost and high resale value of the Honda without a care for how it went around corners or how the doors sounded when they closed. However, we were both buying on the value side of the equation but buying quite different offerings for quite different reasons.

Let's expand this thought. A company might continue to buy insurance from a given broker due to the perception that this person is familiar with their business and has provided excellent service. When asked, they will often say that they "value the business relationship," but what does that really mean? The real value is the knowledge that particular broker has of their business and the service she has provided over a significant length of time. This underscores that buying style is based on perception. That perception may be logical and based on deep analysis, or it may simply be a gut feeling. Either way, the perception in the mind of the buyer is no less strong.

In the case of this insurance broker, the customer perceives it would be difficult for an alternative broker to quickly and easily understand their business, which could result in a reduced level of service. This may be false, but the customer perceives it to be true. Or maybe the customer simply believes it would be too aggravating to find another broker. In either case, they remain with the same broker, buying on the value side of the axis because they don't want the perceived cost, time, and risk of searching for and going with someone else.

So the value that drives someone to buy a particular offering without considering possible alternatives can be many things. Perhaps it offers a certain feature or functionality, perhaps they have experienced a relationship or level of service, or maybe they rate the expertise of a certain supplier as unique. Interestingly enough, it might also be the price.

Price is an intriguing component of the buying journey because it is usually associated with a commodity style of purchase that would most often be at the choice end of the scale. It is frequently surprising to our clients that we list price as a possible factor at the value end of the scale. This happens when the customer views a particular brand as always having the "best price." Many people will shop at Costco due to the perception that they offer the best prices; however, they rarely comparison shop. Such believers in the brand, even when shown that particular items cost less in other stores, may put that down to one-offs and continue to shop at their chosen outlet with the perception that, generally speaking, the "price is right."

Once again, I can't emphasize enough how this is a polarized scale. Buyers either believe they have a *choice* for what they require or believe a unique *value* is associated with a particular offering, resulting in them buying it without seriously considering alternatives.

SOLUTION VERSUS PRODUCT

The second of the two polarized scales again deals with the buyer's *perception* of what is actually required. On the *solution* side of the equation, the buyer knows they need to enter into a buying journey and acquire something, but they are unsure precisely what it is they require. They will be looking for someone to advise them on their acquisition. In essence, they have a problem and are looking for a solution. It may be that they lack the knowledge or expertise to know what they want or they simply don't have the time to find out what is required.

At the other end of this polarized scale, you have the buyer who knows exactly what *product* they need. While they may require a number of products and services, they perceive they have the knowledge and expertise to determine exactly what they need. Once again, there is no middle ground—either the buyer perceives they know what they need or they want help in determining what they need.

Take somebody buying new tires for his car. The solution buyer goes to his favorite tire supplier or the dealer where he bought his car and simply tells them he needs new tires. There may be some discussion about brands

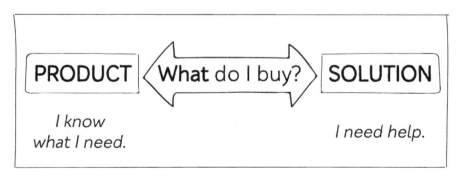

ILLUSTRATION 7.2. Buying style: What do I buy?

or sizes, but the buyer is essentially going with the supplier's recommendations for providing a solution. The product buyer knows exactly the brand, size, and tread pattern of tire he needs and will therefore go directly to acquire that offering. He may well shop around to see who can provide him with the best price, or he may go to a favorite and trusted provider, but again, he knows exactly what he wants.

One possibly confusing approach to buying is where the buyer wants to self-educate. They deliberately set out to understand their options and then make the decision themselves on what they should acquire. They may have the appearance of a solution buyer, but that is not the case. The solution buyer outsources the decision of what to buy to someone else. It is never their intent to develop the knowledge or expertise required to understand the alternatives and make the decision as to what to buy. They essentially rely on someone they consider to be an expert. The individual who sets out to develop the knowledge and expertise they perceive as necessary is a product style of buyer.

Go to the local hardware store and you will see this in action. Two people have an ailing air conditioner. The classic product buyer knows exactly what she needs; she goes to the appropriate aisle, collects the required parts, and heads to the checkout. The uninformed product buyer is relatively ignorant of the task and thereby seems like a solution buyer, but he has decided to self-educate. He asks all kinds of questions, discusses the symptoms, reviews alternatives, and gleans the knowledge and expertise he needs before buying the necessary parts and tools. What would an actual solution buyer do? The true solution buyer would call the local HVAC servicing company.

THE FOUR-QUADRANT (4Q) BUYING STYLE MODEL

A very interesting thing now happens when you join these two polarized scales together in the classic four cardinal points of a compass format, as shown in illustration 7.3.

Of course, nothing happens until "What to buy" meets "Where to buy," so let's locate the elements and label the quadrants (illustrations 7.3 and 7.4) to show the complete 4Q Buying Style model.

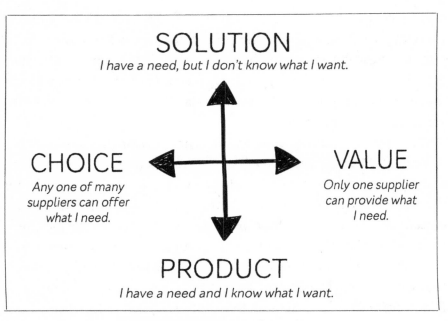

ILLUSTRATION 7.3. Buying style: 4Q elements

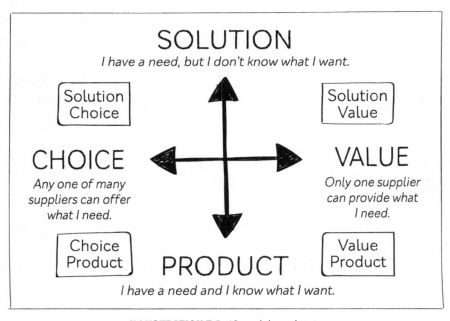

ILLUSTRATION 7.4. 4Q model quadrants

And to make this a little easier to follow and understand, let's replace the labels with taglines in illustration 7.5 to add a little personality to each quadrant. Now let's look at each one in detail.

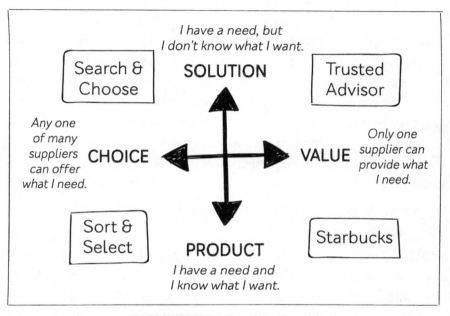

ILLUSTRATION 7.5. Complete 4Q model

BOTTOM LEFT: CHOICE/PRODUCT, "SORT AND SELECT"

In this quadrant, the buyer perceives they know exactly what they need and they have a choice of potential suppliers or offerings. We usually find the classic commodity purchase in this segment. It can also feature the style of buying we refer to as "RFP Land," where the buyer can simply set off various suppliers against one another, often via a request for proposal (RFP) to find the best choice. It may not simply be the price; other factors could come into play, such as delivery, overall terms and conditions, or other factors. None of these factors—at least at this step of the buying journey—is seen as being unique and/or valuable enough to cause the buyer to gain an enduring preference for any particular supplier or offering.

TOP RIGHT: VALUE/SOLUTION, "TRUSTED ADVISOR"

In the diametrically opposite quadrant—and as such a totally opposite buying style—you see the buyer that knows they need help acquiring a solution but also has a favored company or individual to turn to in order to gain assistance and acquire the required offerings. Maybe this is the need for a revised insurance policy, and they turn to their trusted broker, whom they perceive has a unique and valuable knowledge about their business on which they can then base their recommendation.

Or perhaps it is a company looking for help with their IT infrastructure, so they approach a consulting company on whom they have relied for several years. In this buying style, they simply turn to that company to recommend and probably undertake the work required to meet their needs. In this way, they outsource the decisions about what they need to their supplier. This type of relationship is often known as the "trusted advisor"—ironically a term that is likely the most misused in all of sales and selling. However, in this case, it is an apt and accurate description of the buying style.

TOP LEFT: SOLUTION/CHOICE, "SEARCH AND CHOOSE"

In this buying style, you'll find a buyer that knows they need help in figuring out what is required, but at the same time, they perceive they have a choice in terms of whom they turn to. An example would be someone who has come into a sizeable inheritance or won the lottery. While this rather nice windfall doesn't offer them financial independence, they have never had such an asset. They know they need assistance in minimizing income tax and investing their newfound wealth, but they perceive that many accountants and wealth managers could help them. Their buying journey may comprise an hour on Google looking for highly rated individuals in their area and then calling them to see who could meet with them right away.

BOTTOM RIGHT: PRODUCT/VALUE, "STARBUCKS"

This buying style is typified by the buyer who knows exactly what they want and also has a preference for a particular supplier or offering that they perceive offers them a unique value. As discussed, this unique value can come in many forms. We like to call this the "Starbucks" quadrant because, in the United States and elsewhere, the Starbucks brand has achieved dizzying heights of "owning" a quadrant and a segment of the market.

For those whose perception (or should I say belief) is entrenched in the Starbucks promise, their buying journey goes something like this: "It's 7 a.m., and I know I need coffee. I don't need anyone to consult with or advise me—I need coffee! I'm off to Starbucks." These buyers are quite willing to drive blocks out of their way, stand in a long line, and go through a complex ordering process in what seems to some like a foreign language in order to get what is (to them, anyway) a singularly special cup of coffee.

4Q IN THE REAL WORLD

The four quadrants of the 4Q Buying Style model comprise the two polarized scales of choice versus value and product versus solution and clearly demonstrate how the buyer perceives their buying journey. This perception is personal and individualized. Some buyers will approach the very same buying journey with a different buying style. To show this better, let's go back to that person buying new tires.

BUYER A: SORT AND SELECT

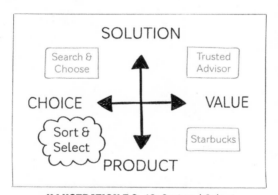

ILLUSTRATION 7.6. 4Q: Sort and Select

Buyer A has done his research online and knows exactly what tires he wants for his car. He then searches for different options, perhaps even using the suppliers that sell the tires online and ship them to a local dealer, who will install them for a fixed and known price. Price is usually the deciding factor, though not always.

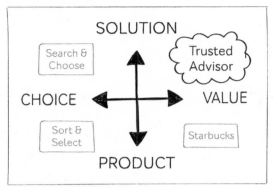

ILLUSTRATION 7.7. 4Q: Trusted Advisor

Buyer B drives to her dealer or favorite tire shop, which she trusts, likely based on a history of service. She simply asks them to select what they think is best for the car, install the new tires, and give her a call when it's ready to pick up.

BUYER C: SEARCH AND CHOOSE

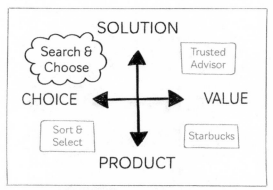

ILLUSTRATION 7.8. 4Q: Search and Choose

Buyer C knows he needs new tires but doesn't know the details of what he needs. He calls around to the local service centers to see who could help him that afternoon. Once he's found someone who can help him that day, he drives over there and goes with what is recommended.

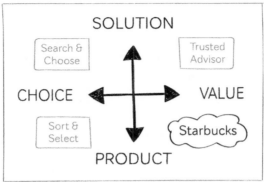

ILLUSTRATION 7.9. 4Q: Starbucks

Buyer D knows what she wants and has a tire shop she's been going to for years. She calls them and tells them she wants a full set of Goodyear Eagle F1 Asymmetric 225/40R18 tires. She then makes an appointment to go over there when the tires arrive and they have the time to install them.

Four different individuals buy the same offering four different ways. No one is right or wrong; they simply have four different buying styles. This doesn't imply that each and every offering can be bought in all four ways, but hopefully it serves to underscore that there are four distinct buying styles and the perception of the buyer dictates their buying style.

CHANGING BUYING STYLE DURING THE BUYING JOURNEY

Buyers don't use the language of the 4Q model. They don't say, for example, "I approach my buying as a top-right buyer." They do, however, use a language that makes the buying style very easy to decode. They will say things such as "I knew I needed new tires, so I went to the dealer down the road that I've been going to for years. We know them, and they've looked after us really well." It's not difficult to decode the buying style for a buyer, but one point of interest is how the buying style can change over the course of the Customer Buying Journey.

We had a client who was in the business of implementing a particular type of application based on the Oracle platform. They had specialized in just this one area and only on Oracle. They had a rigorous approach to software development and had significantly invested in training their team in their own approaches and methods. This had paid off handsomely for them, as they had a great track record in an industry notorious for cost and time overruns.

Almost all their clients had approached the buying journey believing they had a choice. They perceived that many software developers could do the job and would ultimately issue a competitive RFP to see which company's bid was the most favorable. However, as they explored the options, they would invariably come across our client. Once buyers started talking to them about their approaches, they clearly stood out from the crowd.

We heard time and time again how they had "found" this company that only focused on this one area, that they had a great approach to software development and a broad range of very happy customers who were only too happy to provide glowing testimonials. The more the buyer understood about their approach, the more our client became viewed as unique in what they did. We repeatedly heard from their buyers that they found no viable alternatives, and in most cases, they didn't even bother with a competitive RFP. In this case, as the buyer moved through their buying journey, they shifted from their early perception of being a choice buyer to become a value buyer.

In the same way, buyers can shift across either of the two polarized scales and around the 4Q model. We worked with a very large software company that sells drafting and design software. Their buyers were very well informed and generally bought their software as a product buyer. They knew what they wanted and were able to dictate to the various distributors exactly what they wanted and would then shop based on price. However, as the software application moved from two-dimensional to three-dimensional functionality, an interesting thing happened. The new software functionality generated more than a few differences in its use and application. For example, designers would now be able to use digital software for 3D design, a much more complex process. Furthermore, what these companies could then offer their own customers changed, as they could now offer 3D rendering and modeling.

Overall, this meant that work processes needed to change across their business, users needed additional training, and their very business and what they did for their customers experienced a significant upheaval. All of a sudden, buying software was no longer a simple case of buying some new licenses. Customers moved from product buyers to solution buyers as they now looked for a distributor who could help them with a series of support, training, and consulting services. They needed to rely on their distributor's knowledge of how to best use the software application in their business and indeed what products and services they needed to best leverage this new capability. Because of this possible change in buying style across the buying journey, we always recommend that people examine the predominant buying style at each step of the buying journey.

MARKET DEFINITION ALERT

It is very important here to emphasize a core belief of mine derived from our years of research. We find that for a given market when buying a particular offering, there is a predominant and predictable buying style for each step of the buying journey. As previously stated, we see *the definition of a market as being buyers with a similar buying DNA.* While this may seem a bit esoteric when discussing buyers and their styles and habits, it becomes a very clear and elemental factor on the other side of the great divide when we look at marketing and selling to these buyers. It is important to reflect on this; I am saying that if two buyers look to acquire the same offering but have different buying styles, they represent two distinct markets.

Let's go back to the example of buying car tires. Buyers who know what they want and shop based on price (i.e., choice/product) and those who take their cars to a dealer and ask them to put on new tires (solution/value) are not considered a singular market. Obviously, both types of buyers are buying car tires, and they may even be the same brand and size, but the buying journey DNA is different. They have a differing buying style and quite probably different buying steps in the overall buying journey, and this in itself is enough to categorize them as a different market. Although there is often confusion and perhaps ambiguity in defining a market, I always come back to the foundational rule that *buyers within a market, when buying a particular offering, will buy in remarkably similar ways.* In other words, they share the same buying journey DNA.

KEY PLAYERS WITH DIFFERENT BUYING STYLES

As you saw when I discussed the *key players* component of the DNA, in the majority of situations, more than one person is involved in the overall

Customer Buying Journey. This then introduced another area of the DNA that needs to be decoded: due to different perceptions, different individuals within a given buying journey might adopt differing buying styles. Although we see this dynamic in a number of different ways, one of the most fascinating areas is in the strategic sourcing of products and services by the materials management or professional procurement group of an organization.

The background and role of these individuals lead them to highly desire that every Customer Buying Journey ultimately becomes a product/choice decision. They want to see every acquisition go into RFP Land so that they can dictate what they want to a series of potential suppliers and make the decision based on price, delivery, service, and perhaps a few other quantified variables. They put each and every requirement out to tender, and the vetted and invited suppliers then get to bid against each other. The eventual winner is then the supplier who bids at the lowest price.

This is all well and good when there really is parity among the various suppliers, but perhaps the VP of engineering at the company perceives one supplier as more innovative and wants to forge a more strategic relationship. Perhaps this VP of engineering sees that this particular supplier could assist with future research and development and that he could leverage their know-how. Now you have a key player in the equation who views the buying journey as possibly a solution/value buying style. In this case, you now have two individuals with diametrically different positions in the 4Q model. You will see what this means to the supplier when I show some specific instances of strategy and market engagement in our two case studies, but for now, I want to stress how different players engaged in the same buying journey might have differing buying styles.

To resolve the complexities of having key players with differing buying styles, we use the term *predominant* buying style—defined as the style the organization is most likely to adopt. In the example above, if the procurement department usually issues a competitive RFP regardless of what the VP of engineering may wish, then the predominant buying style is choice/product, at least for that step in the overall buying journey. If, on the other hand, the VP of engineering usually convinces the organization of the value of a strategic relationship with a particular supplier, then the predominant buying style would be value/solution.

MARKET DEVELOPMENT

It is important to note how markets develop, or what we call the "natural gravity" of the 4Q model. When a new category of offering is launched, it tends to be bought in the top-right, solution/value quadrant. This is simply because, as a new category of offering, the buyer does not understand it very well; therefore, they would tend to buy on the solution side of the product/solution axis. Furthermore, as a new category of offering, there is likely only one provider, which then implies that buyers would buy as value and not choice.

Two dimensions of the gravity will usually end up with that category of offering falling from the top right quadrant to the bottom left. First, as other companies emerge on the scene with comparative offerings, buyers will have a choice that will move them from the right-hand side of the model to the left. Then, as buyers gain more knowledge and experience of the offering, they will tend to move from the top to the bottom of the quadrants as they move from being solution buyers to product buyers.

When our own clients explore this concept of market development and the gravitational forces across the 4Q model, they are tempted to suggest that buyers are somewhere in a transitional state, and thus they plot them in different places in the 4Q model. But this cannot happen. Although a market can be in a transitionary state—for example, moving from value to choice—an individual buyer cannot be. Each axis of the 4Q model is polar: a buyer is in either one state or the other. It is not possible for an individual buyer to have a buying style somewhere in between on the axis—either they believe they have a choice or they don't, and either they believe they know what they want or they don't.

WHAT'S RIGHT AND WHAT'S WRONG

It is very important to firmly establish that no buyer or buying style is right or wrong or more or less desirable. In our work, we often see a tendency to classify one buying style as superior to others, but this is not the case. When I turn to strategy, you will see how mistakes can be and often are made in terms of aligning the selling to the buying. But at this stage, you want to make sure that there is never an impression that one buying style is better than another.

TAKEAWAYS

⇒ There are two scales on which buyers will make their decisions of what to buy and who to buy from. Both are polarized binary scales with nothing in between.

⇒ The buying style is based on the following buyer *perceptions*:

- ◦ Either buyers believe they either have a choice of supplier /offerings or they believe there is only one particular supplier/offering that possesses a unique attribute that would cause them to buy it over any alternative.

- ◦ Either buyers believe they either possess the knowledge and expertise to determine what to buy or they believe they need the assistance of a supplier.

⇒ These two polar scales, when combined, give rise to the 4Q model, which defines the four styles in which buyers buy.

⇒ Different individuals with differing buying styles may buy the same offering, *in which case they are different markets*.

⇒ The buying style may change as a buyer moves through their Customer Buying Journey, but in most cases, this change occurs in a consistent and predictable manner.

⇒ The buying style for key players in a single buying journey may be different.

⇒ There is no right or wrong buying style.

CHAPTER 8

STRAND 5: VALUE DRIVERS

T HE NEXT STRAND of the Customer Buying Journey DNA to be decoded and mapped is the *value drivers*. These are the reasons someone would actually get into, and progress through, a buying journey. Value drivers are the pot of gold; they provide the motivation to start and the fuel to continue and successfully complete the buying journey.

NEEDS VERSUS WANTS

When we work with our clients, value drivers represent an area where they are most tempted to cross the divide over to the sales and marketing supply side of the equation and start thinking about what is being offered and why someone should need it. But at this point, you must firmly put and keep yourself in the buyers' shoes and consider what they want. When talking about the supply side, I will use the common term *value propositions* to describe why a supplier believes a prospective customer would want their offering. Here, however, the focus is on the buyer's perspective, so I will therefore use the term *value drivers*.

Before leaving the topic of the supplier's view versus the buyer's view, let's briefly touch on another important aspect. When we talk to buyers about what they hope to gain from entering into their buying journey, we hear what they *want*. And what they want may be very different from what they *need*. I myself might want another glass of wine, but perhaps what I need is a healthier diet. Keep in mind that buyers are motivated more by what they want than what they need. Wants and needs may indeed come together; however, when we talk to buyers, it is clear that their perception of what they want drives their motivation for investing in a buying journey.

THE PARADOX WITH STRATEGIC VALUE DRIVERS

You might think that when we talk to buyers who share with us their motivations for buying that we would hear strategic "high-order" objectives such as their desire for their company to become more globally competitive or reduce costs across their operations. This, however, is rarely the case. Instead, those strategic objectives very quickly cascade down into various initiatives becoming a series of projects or more tactical goals. Let's look at an example of this that we came across in the health care field.

A hospital executive had decided, and for good reason, that she was going to focus on and invest in the reduction of hospital-acquired infections (HAIs)—surely a major-league, high-order objective. However, at the same time as the hospital's executive committee sanctioned this action, they also agreed that three initiatives, or subsets, would come under the banner of reducing HAIs. Those three initiatives were ensuring that all staff adopted a rigorous hand cleansing process, replacing the HVAC system with a new one that included active filtration, and introducing a policy to ensure the appropriate use of antibiotics.

These three initiatives then cascaded down again into a series of more tactical goals. For example, they implemented the hand-cleansing initiative through a survey of current practices, a series of communications educating both staff and patients on the risks of incorrect or incomplete hand cleansing, and a series of posters displayed across the facility. When we asked buyers why they were looking to acquire certain offerings, they did not say that their value driver was to reduce hospital-acquired infections. They said they wanted to educate staff on the risks of insufficient hand cleansing or inform patients that it's okay to ask staff if they had washed their hands.

Now consider if this hospital group had not known what to do but had just agreed that they needed to focus on HAI reduction. They then may have entered into a buying journey looking for a supplier that could help them achieve this overall goal. But this is rarely the case. In most cases, the buyer breaks down these high-order objectives into a series of more tactical initiatives, and hence the value drivers tend to be more commonly associated with these tactical initiatives than the high-order goals. And sometimes we would hear how an overall secondary initiative—such as hand cleansing—contributes to the higher-order goal, but the higher-order goal was not the real value driver for the buying journey.

The real key to decoding the value drivers is to understand exactly what the owners of the Customer Buying Journey want to gain as a result of their efforts.

Sure, they may know that what they are acquiring will ultimately contribute to a higher objective and perhaps even increase the overall value of their organization, but these are rarely the true motivators for them. In part 2 of the book, I will discuss the massive implications of this aspect of the buying journey when we switch context and look at what this means to the supplier in terms of strategy, sales, and marketing. But for now, let's stay firmly rooted in understanding how buyers buy.

VALUE DRIVERS CHANGING ACROSS THE CUSTOMER BUYING JOURNEY

Just as the other strands of the Customer Buying Journey DNA may change as a buyer goes through the stages of their journey, so can the value drivers. In many ways, a buying journey can be a voyage of discovery for the buyer. This is less the case when the buying style is in the bottom two quadrants—product as opposed to solution. In this case, the buyer usually perceives that they know what they need and is therefore less likely to gain new knowledge and have the value drivers change or evolve over the course of the buying journey. But it is important to note that even a product-style buyer can still gain new knowledge that could cause the value drivers to change or evolve and even their buying style to change.

Let's go back to an individual buying tires. Maybe he first approaches the buying journey with the perception that cost alone is his value driver. He's simply looking for the most inexpensive tires that the dealer can put on the car. In this case, let's say that he goes to the dealer and asks to have some cheap tires installed on the car. The dealer in this example is enlightened and says that while they would be happy to do so, perhaps the buyer should consider the safety and noise benefits of a more expensive tire. Perhaps they then share a credible report that rates tires in terms of their stopping distance on a wet surface and their noise level on dry pavement. At that point, the buyer has gained new knowledge. Yes, he knew tires had some differences, but he never appreciated the significance of those differences and what they could mean for his family's personal safety and comfort. All of a sudden, his value drivers may have changed from simply price to becoming a combination of price balanced against safety and comfort.

Any buying journey can be seen as a voyage of discovery, and during that journey, the value drivers are likely to change. Of course, this may well be the result of interaction with a potential supplier's sales and marketing activities, which we will look at more closely when we consider the buying equation from the other side.

FOCUSED VALUE DRIVERS

When we talk to buyers about what they hope to gain from a certain buying journey, another interesting fact emerges: they usually have only one or two real motivators. This is especially true at each end of the buying journey. When an individual or group is at the front end of their buying journey, they tend to have a clear focus on what they want. In the same way, when we talk to buyers who are close to or have made their acquisition, they have clarity about what they hope to gain. We rarely find buyers at this stage who list more than two, possibly three, value drivers. It's quite likely that if we prompt them, they may come back with a secondary list of benefits they hope to gain because of their acquisition, but they almost invariably focus on just one or two of the good things they hope to gain through their acquisition.

In the middle stages of the buying journey, there may not be such clarity, largely due to the learning that is going on. During these middle stages, the buyer is discovering new aspects of possible approaches. The scope of what they are looking for may be changing, and indeed their perception of the possibilities can change. However, as they move toward the end of the journey, a focus develops. In many ways, it has to or else confusion may reign and the buying journey could slow or stop.

TANGIBLE AND INTANGIBLE VALUE DRIVERS

When looking to understand what really motivates a buyer to start and move through a buying journey, another interesting fact emerges. Although we like to think that acquisitions always produce tangible results, we have seen many situations where buying journeys are driven as much, or even more, by intangible drivers. The list of such intangible value drivers is long and might include such things as prestige, peer pressure, or just plain curiosity. We have found examples in which the value driver for a buying journey was simply to be seen to be doing something. In this case, the results of the acquisition really didn't matter, but by entering into a buying journey and making an acquisition, stakeholders would see a level of activity that signaled progress.

Many individuals in an organizational setting are motivated to want what they think their boss wants or what will get them recognition or rewards as opposed to losing their job. And that motivation works both ways, as few people are willing to put their jobs on the line for a particular acquisition even if they sincerely believe it would be the right thing for their organization to do.

The more we talked to buyers, the more we realized the importance of some of these intangible value drivers. In conversations, they rarely surfaced, at least not at first. We would always hear the supporting reasons for a particular acquisition expressed in highly tangible and logical business terms. However, as we dug deeper into many of these cases, intangible value drivers not only started to appear but invariably played a key role in the overall Customer Buying Journey. At times, tangible, businesslike value drivers seemed more like window dressing for a somewhat nebulous buying decision in order to make it more palatable to other stakeholders in the process.

TAKEAWAYS

⇒ Value drivers motivate buyers through their Customer Buying Journey; they are what buyers hope to gain as a result of that buying journey.

⇒ The value drivers have to be sufficiently compelling to outweigh the costs, risks, and change associated with acquiring and using the offering.

⇒ Most buyers only have a few value drivers on which they base their decisions. These are the primary value drivers. Although the buyer may be aware of other benefits associated with their choice, they tend to focus and make decisions simply based on these primary value drivers.

CHAPTER 9

STRAND 6: BUYING CONCERNS

THE FINAL STRAND of the Customer Buying Journey DNA is the *buying concerns*: inhibitors that can slow down or stop a buying journey. This area arose not only from our work and research in talking to hundreds of buyers but also from talking to a like number of sellers. Understandably, the selling side was very interested in why customers weren't buying. Suppliers truly believed their offerings would deliver value to their prospective customers, yet the customers weren't buying. Invariably, their first thought was that for whatever reason, the buyers did not understand their offering and its inherent value. Yet when we talked to those potential buyers, we discovered that not only did they understand the offering, but they also believed in the value it would deliver to their organization.

I must admit that this was somewhat of an epiphany to me at the time. How could someone be aware of and even professionally evaluate an offering that would deliver value to them yet not invest in that offering? This challenged my basic understanding of sales and marketing and much of what I had learned in my sales career. It challenged my basic ideas of business.

One of the earliest examples of observing this paradox up close was when we were working with Alliance Medical (as they were called at that time). Alliance was an early entrant into the world of medical equipment reprocessing, or stringently applied reprocessing of selected used medical equipment, thereby allowing hospitals to safely and legally reuse items that would otherwise have been discarded. The cost of this service represented some 60 percent of the cost of replacement and thus could potentially save a hospital 40 percent for each use. In terms of positioning and selling, no one would fault you for thinking of this as a no-brainer. However, I well recall the CFO asking me, "Martyn, what's wrong with our sales force? All they have to do is show the hospitals that by using our service, they would save money—guaranteed. I mean, it's as if we were offering twenty-dollar bills for twelve bucks—who wouldn't buy?"

Indeed, who wouldn't? We conducted our usual market research by closely examining the buying process by talking to hospital CFOs. We asked if they believed they would save money by using our client's services. Yes, they answered. Did they believe they would reduce toxic waste? Again, yes. So based on these responses, we asked the biggie: "If you believe that by investing in this service you will reduce costs for the hospital, why don't you buy?" The answer was simple: "You have to understand that this is only one of many ways we can reduce costs."

They shared with us that they were not short of initiatives and ideas to reduce costs. And they had no doubt that one day they would indeed consider using reprocessing services, but at this particular time, they had other priorities. One CFO told us she had salespeople approaching her practically every day, and she believed that most of them had good offerings. But she and her team only had so many hours in a day, and they turned the vast majority of them away. The more we talked to buyers, the more the same story emerged. They were aware of many offerings that they believed would provide some aspect of value in return for money invested, yet for a number of reasons, they either didn't get into a buying journey or, once in, failed to make progress to a successful conclusion.

The more we looked at this challenge, the greater its significance became. We came to realize that one of the most important aspects of decoding the DNA of the Customer Buying Journey was to figure out exactly what stopped or slowed down a buying journey. While the *value drivers* provided the momentum for a buyer to move through a buying journey, the buying concerns created the drag.

The second revelation to come from this research was that in a given market, when buying a specific offering, we saw the same buying concerns among different buyers. Organization after organization were getting hung up on the same issues, all of which only reinforced our steadily evolving theory—*that buyers in a particular market, when looking to acquire a certain offering, behave in remarkably similar ways.* This only served to underscore the tremendous value of decoding the DNA of the Customer Buying Journey for a particular market.

THE NINE FACES OF BUYING CONCERNS

Once we realized the critical and disruptive influence of the buying concerns, we immediately set to work tracking and documenting these elements that slow down, impair, or even prevent the buying journey from starting in the first place. We created a catalog of all the possible barriers that could stop a customer from buying something they knew to be of value to them.

After much sifting and sorting, we were able to condense our findings into a list of nine categories. We now use this list to help decode the DNA, map the Customer Buying Journey, and serve as our overall checklist. Let's explore each one in turn.

BUYING CONCERNS

1. Process
2. Priority
3. Individual
4. Organizational
5. Alternatives
6. Business
7. Implications
8. Fit
9. Change

1. PROCESS

This category refers to the actual process—purchasing, sourcing, and so on—within a buying organization set up expressly for the acquisition of products and services. That this could be an area of concern may sound obvious or even trivial, but I can attest to it to being far from such. The potential for concern is usually parallel to the size of the buyer, as this is far more significant to larger organizations than individual buyers or small operations. While it may be stating the obvious, an organization needs a process to buy something. If there is no such process apparent to the buyer, this in itself can be a major buying concern. Factors the buyer needs to consider include who needs to be involved, how the funds are allocated, and how the acquisition will be made.

This is rarely an issue if an organization is simply looking to buy something in the same way they have bought before but now from a different supplier.

But consider if they are contemplating the acquisition of a capital item they have previously rented. Maybe the business case is there to justify the capital cost over the rental amounts, but how would the organization actually go about acquiring something of that significance? Probably the CEO or CFO would dictate this, but to the buyers themselves, it is not always apparent what the process would be. The process could appear to be so fraught with difficulty and the unknown that it simply does not seem worthwhile.

In another instance, we worked with a company that had developed a breakthrough technical textile. This particular textile had two significant qualities: first, it was antimicrobial, and second, it was liquid repellent. This textile was used to create medical scrubs—the coveralls that most health care workers wear. When comparing such scrubs to the standard textiles, it would seem once again like a no-brainer decision. But when we looked into the hospital's buying journey, among the buying concerns we found was the lack of an apparent process to buy such technically advanced health care clothing. Yes, they bought scrubs, and they had a well-defined process for that, but this didn't fit that process. The usual way we found was that they bought scrubs both as a highly commoditized item (i.e., the cheaper the better) and usually as a component of the overall laundry supply, and often even rented. The new technical scrubs were apparently not available via the established supply chain, and this became a critical buying concern that would indeed stop or slow down the buying journey.

2. PRIORITY

When talking to buyers, we found numerous examples of potential purchases that they believed would bring value, but they just weren't a priority at that time. Can those priorities be changed? Yes, but we found this to be far from common unless some unanticipated major event acts upon the company. Perhaps it is an acquisition, a merger, or external regulatory issues, but it is certainly not a wishful buyer within the company or a hungry sales rep without.

One of the factors we saw that slowed or stopped a Customer Buying Journey is a condition we describe as "fully deployed resources." When an organization is in such a state, no more time, money, or people are available for further investment. The company has already chosen and acted on its priorities and has no room for further investment, *no matter how compelling*. The sophisticated buyer is looking at not just the resources required for acquisition but also the resources required for successful adoption.

In most cases, any benefit associated with acquiring a particular offering comes not from simply acquiring it but from its successful adoption and continued use. This is one of the primary reasons you must consider the total end-to-end Customer Buying Journey and not simply the acquisition. The customer will invariably be equally or more concerned about the adoption than the acquisition. They will know if they have the capacity and resources to fully implement and adopt the offering and thus gain their return and if it is a current priority for them to do so.

3. INDIVIDUAL

This buying concern focuses on the individual who is "carrying the ball" at any stage of a buying journey. This individual may change across the steps, but every Customer Buying Journey is dependent on an individual to move it forward. Also note that this isn't necessarily what used to be termed the "decision maker"; rather, it is the person who needs to own or sponsor the journey at any particular point in the overall process. This individual needs to undertake certain activities to positively move the process forward in the organization. Those activities are wide ranging and include such aspects as the following:

- convincing others of the merits of the proposed acquisition
- approving funds
- gaining more information
- looking at alternative approaches
- creating an implementation plan
- analyzing aspects of the acquisition or use of the offering
- testing the offering
- creating a comparison of the offering to current or alternatives approaches
- handling objections across the organization
- creating and presenting a business case
- scheduling a meeting of key individuals
- *deciding to move forward* in the buying journey

The list goes on, and often overwhelmingly. And if that individual delays or fails to achieve any one of the required activities, then the buying journey can grind to a temporary or even permanent halt. It is therefore imperative that you consider this individual or set of individuals when decoding the overall buying journey. You must constantly be aware of their own personal motivations and concerns with respect to the activities they must undertake and the sponsorship they must provide. Clearly, their motivation to move the ball forward rests with their perception that the benefits gained will outweigh the effort and risk.

4. ORGANIZATIONAL

We have termed the fourth buying concern *organizational*; however, this area could equally be called *political*. These are all the political barriers, activities, objections, and concerns that are likely to come up across the organization that can slow or stop the progress of the buying journey.

A dynamic network of individuals makes buying decisions in today's world, and politics is what often happens when a group of individuals becomes involved in any activity or process. Each person is going to bring different agendas, motivations, perspectives, and perceptions. This is obviously less important when only one or two individuals are involved in a Customer Buying Journey, but that is rarely the case. Most buying journeys include a far wider array of players than at first thought.

Once again, we found that these buying concerns were common across a particular market when considering a specific offering. For example, infection prevention committees are very likely to respond in a similar way, across different hospitals, when faced with a new offering for a certain aspect of infection control. Likewise, we could see that quality control officers in manufacturing companies are likely to share similar concerns and have similar agendas when faced with changing suppliers for key components of their raw materials.

5. ALTERNATIVES

This buying concern refers to any and all alternatives an organization may consider before they move forward with a particular acquisition. This does not include alternatives for the resources used to acquire and adopt a certain offering, as those are already categorized under *priority*. This buying concern focuses only on how the buyer considers alternatives to a particular offering. The easiest to consider are obvious alternative offerings, such as competitive offerings from different suppliers. However, buyers often cast their net much wider than may be expected.

Take a buyer who may be considering the acquisition of a luxury hybrid vehicle. In this case, he may be comparing several clearly competitive alternatives. But in the end, he might decide to buy a much less expensive car—not one in the same category as the luxury hybrids but nonetheless an alternative he could live with. This is illustrative of a trend we have seen develop toward the "good enough" alternative. We have seen numerous examples of buyers who have been considering a certain offering, but at the end of their buying journey, they acquire something that could be considered of a lower quality or having less functionality. But to use their words, it was "good enough." The buyer realizes it is not at the same level of quality, functionality, or prestige, but they think it's good enough to meet their needs.

This can be confusing to suppliers, as they see what they think is an inferior offering being selected over theirs—an offering they might not even see as a competitor, but the buyer obviously viewed it as a viable alternative. I will talk further about the implications of this trend for the supplier when I switch focus from understanding how buyers buy to what suppliers can do about it.

The other alternative usually considered, albeit not always formally, is to do nothing, to stay with the status quo. It is the road not taken, and not only is this alternative often a realistic option, but it is usually an easy one as well. In this case, the buyer does not believe that the benefit is worth the risk, cost, and effort of acquisition and adoption of a new offering. Many buying journeys fail to finish simply due to the relative painlessness associated with just stopping. No, they didn't get something new and probably better, but it didn't hurt, and the price was certainly right. If the status quo is acceptable, it contributes to a lack of motivation to move forward with an alternative approach unless there is a clear gain with little risk.

6. BUSINESS

This buying concern has to do with the fiscal side of the equation—the business case. Is there a complete and compelling business reason to trigger and move forward through a Customer Buying Journey? This may be a simple back-of-the-napkin guesstimate of affordability, all the way to a formal and very comprehensive cost analysis. In all cases, the fundamental concern is if the value outweighs the cost.

Over and above (and sometimes under) the obvious facts and numbers of the business case, we often see intangibles and aspects that are harder to quantify in this equation. If, for example, an organization is to invest in a new automated process, will costs really come down? Or if a hospital invests in a new surgical robot, will more patients come to the facility? What if a company invests in a new marketing campaign—will they reach and acquire more clients? These are vitally important questions, the answers to which are most likely the key reasons for engaging in a buying journey in the first place. And they can be tough to calculate.

Sometimes we can quantify variables with credible studies and benchmarks, but customers might discount these claims for other reasons. The value gained through a certain acquisition may itself not be purely financial. If it's an acquisition that results in prestige or a "feel-good" element, it can be hard to monetize. If being the company with the best location in town or your logo on the side of the sports stadium translates into value, then that is the reward for the expenditure. And for some buyers, that soft value could well be the reward for the acquisition.

For the buying journey to successfully move forward, the business case—however arrived at—must convincingly indicate and bolster the perception that the value gained will exceed the overall cost.

7. IMPLICATIONS

This concern focuses on the implications of acquiring a certain offering—that is, what actually happens when someone buys something. There can be a litany of consequences. Will they have to change their processes or their organization? Will they need to train people? Perhaps they will need to cease doing business with an alternative supplier. Maybe they will need to change their building, their furniture, their floor plan. It is rare that someone buys something without there being downstream implications. We also discovered that usually far more implications are associated with the adoption of an offering, with greater impact on the Customer Buying Journey, than the suppliers were ever aware of.

We found that these concerns could come unannounced out of left field for what might seem trivial reasons. Consider our study of the buying journey for the adoption of a robot in a manufacturing process. For various reasons, the robot's adoption would require some basic training for many workers. But the workers could be trained in fewer than thirty minutes, and the training was quite straightforward. However, we found that in this particular market, training was a sensitive topic due to the unions usually involved, and significant funds and time had already been invested in worker training. So what may have appeared as a minor investment in time and effort translated into a buying concern that significantly slowed and almost stopped the progress of the overall buying journey.

A useful way to think about implications is to consider what the customer has to do in order to gain the ultimate reward for using the offering. Very rarely is the offering itself the complete solution. Unfortunately, the word *solution* has insidiously crept into the sales and marketing lexicon to the point of not just misuse but absurdity. I have seen kitchen sinks marketed as a "complete kitchen workstation solution." In the vast majority of cases, the "total" or "complete" solution being marketed is anything but when realistically viewed from the buyer's perspective. Taking the example of the kitchen sink from the buyer's perspective, the need to think about remodeling their kitchen, new units, electrical, hookups, plumbing, and who knows what else all have to be considered. The solution is not simply buying that new sink, no matter how much the marketers may try to tell you that it is indeed your complete solution. The complete solution must include all the aspects a buyer has to consider, acquire, and do in order to reach their hoped-for end value.

8. FIT

Fit has to do with how a potential acquisition aligns with how and what that company would usually buy. For example, if an organization embraces a cost-conscious culture and consistently looks at every way to save a dollar, then they are unlikely to buy or rent in "Class A" buildings or supply luxury hybrid company vehicles. Illustration 9.1 provides some of the major factors we observed under *fit*. As you can see, buying concerns under the heading of fit can come in many shapes and sizes, but they are usually easy to spot in any particular buying journey. The first part of the illustration deals with tangible aspects of fit and is pretty much self-explanatory. These refer to the "nuts-and-bolts" aspects of how many organizations deal with suppliers in their day-to-day workings. Some intangible aspects of fit might be a bit harder to nail down, however.

ILLUSTRATION 9.1. TANGIBLE AND INTANGIBLE ASPECTS OF FIT

TANGIBLE ASPECTS OF FIT	ONE END OF THE SCALE	THE OTHER END OF THE SCALE
Geography	Local suppliers	Global
Environment	Prioritize eco-friendly offerings	Less value placed on eco-friendly offerings
Suppliers	Like to go with a few suppliers and build long-term and strong relationships	Comfortable with embracing new suppliers
Terms of conducting business	Tend to impose how they deal with suppliers	Flexible with letting the supplier drive the transaction
Standardization	Looking for compliance with standards	Willing to put function above compliance with standards
INTANGIBLE ASPECTS OF FIT	ONE END OF THE SCALE	THE OTHER END OF THE SCALE
Risk	Low risk	Tolerant of higher risk
Life cycle	Tend to go with well-proven approaches	Actively embrace new ideas and offerings
Scope	Tend to go with a phased and small step approach	Tend to go with sweeping visions and commitments to full-scale implementation
Leadership	Happy to follow the crowd	Like to be viewed as leaders in their industry

A good starting point for understanding these intangibles is by taking a close look at the theories of market maturation, which explain much of the associated behavior allied to these aspects. The market maturation curve—and it's a classic bell curve—does a great job of categorizing buyers and how their category affects their motivation to buy or not to buy as a market develops. The concept is originally ascribed to Everett Rogers in his seminal work *Diffusion of Innovations*,[1] first published in 1962. Thanks to Rogers, we now know that different individuals are attracted to acquire new offerings in different stages of the product's life cycle. We all know people who love to get the latest technology, fashion, or fads. And you probably know others who are far more comfortable acquiring only tried and tested offerings. Rogers divided the market into five sequential categories of buyers, as outlined in illustration 9.2.

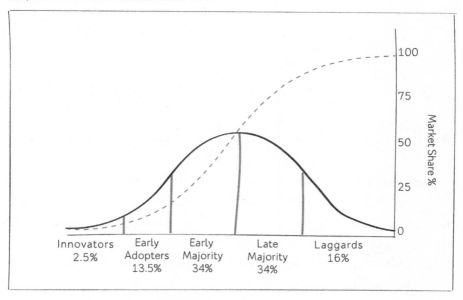

ILLUSTRATION 9.2. The market maturation curve

In the early 1990s, Geoffrey Moore, in his book *Crossing the Chasm*,[2] popularized this approach to classifying the market as it dealt with the acquisition of new software technologies. He redefined the theory as the Technology Adoption Life Cycle and showed how it specifically applies to new software products being launched into the marketplace. This theory has now been adopted and adapted by several sources and has its own Wikipedia page under the definition of "Diffusion of Innovations." Illustration 9.3 is a good amalgam of all these theories, and in it, I have illustrated the five stages of the product life cycle and, against each, the classification of the buyer and their major motivations for adopting a new offering.

ILLUSTRATION 9.3. STAGES OF THE PRODUCT LIFE CYCLE

STAGE	PRODUCT LIFE CYCLE	BUYER CATEGORY	PERCENTAGE OF MARKET	WHY THEY WOULD BUY
1.	Launch	Innovators	2.5	• to try or test something new • to discover how something works • to learn about something new
2.	Introduc-tion	Early adopter	13.5	• to help achieve their vision • to leverage something new • to do something different
3.	Growth	Early majority	34	• to meet a specific need • to gain a specific benefit
4.	Maturity	Late majority	34	• to do what everyone is doing and has proven • when the pain of not acquiring becomes greater than that perceived with acquiring
5.	Decline	Laggard	16	• when there is no other choice

If you overlay the product life cycle (as shown by the dashed line in illustration 9.2), you can see how various categories of buyers acquire these products. But products can get stuck and never make it through the full life cycle due to their lack of appeal to the next category of buyer, and indeed this point is the central theme of Moore's book. For example, the consumer-packaged goods companies will closely monitor the diffusion of their new offerings through these stages. When they believe that most of the early adopters have started buying a product branded as "New"—that is, when they have captured about 16 percent of the market—they will change their branding from emphasizing the product's newness and to emphasizing certain features and benefits they believe will appeal to the early majority.

When we talk to buyers, it is usually very apparent which category they fit into. When we ask them why they started a buying journey and what they were looking for, their language and attitude speak volumes about where they fit on this curve.

When we hear someone talk about her excitement for a new offering and how she wants to understand it, test it, and see how it works with little or no apparent focus on what she was going to do with it, we know we are talking to an *innovator*.

Early adopters behave in a similar way, though with a much greater focus on how the offering will enable them to do something new and different. The focus shifts from the offering itself to what they want to do with it. These people want to be seen as *enablers* of that vision and, in doing so, revolutionize the market, their organization, or their chosen field.

The early majority—a relatively large segment of the total market—are also known as pragmatists, and that's a great term, as they have clear and practical reasons for entering into a buying journey. They want to make something cheaper or faster or improve their current operations. While not afraid of practical change, they have little interest in the giant leaps taken by the early adopters. They are much more concerned with taking sure and positive strides toward their goals.

The late majority, also a significant percentage of the market, tend to be followers and are hesitant to take even tentative steps forward. These individuals are much more likely to buy more mature offerings; they will watch the leaders and then benefit from the early investments of others. They will buy because they see a well-tested, proven offering that will provide safe, risk-free benefits.

Finally, the *laggards* only buy because they have no option. These are people who only adopted email when they realized they were totally isolated from the rest of the world. However, they still have value drivers that are important to understand. In the case of email, they obviously needed to communicate with others, and this need drove them to finally adopt.

Here then are five different groups of buyers, none of which is a majority. So for each buyer in one of those groups who is motivated to buy a product within that segment, the vast majority of buyers are not. For instance, while an early adopter buys a product "to do something different," that same reason will turn off more than 85 percent of the total market. Positives often need to be turned on their heads; indeed, think of the second half of this book's title, *Why They Don't*, because what is a buying motivation for one is conversely a buying concern for many.

Illustration 9.3 demonstrates why the different segments of the market *will* buy something; let's look for a moment at why they *will not*.

ILLUSTRATION 9.4. STAGES OF BUYERS ACROSS MARKET MATURATION

STAGE	CATEGORY OF BUYER	PERCENTAGE OF MARKET	WHY THEY DON'T BUY
1.	Innovator	2.5	• not new and innovative enough to grab their interest • not in the area of interest
2.	Early adopter	13.5	• doesn't appear to directly enable them to do something new and different that is important to them
3.	Early majority	34.0	• not clear how it meets a specific need that they have • not proven and tested • too complex
4.	Late majority	34.0	• not already well accepted in the marketplace • seems difficult • not as simple as plug and play
5.	Laggard	16.0	• not what they have always done the way they have always done it • changes something, anything

Thus the buying concern of fit is extremely important to understand. I will explore what to do about this in part 2 of the book, but for now, like the other elements of buying concerns, the aspect of fit can often be a major factor in defining the target market.

9. CHANGE

Change is the final buying concern, and it can be deadly; this is potential deal-breaker territory. This buying concern has to do with the change that will occur, or at least *the perception of change that will occur*, due to the adoption of the new offering.

Change can come in many guises, from a change in workflow to change in the organization. Despite so many people declaring how they love change, even thrive on it, the fact is that most people fear change. And adopting a new offering—even if it is as simple as just switching a supplier of a commodity product—spells change. However, buyers will rarely declare (admit?) that they are hesitating to buy due to the apparent change they or their organizations will need to endure. They are far more likely to raise what we call "objections of convenience." They may well assert that the price is too high, that they don't have the budget, or that this isn't a good time to buy, but the real root cause of their hesitation is really the fear of change.

We worked with a company that sold a particular type of industrial pump that was being positioned in their specific market against a market leader who had a dominant market share. This pump was undeniably superior and usually cost close to 20 percent less. Although the packaging and usability of the pump were very similar, the operating buttons—all two of them—were on the side rather than on the front of the pump. When people tried the new pump against the traditional market leader, it was perhaps surprising to hear the amount of concern about the positioning of the buttons. To be fair, it did mean that users couldn't walk casually past the pump and see the position of the buttons, but we're really only talking about a quick look to view the buttons on the side. Interestingly, the feedback they gave to the supplier was more in terms of "people don't like them" rather than to admit to something as trivial as the button placement. The root cause of the buying concern was simply the change that people were experiencing in using the pump.

Trivial or not, if people have to change their workflow or do things differently, there is typically an exponentially greater buying concern in the overall buying journey. Some of these concerns are understandable and valid, while others are simply the result of people not wanting to change what they do and how they do it.

It's important not to simply put all this down to people's reluctance to embrace change, because an organization often has very valid reasons for not being ready to endure change. It may be that the organization has just been subjected to significant changes. Perhaps the organization is new and needs to establish some foundational values and ways of working before being subjected to further change. It may be that previous changes were unsuccessful, resulting in more work or a failure to gain the expected rewards.

It doesn't matter if the reasons are valid or imaginary, proven or perceived—the change that an organization thinks it will have to endure due to the acquisition and adoption of a new offering is the buying concern that can significantly slow or stop the Customer Buying Journey.

IMPLICATIONS VERSUS CHANGE

Understandably, we sometimes see confusion between these two categories of buying concerns. When an organization is considering a particular offering, there are downstream implications associated with that acquisition, and there is the change that such an acquisition will lead to. These could be one and the same, but it is very important to discern these as two separate categories of buying concern.

We have defined the difference as follows. Implications are what buyers have to consider when they are in the buying process for a particular offering in order to get what they want from the purchase. These tangibles need to be put into place. Changes, on the other hand, are the softer aspects that will need to happen, such as changes in how people use a particular offering or go about their day-to-day activities. Implications are objective, and change is more subjective—the human side of the equation.

The value in categorizing these two similar buying concerns separately is that they exhibit very different behaviors in the overall buying journey. Implications can be listed by the buyer and most often are. They are, for the most part, highly tangible and can be considered in a logical and objective manner. Changes, on the other hand, are subjective and far more emotional. They are rarely fully explored and are often neither logical nor objective.

For instance, we noticed that in the buying journeys of smaller companies looking for an alternative provider of professional services—perhaps an accountant or an insurance broker—there is an unpleasant downstream requirement. If you go with an alternative provider, you'll have to fire your existing provider. Now, you could consider this buying concern as either an implication or a change. In the first case, if you go with an alternative provider, there is an implication that you terminate the contract with your existing provider. Or considering it the other way, there is a buying concern that the change requires you to fire the existing individual. We found that many small companies continue to do business with someone who they know is providing less-than-acceptable service simply because they do not want to go through the perceived trauma associated with terminating the incumbent. This is illogical, as time and time again we found that they knew perfectly well that the new provider would do a better job, but they simply couldn't face the change process of firing their existing provider. For these reasons, we saw this particular buying concern as change rather than an implication.

TAKEAWAYS

⇒ Buying concerns slow down or stop progress within the Customer Buying Journey.

⇒ Buying concerns are the opposite of the value drivers, and for a Customer Buying Journey to conclude successfully, the value drivers must outweigh the buying concerns.

⇒ There are nine categories of significant buying concerns.

⇒ Some buying concerns are highly tangible and objective, while others are intangible, subjective, and emotional.

⇒ Buyers can hide behind the more tangible concerns to disguise their concerns in other areas.

⇒ Buyers don't always articulate or even fully analyze all the buying concerns; they simply slow down or stop in a buying journey.

COMING UP: TWO CASE STUDIES

Chapters 10 and 12 present two detailed case studies, each one followed by a full analysis in chapters 11 and 13. Please note that both of these studies are fictitious. Although they have been written to reflect real-life scenarios, the companies referred to as the supplier and the buyer in each study do not exist.

As you read the narrative of the two case studies of organizations buying, consider the buying journey DNA. You may even want to make notes on the triggers, the steps of the buying journey, key players, buying style, value drivers, and of course the buying concerns.

CHAPTER 10

CASE STUDY 1

DiaNascent: A BUYER'S TALE

DiaNascent **GLOBAL INC.** (DGI) is a large manufacturer of diagnostic and medical measurement devices. They specialize in instruments that have become everyday hospital and advanced health-care items: EKG machines, heart rate monitors, and the like. They don't do a lot of research and are not really into bringing new and innovative devices to the market. Rather, they specialize in the large-scale manufacturing and supply of these devices to a worldwide market. Not that long ago, DiaNascent had to go shopping.

Eileen Williams is the senior program manager at DiaNascent and has been with them for twelve years. She started her career as a business analyst, but after a few years, she decided to go back to school and get a master's degree. After graduating with her MBA, she joined DiaNascent and has held several positions across the organization.

She is proud of her company as she explains, "Unless you're the type of person who actually notices the brand names on some of those machines they hook you up to when you're in the hospital, you probably haven't heard of us. But trust me, we're a player out there, and I—and my frequent-flyer miles—can personally vouch for that 'global' bit in our name. Where we invest, and where I believe we bring innovation, is in the process of integration and global logistics, which enables us to assemble, test, integrate, and supply our products around the world. We focus on bringing affordable technology to third-world and emerging countries. We sell through a series of large distributors that tend to have a significant market share in the various geographical segments they serve. Our overall operation relies on being able to source or build components across the globe and then package and distribute them to their geo-specific markets. I make it no secret that I like what we do, and I think we help a lot of people."

Eileen is an executive at DiaNascent. She reports directly to the CIO, Alf Witherspoon, who in turn reports to the CEO. Eileen is widely viewed as the 2-IC in the IT organization and seems likely to take over the CIO role, as there's talk of Alf moving on in the not-too-distant future. She is widely liked throughout the organization as a great manager and leader, she's well organized, and she understands a lot about how DGI works. She wasn't joking about the "Global bit," as her work involves a lot of travel. The upside is that this has enabled her to gain a hands-on understanding of the different areas of the organization and the different cultures it operates within. She understands that different local needs exist across the different geographies but also the need for consistent approaches wherever possible.

The projects that Eileen has previously been involved with have all had good track records. She delegates well, takes a keen interest in her team's progress, and always supports them. At the same time, she expects to be fully kept in the loop and advised of any areas that may become problems. She's a good communicator, a good listener, and not afraid of the hard decisions when they need to be made. Not surprisingly, she will not tolerate poor performance: "Most recently I have taken on the responsibility of better integrating and managing our Global Warehousing and Logistics systems. We are a $4 billion operation with major centers in Europe, Asia, and the Americas—overall, we have nine hubs globally. Some three years ago, Ezra Padgett, our senior vice president for operations, commissioned a benchmarking study, as he had voiced some concerns that our overall processes were getting outdated. One of the big global consulting companies undertook a five-month study and confirmed that suspicion, and then some."

As a bit of a corporate backstory, it was widely rumored across the organization that the consult was actually a strategy of Padgett's to gain the funds and resources for a major project he had been talking about for a few years. People used words like *hobbyhorse* and *legacy*, but as Padgett had been one of the three founders of DiaNascent, people always listened to and usually heeded him. An ex-military man (no stars, but most of the other brass) with both a legal and accounting background, he had provided a much-needed element of gravitas to the start-up of DiaNascent Technologies (as it was known at the time), and he was the logical choice to run the company's operations. So it was with his interest, though not overtly so, that the company commissioned the consulting study.

But the apple cart was truly upset when the report came back. It clearly illustrated that things were much worse than Padgett had thought and, though he wished it otherwise, had said. It was a potential two-edged sword indeed. While it justified the cost of the study, it also brought into question the very competence of the organization to fall so far behind in its strategic approaches. However, to Padgett's credit, he quickly grasped the situation, because more importantly, the report enabled DiaNascent to pinpoint and prioritize the areas that represented their biggest opportunities—that is, the areas where they either had screwed up or were falling behind.

Eileen picks up the thread: "When the study was presented to our global operating executive group, they commissioned a cross-functional team representing all hubs to create a five-year plan to move us into the future, and I was appointed to head up the team. The first challenge was that the executive group wanted an initial preliminary plan and budget within sixty days. Needless to say, there was a lot of screaming and kicking, but when the dust settled, we all buckled down and got to it. An overall plan with four phases was duly created, agreed upon, and presented to the executive group. Now we had to find the money to pay for it."

Enter Dave Metzler, finance. Dave has been at DiaNascent for four years and reports directly to the controller. He was assigned to the Global Warehousing and Logistics project from the start and worked alongside Eileen to assemble the overall budget. Says Dave, "I definitely remember the challenges we had with the budget for the new system. It was a big project and represented an important strategic initiative for the company. But we were confident that the investment would reduce overall operating costs by 14 percent and keep us competitive in an ever more challenging industry.

"Basically, we had been falling behind some of our competitors for years, but our customers stayed with us, probably due to our reputation for quality and reliability. But that can only take you so far. That consultant's report had been benchmarked across the industry and clearly put our global operating practices under the spotlight. Eileen and I put together a five-year plan that showed what the total investment would have to be, and we were able to see a payback within that time period. Like I said, we really didn't have a choice; we had to update our systems."

Eileen brings us up to date. "Right now, we are about to complete phase 2 and move into the initial acquisition and rollout of the new software platform to support the vision for our global operations. The total budget for this phase is some $18 million, but it is amazing how quickly that can be consumed. During this phase, we dedicated a great deal of time to selecting the software application we would implement across the globe. It really came down to a choice of two—both big players and both with many successful reference sites—and we chose to go with Syncron International AB. So take that as the background and the context for how we started the second part of our buying journey—to find a company to help us implement the Syncron software."

A BUYING JOURNEY

Interestingly enough, although they were into the second year of the overall project, they hadn't really given much thought to how they would implement the software. Says Eileen, "Sure, we knew it wouldn't be trivial, but at the same time, we also knew that this is a road well traveled. There was no shortage of companies that do this kind of work. We talked to a few in the early stages of the project just to get some budgetary estimates, and we also talked to some software application providers, including Syncron, about how they would approach the job. So we had allocated $1 million of the budget to cover this phase and put the initial time required at about eight months. That seemed reasonable, and we had other fish to fry at the time, so we were hoping that this estimate would not be too far off the mark."

But now the time had come to turn these speculative plans into reality. Eileen delegated the task to one of her IT project managers, Sue Harris, to take a sweep of the marketplace and then report back on her findings. It was also pretty much implied that barring any unforeseen reasons, Harris would inherit the project and make sure that everything came together.

Sue is a project manager by job description and a driver by nature. Detail oriented, she has a great memory and is known for always being on top of her projects. Suppliers sometimes find her a bit distant, as she is so focused on her projects and has zero time for "sales talk." She is very straightforward but never forgets that suppliers often try to spin things their way. Sometimes her team members find her a bit scratchy, as she tends to be very firm with what she wants and expects. But overall, she works well across the organization. She always tries to make sure that the right people are involved in the right way—and at the same time, she won't let herself get sidetracked or involved with people when there is no clear value in doing so. And nobody questions her results. Sue and Eileen have worked together on several earlier projects and have developed a very good relationship. Eileen trusts her, and in turn, Sue knows exactly how to work with Eileen: keep her in the loop and out of the details. Sue's priorities are simple: stay focused and get the results.

Here's Sue: "I have worked at DGI for five years now. I'm IT to the bone, and I've managed a number of large-scale projects. Issuing RFIs [requests for information] and evaluating suppliers is something I've done a lot of. I don't mind some of the work, as it keeps me up to date with what's out there and who is doing what, but I have to be honest—a lot of it is just grinding away at proposals and spreadsheets. But, hey, we've got a project here, and Eileen asked me to take a look at various suppliers that could help us with the implementation of our new Syncron system. She and her team had taken a cursory look about eighteen months ago, so she'd already given me a partial list of possible companies, including Syncron themselves. So this was not a big puzzle to solve—it's the type of thing I've done before, and there are lots of suppliers out there.

"For me, the first task is always to validate the team's requirements and document them in a manner suitable for the RFI. We send out RFIs every few months, and basically they get us the information we need to get a list of possible suppliers. We give them the details of who we are and what we need, and they respond to a series of questions that lets us evaluate their approaches, abilities, and costs. I took Eileen's list, plus I did some research to find other suppliers. At this stage, the more names we find, the better—at least in some ways. I always try to get what I call a 'starter list' and then prune it down to about six to eight companies that I think would be a good fit, largely by looking at their existing client lists. We're a big global org, so obviously we needed a supplier that was used to the ins and outs of doing business with a company our size across multiple time zones, languages, and cultures. I did some straightforward Google searches and also reached out to some of my sources. I have a few colleagues in similar positions in other companies, and we rely on each other for this sort of information. I also have a team member who is very active in one of our business associations, so I checked in with him. Two other interesting sources proved to be a consultant we used last year on another project who works on these types of projects all the time and another team member who had been to a Syncron users forum a few months back and had since been contacted by a company called Orion Tech.

"Altogether, we amassed a list of fourteen companies. As I would have thought, we pared it down pretty quickly to a list of eight that we thought could handle what we required. So the next step was to contact each company and ask them to respond to this specific RFI. And of course, while all this was going on, we needed a specific budget."

Back to Dave Metzler: "When it came to the implementation phase of the new application, we had budgeted about a $1 million for that part of the project. We thought that number would be about right based on some early assessments and by talking to Syncron themselves. To be honest, I had thought that Syncron would simply do it themselves. After all, it is their application, and I would have thought that they would have had the resources and ability to do this.

"But obviously we wanted to make sure that it went well and stayed on time and on budget. I imagine everyone probably says that, but we recently had two smaller projects go off the rails: one that was late and the other one late and over budget. And that consultancy report really rocked the boat. I think Alf Witherspoon's job was probably on the line over this, maybe even Eileen's, and for sure Ezra Padgett didn't need any more egg on his face. There definitely was an incredible amount of attention put on this project to make sure that we had a plan and a budget and would then stick with both. At the same time, of course, the team had to make sure that the implementation was successful and that we ended up with the expected business results and not a basketful of excuses. I think that's why so much time was spent on making sure we had the right partner to help us implement the Syncron system."

So Sue had her budget, but it came with lots of pressure. It was time to cover all the bases, as she explains: "Another important thing is that before issuing the RFI, we had to internally consult with both Legal and Strategic Sourcing. Legal, quite frankly, is fairly easy—they just want to make sure we're not exposing the company to any undue risks or implying any commitments to these suppliers. By using templates from previous RFIs, we were able to please them with no real hassle.

"Strategic Sourcing, on the other hand, is a whole different ballgame. They always want to get involved, and Evan Day—they call him the 'Sourcerer' over there—had worked phase 1 with Eileen and was probably going to work with us on this. Strategic Sourcing is pretty wild and kind of anal at the same time, if you know what I mean. They think they should select the targets of the RFI, and they even want to write the RFI. Then they want to make sure we're getting as much competition as possible so that we wind up with a list of players with whom we—and I think Evan Day uses the royal 'we'—could then put the hammer down, which in source-speak means 'reduce always, steal when possible.' Maybe I exaggerate. Anyway, Evan and I have danced this dance before, and we've always managed to collaborate sufficiently so that at the end of the day, all our needs get met. I'll let him tell his side of the story."

Evan Day is a veteran purchasing professional—a top gun with big boots over at Strategic Sourcing. He came up through the ranks negotiating and contracting with a wide selection of suppliers selling a wide selection of offerings. But behind the swagger, he's a very canny negotiator and keeps his cards close to his chest. At the same time, he is straightforward and would never mislead anyone. He calls it very much as it is. When the shift across the industry happened a few years ago—and indeed the name changed from Purchasing to Strategic Sourcing—he was in the vanguard and very supportive. He always believed that companies could save significant money by using more strategic purchasing practices. He often equates the money he saves the company to the number of jobs that could be kept. He goes on a bit about that, actually. He also has a 2.5 percent bonus plan that he recently negotiated up from 2 percent on Sourcing dollars saved, so you could say he's an all-arounder when it comes to motivation.

He works with many individuals across the organization but is often frustrated that some—even senior individuals—can compromise his work by becoming too enamored of particular suppliers and their offerings. In these situations, it is hard for him to bring in competitive bids and negotiate a better deal. He has written a number of articles for *Purchasing Power Magazine* and is often a featured speaker at their annual conference. He presented a paper at last year's conference on "Saving Dollars, Saving Jobs."

Here's the man: "Evan Day here, Strategic Sourcing, DiaNascent Global Inc. My background? More than twenty-five years in Purchasing and Vendor Management, and I've been here at DGI for the last four years. You know, in these four years alone, I have saved this organization more than $8 million. I'll take half of that, thank you—well, no, actually, it's just a fraction of that. I do get a quarterly bonus based on the amount I'm able to save the company in the difference between budgeted and forecasted prices and the contract price I negotiate. But believe me, it's not a Porsche bonus—more like a nice ski-weekend-for-the-family bonus. My real kick is the OK Corral shootouts with the suppliers."

Evan is never shy about pointing out that he wishes more people could see how much money the company could save by simply cutting better deals. "When I see that we are laying folks off, I think that if we cut better deals, we could maybe save some of those jobs. I guess that's why I get so frustrated with people who simply reach out and start talking to our suppliers and potential suppliers. Each of those conversations should be carefully managed so we can get the best deals. That's the whole point of the word 'strategic' in Strategic Sourcing—we simply have to be more deliberate in how we deal with our suppliers. Really, there's hardly anything in this world that is unique. We could and should always find alternative providers and then see who can provide the best all-around deal for us. And I'm not just talking about dollars but other things as well: quality, reliability, and generally how they look after us."

Evan sometimes pays for his open confidence—he's got a swagger, and he's proud of his nickname. "Yeah, people get on my case from time to time, but I don't worry about it because I'm very serious about my work.

I've always got three numbers in my head for any one project—what the price wants to be, what the price should be, and what the price will be. The first one is what the supplier tries to sell it for, and the third one is what we finally get it for. The one in between—what the price should be—is where I do my real work." Indeed, Evan's research, experience, contacts, and the other tools he uses to calculate the true realistic value of the offering at hand let him negotiate—and negotiate hard—in the good faith he's known for. And the closer price three gets to price two, the happier the Sourcerer is. "I wouldn't usually get involved with a project this size, but I'd already worked with Eileen Williams on the initial Syncron acquisition phase. We did some good work on that one, and Eileen asked if I'd keep an eye out for a call about phase 2. And indeed, Sue Harris called and got me involved in the implementation end of the project. As always, I would have liked to have been involved earlier, but that's the way it often is. But Sue was good. I've worked with her before, and at least she got me into the process before the RFI went out. That makes all the difference, because if you're not careful, RFIs can be written in a way that really favors just one or two companies, and then they can charge whatever they like. I wanted to make sure the RFI was open enough so that a number of possible suppliers would bid on it and in fact encourage some that could perhaps just do parts of it to also bid. You know, there are now some great companies in India and Eastern Europe offering technical services for a fraction of the cost of our onshore companies. I know they may not be able to do everything we need, but why not give them a shot at some of it and get the larger, more expensive global companies for the more complex areas? I'm just sayin', there are lots of suppliers out there who'd love to do a deal with DGI."

Sue again: "I know you just talked to Evan—he probably told you about how he is saving money to save jobs. I'm not sure about that, but Evan's okay and a good guy to work with, and we manage to keep things moving along. So, anyway, we issue this RFI to seven companies plus Syncron themselves. Just so you know, we had previously only talked to Syncron and one of the others. The RFI is essentially a way for us to get information and assess various suppliers and their approaches, and it's always interesting to see how these companies respond. They generally want to come in here and talk to our executives to let them—as they say—'conduct their own discovery.' I mean, spare me.

"It's my job and the job of our team to document what *we need* and then ask them to respond to those requirements as per *our schedule*, not theirs. It can be very frustrating when they want to override the process. Even more frustrating is if you do let them in the door, they usually just do a standard sales pitch, and they all sound the same to me. One of the potential suppliers even called Alf Witherspoon's office trying to set up a direct meeting with him. Funny thing is that his exec assistant and I are good friends, so she just transferred the call to me. Amazing how you can see a red face over the phone, but I have to admit this guy did a pretty good job tap-dancing his way out of the embarrassment of getting caught out. Made my day, I can tell you.

"Anyway, we finally managed to get all the responses in from the eight potential suppliers. We immediately discounted one, as they really didn't have the depth of resources we were looking for. We then invited the others in, each for a three-hour session to go through their approaches in more detail. Here's where things became interesting for us. As I mentioned earlier, we do this kind of thing a lot, and we know that suppliers usually come in and give us their sales pitch, which so often sounds similar. However, on this occasion, there was one obvious exception: Orion Technologies. They must have spent the first hour of their time asking us some really thought-provoking questions. They used examples of projects they had previously worked on to share with us what they considered to be the critical factors for success in an implementation project like this. The one area where they really caught our attention was the training for end users and the associated change management. They convinced us that although we could do a great job of installing a top-rated software application, if the users weren't properly trained and motivated to use the new system, *we would very likely fail* to meet our business goals. Well, that got my attention. Unfortunately, they were also the most expensive and well beyond our provisional budget.

"Two other suppliers scored a lot of points, and they were both bidding with numbers that fell within the budget. So now we had a short list of three. Here's a brief summary Eileen and I put together, cc'd to Evan Day in Sourcing and Dave Metzler in Finance."

Orion Technologies, Fort Lauderdale, FL

- Andy Lowe, Regional Sales Manager
  - Anna Gargarich, Client Support Manager
- major claims
  - specialize in Syncron
  - great project management
  - only star players on their team
  - track record of success
  - executive assigned to every project
  - global
  - innovative methods for end-user training and change management
- total bid
  - **$1.3m**
  - 9 months

IEG, Mumbai, India

- Paula Cox, Regional Manager
  - Sri Raj, Development Manager
- major claims
  - specialize in Syncron
  - great project management
  - global
  - track record of success
  - their own project management system to track and report on everything
  - guaranteed money-back success
- total bid
  - **$760k**
  - 6 months

L&M Systems, Newark, NJ

- Henrik Andersson, Account Manager
  - Steve Frank, Tech Support
- major claims
  - large company with a dedicated Syncron practice

- global
- track record of success
- proven approach to project management
- invest in hiring the best and then a continual investment in their training
- certify all team members at least annually
- total bid
  - **$950k**
  - 9 months

Eileen had been in contact with Sue throughout this phase and with her cast the deciding ballots in the selection of the short-listed suppliers. Here are some of Eileen's thoughts: "We were pretty confident that all three suppliers could do the installation and get all the technical bits right. Especially IEG—absolute tech wizards. I got the feeling that Sue could've hung out with them forever. We do a lot of business in India, and we had a bit of a track record with them for some relatively minor maintenance stuff, so confidence in their technical ability was not an issue. We were all quite impressed with their regional manager, Paula Cox. She was very professional and obviously had a lot of experience in the industry. She asked great questions and was able to quickly pick up on what was important to the team and some of the nuances of our situation. The proposal she presented was very detailed and addressed all that was asked of the suppliers. Their money-back Guaranteed Success program, where they don't charge for any overruns that are their fault, was initially very interesting and a claim of their confidence in their abilities. But we realized that at the end of the day, we wanted a successful project, not our money back with a dodgy system.

"We considered the possibility of IEG doing the install and Orion providing end-user training and change management—food for thought that would be worth looking into. Of course, the IEG price was right—the lowest of the three—and we all felt they could probably even bring it home under budget and in less time. The big downside, though, was the lack of end-user training. Even with the lower price, could we get the user training done from the leftover dollars from this deal? We did a lot of head-scratching on this one, and if Orion hadn't schooled us so well on end-user training and change management, IEG would have been the front runner.

"Then there's L&M—what can you say? Very big, very solid company with impressive credentials—so big, though, that we would have been one of their smaller clients, and we felt this could be a bit more of a risk. They were definitely a strong contender overall, but we never felt they really needed the business or would partner with us through all the ups and downs any project like this is going to run into. And Sue felt the tech support guy didn't take the time to really listen or understand our needs—he seemed more interested in talking about all their internal approaches to certifying their team members and their approach to project management. Although this was seen as important, we would have felt more confident if he'd listened more to what we were sharing."

Sue Harris takes up the assessment: "For me, it was Orion that was really on the ball. They shared some really innovative ways to look at end-user training. For example, creating custom videos—you know, like on YouTube—that our users could access at any time to quickly explain how to use the various features and functions. To be honest, they blew us away with their capabilities and approaches in not just installing the technology but ensuring we were successful. The only trouble was that we hadn't included the dollars for this type of training in our original budget. But we could see that we needed to focus more on the user training aspect of the project. And it wasn't so much that we hadn't thought of it, but we weren't aware of some of the newer approaches that Orion Tech was offering. They also shared how we really had to create an overall approach to change management. They said we couldn't simply switch on the new system and expect users around the world to start using it. This too made a load of sense. Strange how we really knew this from previous experience but hadn't had any structured way to look at it before Orion shared their thinking with us."

Eileen adds her thoughts: "Orion really turned our heads around—very solid company, excellent references, and really focused on the success of the overall project, not just the technical implementation. The inclusion and importance of end-user training and change management were seen as not just another key but the most important key to the success of the project. Right from the start, we all felt comfortable with Orion. They had this ability to ask insightful questions and get inside our heads about the project. Their client support manager, Anna Gargarich, was able to share a lot of insight into what makes projects like these successful—including, of course, the need to ensure that the end users were motivated to use the new system and trained to do so."

Sue now wanted to test the water with the other two suppliers. "After our initial meeting with Orion, we went back to both IEG and L&M Technologies and asked them about their approaches to end-user training. We deliberately did not mention change management; we wanted to see if either of them would bring it up. It sort of surprised me that both companies said they could do the training, but neither one demonstrated the innovation we had seen from Orion. IEG raised the topic, but we felt it was not something they had any real depth of understanding in. It makes sense in some ways, as these were technical implementation companies; their teams are composed of technical people, and I think their primary end goal is a successful technical implementation. If truth be told, that's also what we had been thinking. But Orion shifted our mind-set, and the focus was then placed on not just a successful technical implementation but a successful business implementation."

It's not hard to see that both Eileen and Sue had been impressed with Orion. But the big issue now was money. Eileen knew that before they could turn Evan Day loose on any supplier, they needed to rethink the budget. In the meantime, Sue had been busy. She explains, "We had been following up on references and doing all the usual due diligence you would do with a short list of three companies. I think we knew that we would like to go with Orion, but Eileen was still working on the budget at that time. So I thought it was time to get Evan involved to see if he could work some magic with the current budget."

Says Evan, "The team had come a long way down the road before I became involved again from the Strategic Sourcing side of the equation. Before my first meeting with anyone, Sue had told me that they had a short list of three possible providers but that they had a strong preference for Orion Tech. When I looked at the proposals, I thought it a bit strange, as Orion was clearly the most expensive, and I know how sensitive to costs we are. I met with Sue and Eileen and quickly understood that the three proposals were not equal. Orion had included the costs for additional consulting services in the areas of change management and end-user training. They wanted Orion Tech to do this additional consulting and then create a series of training videos for us. I got it. And this is the kind of stuff I can often help with.

"I was thinking we could get Orion to do the training aspects of the program but go to one of the cheaper offshore companies to do the technical implementation. For example, IEG was a load cheaper than Orion and very solid with the technology stuff. I talked to Sue and Eileen about this approach and how it could solve the budget issue. They were lukewarm because they really liked Orion—see what I mean about nonsourcing people talking to suppliers and falling in love? But at the end of the day, if they couldn't find the budget and I could find a cheaper solution, then we all win, right?"

It all kept coming back to the money, and that meant Eileen had to go back to Dave Metzler in finance. Dave and Eileen had done their primary job well and had realized the importance of the project's success, but now they needed more money.

Says Dave, "Thanks to Orion Tech—and I don't mean that sarcastically—we realized that the entire issue of end-user training and motivation to use the new system was critical to our success. I think before talking to Orion, we were somehow thinking that we could flick the 'On' switch and everything would be fine. But Orion connected us to others who had done similar implementations, and it became obvious that we had underestimated the importance of this training and overall change management. And yes, we had also underestimated the costs. I worked with Eileen to see how we could accommodate the additional costs."

For Dave, this was a tough one. "We can only do so much of this. We only have so much money, and the exec group would be in no mood to fund another cost overrun. I don't think I would have wanted to be anywhere near the meeting if the team had had to ask for more money. Even with a great argument based on the need to do this additional training, I think there would have been no tolerance for such a situation, and I'm pretty sure jobs would have been lost.

"There were some tense meetings, but finally we were able to move some budget from other areas to accommodate the additional funding. I'm pleased we were able to work it all out within the scope of the original budget. It did mean, though, that we had used up our contingency—no more blood out of that stone. I'm sure Eileen and her team will understand, though, so I think we are back on track with a very tightly managed project. Let's hope Evan Day can pull off some of his magic."

Says Eileen, "Dave Metzler was a great partner on this. He was able to support us as we redeployed budget dollars to cover the additional user training and focus on the change management aspects of the implementation. He and I had numerous meetings on the topic while Sue kept pushing ahead with the overall project. Orion Tech had certainly put us in a spin, but it was a good spin, if there is such a thing. All the way along, we knew that we had to place the focus on implementing this software on time and on budget. But of course, we also knew that we had to be successful and get the expected business results of reducing our global operating costs. Orion really helped us see that we needed to ensure that our end users would all be able and indeed would want to use the new system successfully."

The amended budget, now a tightly wound one with no room for error, would be tossed back to Sue Harris. She would have the money with the proviso that pretty much all her contingency funds were gone. And she still had a card—hopefully an ace, certainly wild—up her sleeve in the person of Evan Day. The budget had been approved a couple of days prior to Sue and Evan's first negotiation session with Orion, so Eileen talked to them both and they agreed to give Evan at least a chance to run his split-solution idea past Orion. They wouldn't push too hard, knowing they had the funding in their back pockets, and Evan was finally going to get some face time with the suppliers.

Says Evan, "Sue had called Orion and arranged the meeting with their regional sales manager, Andy Lowe, and their client support manager, Anna Gargarich. I knew we were going to discuss breaking their proposal into two components: one that was the technical development and implementation and the other focusing on the change management consulting and end-user training. I don't think that was on their agenda, but they figured out pretty quickly where it was going. And they didn't like it at all. They said it would be extremely difficult to pull these two facets apart. Andy went on to specifically warn of the negative impact that splitting the solution would have on the change management aspects of the installation. And of course, that struck home, because it was primarily Orion's insight into change management that had made them the clear frontrunner throughout our buying journey."

Sue expands on the meeting: "Andy Lowe explained that they create the training videos as they are developing the application, and if they were forced to do the two tasks separately, the costs would actually go up. Evan and I explored the topic with them further, but we both concluded that (a) they knew what they were doing and (b) the concept of breaking the solution up into components was not going to fly. Jeopardizing the change management was a deal-breaker for me. We had the money, so I couldn't see the point in pushing this any further, and I was hoping that Evan was of the same mind."

Evan concludes, "Can you believe Sue actually kicked me under the table? Anyway, I knew it was time. I said to Andy, 'You're probably right, and we're probably good with this—let's talk next week.'"

THE HOME STRETCH

Sue recalls, "Our meetings with Orion after that pretty much just focused on the details, timing, terms and conditions, and so on. I kept the two other suppliers in the game for a while, and hopefully that helped keep the Orion gang on their toes. We were able to fine-tune a few areas and ended up with numbers that seemed fair and reasonable for everyone. We were also given the go-ahead to build some incentive payments into the contract to reward them for delivering on time and on budget. It then only took a couple of weeks to get the contract reviewed by the legal beagles and then get signatures on lines. That was fun—watching Evan sign a PO for 1.3 big ones. Eileen and I were both happy, and I believe we protected the organization's interests and picked the right partner."

Eileen Williams was glad to see such a successful conclusion of DGI's Buying Journey. "As senior program manager, I am very pleased to share that we came in on time and on budget. Sue and her team did a great job in planning and executing the Syncron implementation project, and yes, I got to keep my job. It's interesting how there was so much focus on coming in on time and on budget, probably due to some unfortunate history when that didn't always happen. It was also encouraging to see how the team handled adversity when some unexpected issues jumped into the project.

"But when all is said and done, the most important point isn't just the time and the money but also that the desired and required business results were achieved. And I am very happy to say that this was the case with this project. I am so pleased that we put the focus on the change management and end-user training aspects of the project. I'm convinced that if we hadn't invested in those areas, we would not have been successful. Even though it was obvious to us that the new system would return benefits to the overall organization, it was not so obvious to our people around the world and why they had to change what they had been doing for years.

"We were asking those who had always worked in a particular way to change—to move from using calculators and notebooks to inputting data into the system, to change from walking around a warehouse and counting stock to using RFID and scanners. And it's great to now walk into any of our warehouses around the world and see common systems that are accepted as world-class being used by our people. It's also great to work for a company that remains competitive and has experienced above-average industry growth in the last two years."

CHAPTER 11

DiaNascent CASE STUDY ANALYSIS

MAPPING THE CUSTOMER BUYING JOURNEY OF DiaNascent

WE WILL NOW map the Customer Buying Journey and decode the associated DNA for this case of Orion Tech selling implementation services of Syncron software. Of course, in real life, we would not base such an analysis on just one case; we would study many more and look for similarities. Furthermore, mapping a buying journey in real life would be more complex than in this one example, but for the sake of this case study, DiaNascent should serve to illustrate the concept. The following analysis is somewhat generalized to illustrate what the overall buying journey should look like for Orion Tech.

DNA STRAND 1: TRIGGERS AND DEPENDENCIES
- Dependencies
  - the need to invest in the Syncron system for warehouse management and logistics
  - the belief that the company does not possess the in-house skills/knowledge/expertise to implement the software with their own resources
- Triggers
  - a need to find an external supplier to implement the Syncron software

DNA STRAND 2: STEPS

ILLUSTRATION 11.1. DiaNascent: STEPS AND BUYING ACTIVITIES

STEPS	KEY ACTIVITIES	TOUCH POINTS (WITH POTENTIAL SUPPLIERS)
1. Initial Scope	• scope project • create an overall multiyear plan • appoint key players/determine roles • assess third-party providers	
2. Market Assessment	• validate and document requirements • talk to colleagues and trusted sources • read case studies and trade magazine reviews • create a list of possible providers • conduct initial research on potential providers	• search websites • read case studies
3. Request for Information (RFI)	• cut starter list to list of providers to receive an RFI • liaise with Legal and Strategic Sourcing • create an RFI document • publish and send RFI to possible providers • meet with possible providers to understand their approaches and competencies	• connect with suppliers • send RFI • respond to questions regarding the RFI • host supplier presentations
4. Explore Alternatives	• create a short list of viable providers • validate the provider's approaches • assess different approaches • finalize approach, priorities, and requirements • validate/change budget, timelines, resources	• work with representatives of shortlisted suppliers
5. Finalize Approach	• conduct due diligence on shortlisted providers • meet with possible providers to finalize their approach, plans, and proposals • check references • finalize overall approach to the implementation project	• work with representatives of shortlisted suppliers

(continued)

ILLUSTRATION 11.1 *(continued)*

STEPS	KEY ACTIVITIES	TOUCH POINTS (WITH POTENTIAL SUPPLIERS)
6. Contract	• meet with possible supplier(s) • clarify details/approaches • request final proposal/pricing • determine and assess alternative sourcing approaches • review terms and conditions • negotiate • perform legal review • complete contracts	• work with representatives of shortlisted suppliers
7. Implement	• initiate project • hold project review meetings • report on progress • manage problems	• manage all aspects of the delivery of services • review progress • review results

DNA STRAND 3: KEY PLAYERS

The senior program manager is responsible for initiating the overall Customer Buying Journey and framing the overall project. With help from finance, an overall budget and plan are created. At the end of this first step in the buying journey, the responsibility to select and work with an implementation partner is delegated to the project manager, who is ultimately responsible for this technical implementation of the overall project. Under the direction of the senior program manager, the project manager conducts the initial Market Assessment. The Request for Information (RFI) is created with the involvement of the Strategic Sourcing department. The project manager is then responsible for evaluating the responses from the RFI and determining a short list of viable approaches. As the approach is being finalized, the senior program manager is advised of the directions and, together with Finance, approves the directions and budget. Strategic Sourcing then returns to negotiate and finalize the contract. As the project moves into implementation, it is once again the role of the project manager to lead this step in the overall buying journey (see illustration 11.2).

ILLUSTRATION 11.2. DiaNascent: **KEY PLAYERS BY STEP**

STEPS/ROLES	SENIOR PROGRAM MANAGER *EILEEN WILLIAMS*	PROJECT MANAGER *SUSAN HARRIS*	FINANCE COORDINATOR *DAVE METZLER*	STRATEGIC SOURCING *EVAN DAY*
1. Initial Scope	LEAD	Some	Some	
2. Market Assessment	Major	LEAD		
3. Request for Information (RFI)		LEAD		
4. Explore Alternatives		LEAD		
5. Finalize Approach	Major	LEAD	Some	
6. Contract		LEAD		Key
7. Implement	Some	LEAD		

DNA STRAND 4: BUYING STYLE

In the initial steps of the Customer Buying Journey, DiaNascent believed that they knew exactly what they wanted—resources to implement and globally install their new Syncron system—and that several companies could help them. We would typify this buying style as choice/product, "Sort and Select." However, due to their interaction with Orion Tech in their search for possible providers, their beliefs changed.

First, Orion highlighted the need to recognize the importance of end-user training and then consider the change management aspects associated with implementing such a system. This moved the buying style from product to solution, wherein DiaNascent no longer perceived that they knew what they wanted; they were now dependent on Orion to share with them how to be successful in implementing software applications such as Syncron.

Second, Orion showed them some very innovative ways in which to conduct the end-user training. This moved the buying style from choice to value in that Orion was unique in their ability to provide this training,

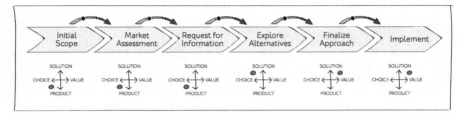

ILLUSTRATION 11.3. DiaNascent buying journey

which DiaNascent now considered crucial to the project's success. DiaNascent initially didn't see Orion as the only possible provider of these services until they tested other possible providers, all of which helped illustrate the uniqueness of Orion's offering. We therefore see the switch from choice to value in step 5 of the Customer Buying Journey when it truly emerged that Orion was unique in their ability to provide this valued element of the required solution.

DNA STRAND 5: VALUE DRIVERS

Although the overall value DiaNascent sought in the Syncron project was global competitiveness and reduction of operating costs, these are not directly associated with the implementation project and the selection of a supplier of implementation services. The *value drivers* of the buying journey for the implementation partner are more as shown in illustration 11.4.

During the early steps of the buying journey, the value drivers for the selection of a supplier for implementation services of the Syncron software were firmly placed on being able to remain within the expected budget and plan. Obviously, there was also the focus on ensuring that the selected supplier could deliver a successful project.

Then, as a result of the discussions with Orion, the value drivers were augmented by the growing awareness of the impact that end-user training and associated change management could have on the project. Orion helped educate the DiaNascent team that these aspects were critical to the success of the project, and thus they became adjuncts to the previous value driver of having a successful project.

At the contracting stage, the value drivers became more economically focused. At this point, DiaNascent had essentially selected Orion

ILLUSTRATION 11.4. DiaNascent: VALUE DRIVERS BY STEP

STEPS	VALUE DRIVERS
1. Initial Scope	• ability to manage cost and time
2. Market Assessment	• successful project
3. Request for Information (RFI)	
4. Explore Alternatives	• ability to manage cost and time
5. Finalize Approach	• successful project
	• effective end-user training and change management
6. Contract	• getting what's required but with good pricing, terms, and conditions
	• successful project
	• effective end-user training and change management
7. Implement	• successful project
	• gain the expected business outcomes
	• ability to manage cost and time

Technologies as their provider. For this step of the journey, the value driver was primarily the ability to negotiate the right deal.

Finally, as the Customer Buying Journey moves into the final step of implementation, the value drivers become associated with the successful management and delivery of the project.

DNA STRAND 6: BUYING CONCERNS

Illustration 11.5 represents the friction across the Customer Buying Journey steps. Light gray illustrates any aspect that may slow down the journey, while dark gray is something that could stop the buying journey.

This Customer Buying Journey has remarkably little friction or *buying concerns*. This is primarily because once an organization has made a commitment to implement an application such as Syncron and they realize that they need outside help, there is little to slow down or stop such a buying journey. A process is in place, as it is a subset of the overall project and it clearly is a priority, as without such an implementation service, the much larger investment in software will never be utilized.

ILLUSTRATION 11.5. DiaNascent BUYING CONCERNS BY STEP

STEP/BUYING CONCERN	PROCESS	PRIORITY	INDIVIDUAL	ORGANIZATIONAL	ALTERNATIVES	BUSINESS IMPLICATIONS	FIT	CHANGE
1. Initial Scope				▓ (could slow down)	▓ (could slow down)			
2. Market Assessment					▓ (could slow down)			
3. Request for Information					▓ (could slow down)	■ (would likely stop)		
4. Explore Alternatives				▓ (could slow down)				
5. Finalize Approach				▓ (could slow down)	▓ (could slow down)			
6. Contract	▓ (could slow down)			▓ (could slow down)	▓ (could slow down)			
7. Implement								

KEY

■ A buying concern that would likely stop the buying journey

▓ A buying concern that could slow down and possibly stop the buying journey

Not a significant concern

The project manager, who is the lead individual to be considered under the buying concern of "individual," is highly motivated to find and engage a good implementation partner. As a duo, Eileen Williams and Sue Harris display a mutual motivation to successfully conclude the buying journey.

There were a few considerations under the area of "organizational." Early in the process, it was unclear how they would proceed, with an implication that they would simply go with Syncron, the chosen supplier of the software package itself. In the later stages, pressure could come from other parts of the organization, especially from Strategic Sourcing, to go with a lower-cost alternative. The only real danger of stopping the buying journey is in the "business" category. Orion Technologies rely on their expertise in end-user training and change management to differentiate them from others, but these services come at a price. Budgets are typically set earlier in the overall buying journey, so this additional, albeit valuable, service represents a significant increase in price. Some buyers may not be able to accommodate such an increased burden on the budget and thus could favor an alternative provider or approach. There are no apparent issues with the final three categories of implication, fit, and change.

SUMMARY

As all Customer Buying Journey DNA analyses should, this case study focuses on one particular offering into one particular market.

The market is global companies who

- are concerned with multilocation warehousing and logistical operations
- have determined that they need to automate their operations and who have chosen to implement the Syncron application
- have determined that they need third-party assistance in the implementation of that software
- have the capability to view end-user training and change management approaches as vital to the success of the project yet do not believe that they have the expertise to handle these aspects of the project in-house

The offering is

- implementation services for the Syncron application package
- aimed at more complex, larger, multinational implementations
- inclusive of innovative end-user training and change management consulting services

Note that there would be a different buying journey for simply technical implementation services. In such cases, the buying style may remain one that we would classify as product/commodity, and thus the buying journey would likely result in choosing the cheapest provider with good credentials.

Not all prospects for Orion Technologies would embrace this buying journey. Some prospects may not value the end-user training and change management services or may believe that they have the expertise to do these aspects of the overall project themselves. Most importantly, in these two cases, you should classify such prospects as a different market. This is why the last bullet in defining the market is so key to this particular Customer Buying Journey. A host of companies might never see the value of end-user training, but the point is that those companies, by definition, are not this market and will not follow this particular buying journey. I will discuss the implications this would have for a company like Orion in part 2 of the book, but for now, the focus remains on understanding the Customer Buying Journey.

CHAPTER 12

CASE STUDY 2

CCHN: DOES THE GLOVE FIT?

ARTICLE IN *HEALTHCARE WORKER MONTHLY*

A "HANDY" NEW DEVELOPMENT THAT'S COMING YOUR WAY

We recently spent a few hours with Dave Shepard, CEO of Digex Corporation, talking about a new technology in an area very familiar and close to all health care workers—the surgical glove. Now, gloves are something we use every day; in fact, many of us use them several times a day. We rarely think about it as we pull on our latex or vinyl gloves. But after talking to Shepard, you may find that you start giving it more than just a passing thought.

Sure, we all know we use those gloves to protect ourselves and our patients from the spread of pathogens. But what many may not be aware of is that the inside of that very glove can be an ideal breeding ground for exactly what we are trying to prevent. Citing an FDA White Paper, Shepard notes that the warm and damp environment inside the gloves is an inherently effective incubator for pathogens. Compounding this is evidence to suggest that wearing gloves gives some health care workers a false sense of security, leading to a reduced emphasis on hand cleansing. It has also been found that some health care workers may even wear the same gloves between different patients. While we hope none of our readers would practice such behavior, it's hard to deny the data.

To address these concerns, Digex is bringing to market a breakthrough in technology and perhaps a revolution in how we think of gloves, pathogens, and cross contamination. After several years of research and trials, Digex has now gained certification for an approach that brings "nano-technology" to this everyday disposable item.

For those who are not overly familiar with the term, nanotechnology is the science of the very small. Take the proverbial human hair, which is approximately 60,000–70,000 nanometers in thickness, and you start to get the idea. The gloves are manufactured using this technology that allows for exponentially finer tolerances and margins in building microbial barriers to pathogens. They have been laboratory tested to reduce the bioburden on gloves by over 99 percent, resulting in significantly reduced cross contamination. Not only that, but they offer a superior feel over our traditional latex and vinyl gloves. Shepard shared that in blind testing, nine out of ten health care workers chose the Digex glove over latex or vinyl for their superior tactile feel. And yes, we tried them—perhaps not under true laboratory testing rigor, but we did find a difference, and we liked them.

Anything that helps protect us and our patients is always a very welcome advancement. We have been wearing essentially the same gloves now for decades. Other professionals have enjoyed the benefit of high-technology protection. Police have Kevlar, firefighters have Nomex, winter athletes have Gore-Tex, so maybe finally we are getting our own piece of high-tech with Digex. Soon we may all be wearing these new nanotechnology gloves. We certainly hope so.

CITY CORE HEALTHCARE NETWORK

Rob Summers is an emergency room (ER) doctor with the City Core Health-Care Network (CCHN). CCHN is a network of six hospitals across the Midwest with an average of three hundred beds each providing general and specialist care to the local population. For Rob, it's been almost ten years since he's joined CCHN right out of med school. He's had a few opportunities to move into other areas, and indeed to other organizations, but he likes CCHN and truly believes in what they do. Says Rob, "Contrary to stories I hear about other organizations, there seems to be a distinct lack of politics around here, and I like the focus we have. Patients, and the care we deliver to them, are the absolute number-one concern. You may not like to hear this, but it isn't always that way. Sadly, other things can get in the way. But here at CCHN, we seem to have our priorities right."

Rob had seen the article about the Digex gloves and although it didn't immediately trigger any reaction, it was the sort of thing that always interested him. "I guess I've been responsible for bringing in several new approaches and even some different equipment into our organization. I like to keep abreast of what's happening out there. Health care is always advancing, always changing, and you can't afford to simply stay with what you know and what you've always done. That's how this whole thing with Digex started. It was a while ago now, but I'd read that article in *HealthCare Worker Monthly* about this new nanotechnology glove that claimed to cut down on infections in a big way. Sounded good, right? Too good, perhaps? Well, that's what quite a few people thought. After all, it's people's lives we deal with here, so due diligence takes on a whole new meaning. And even in medicine generally, where advances in technology are a given, lots of people still don't like change. I had no idea about the actual value or efficacy of the Digex glove, but the article caught my eye.

"Now, the ER can be a dirty place. We don't get many patients who've had a chance to shower and change before coming in. We get accidents from the home, the job site, and especially the roads. And once triage has been sorted and treatment started, we always have a lot of cleaning up to do. So we are really aware of pathogens—germs to most folks—and how to prevent them from complicating the already difficult job of putting our patients back together. I'm not sure if you know, but the CDC[1] tells us that more than two million people in the US are sickened every year with antibiotic-resistant infections, with at least seventy-five thousand dying as a result. In fact, hospital-acquired infections (HAIs) kill more people in this country than AIDS, breast cancer, and auto accidents combined.

"And now we're seeing these superbugs like MRSA[2] emerge, and according to those who know, antibiotic-resistant HAIs are on the rise. So it's a topic very much on our minds. Of course, to no one's surprise, there is no shortage of sales and marketing people knocking on our door just about every day with claims of being able to dramatically reduce these infections. A pity, I suppose, as something worthwhile may be out there, but we just don't have the time to sort through it all.

"To get back to the gloves, how did this all start? Like I said, I read that article, and shortly after I was at a trade show and walked past the Digex booth. The name rang a bell, so I stopped by to see what they were up to. I talked to their reps and tried on the gloves. I did think at the time that they were different; somehow, they felt thinner yet stronger as well. And their claims to reduce the bioload on gloves and thus cross contamination were very interesting. But you know how it is—everyone at these trade shows is claiming huge breakthroughs in technology, especially in the area of infection prevention. At this one show alone, there were dozens of offerings all claiming to reduce HAIs. Anyway, I gave them my card, and I guess because I'm the head doc in the ER, I warranted a follow-up. They called, and I agreed to meet with their rep, although I warned them my time really isn't my own in the ER, so I have to go with the moment and see what happens.

"The rep for Digex dropped in—his name escapes me, but I probably have his card somewhere. Nice guy, seemed to know what he was talking about. He asked me about our own practices at CCHN and what gloves we use. I found a dispenser and showed him what we currently use, but I had no idea what we paid for them. I told him he would have to talk to our people in procurement. But as he pointed out, he wasn't looking to compete against what we use today—he wanted to introduce a totally new approach to the organization. His data on pathogens that can breed on the inside of the glove and even exist on the outside of a glove were quite frankly more than a little eye-opening. He did a very persuasive and entertaining demo where he turned one of their gloves into what looked like a cow's udder full of very hot water. Lots of fun, but unfortunately, I had little more than a few minutes to chat with him. He understood, and before going, he brought up the idea of a real-world trial in the ER. I was open to that, but we both knew I couldn't just start using these gloves on my own.

"So he left me with a load of information and the offer to set up a fourteen-day trial where he would come in, talk to our staff about the new technology, and allow us to have unlimited use for two weeks. In return, he wanted everyone to complete a short survey summarizing their thoughts and comparing the Digex gloves to our normal surgical gloves. I must admit the technology intrigued me, and anything we can do to reduce infection is always a priority in my mind. Plus I liked these gloves—they were simple, they seemed to provide a better tactile feel, and if they truly reduced infection, then what do we have to lose? Granted, they cost more, but the rep—here, I found his card—Ted Alderson was very convincing that in reducing infections, they will actually save us money in the long run. I'm not sure about that; I'll leave that to others to sort through.

"I sent an email to my colleague Bret Rogers, our chief medical officer (CMO), and asked him for his opinion and if it would be okay to start a trial in the ER. Bret and I know each other quite well, and he got back to me right away. Not surprisingly, he had no issues with me going ahead as long as we were making no financial or commercial commitments and we had assurances that the basic biosecurity of the Digex glove was at least as good as what we were currently using. He also stipulated that I should coordinate with Stephanie Wong, our Infection Prevention and Control specialist—IP for short.

"I've gotten to know Stephanie quite well over the years, and from the point of view of getting the trial going, having her involved was both good news and bad news. Stephanie is a real expert when it comes to infection prevention; it's a driving motivation for much of her efforts with the IP group at CCHN. But as befits the position and responsibility she holds, she has to be rationally skeptical of all claims made by manufacturers. She wouldn't be there if she didn't have a very sensitive and practical nose for hype and hogwash. And besides, it's not my place to try to convince her that these gloves are going to reduce infection—Digex will have to work that one. I just felt that this two-week trial was a good opportunity to find out a bit more. So I met with her over coffee one morning, and I'll let her pick up the story at this point."

Stephanie Wong is a registered nurse (RN) with fifteen years at CCHN and heads up the Infection Prevention and Control team. While she finds it a fascinating and at times very rewarding role, it can also be quite frustrating. Stephanie explains, "Hospital and health care–acquired infections are a constant and insidious problem and much in the spotlight these days, and deservedly so. Of course, where there are problems, there are always those whose job it is to provide solutions. I am constantly inundated with marketing material for all the great things we can do to reduce infection. And I can tell you that not a week goes by without several salespeople calling me. But I'll be very frank here: very few of them get any further than that. I've even had the CEO send the odd rep my way who managed to get his attention, but sorry, that is no guarantee of any special treatment. And he's fine with that—he knows this is my turf and trusts that I'm working with the right priorities.

"Now, I'm sure there are probably some good ideas out there, but most of it is snake oil. Not only that, but before we start investing in any hard product technology solutions, especially gloves, I just wish everyone around here would get back to basics and *wash their hands properly*. It is amazing to me that we must still remind people when and how often to scrub up. Look at the posters all over the place. And the CDC says unequivocally—and I quote—'Hand-washing is the single most important means of preventing the spread of infection.' It could make the biggest difference of all.

"And it's not just us. I go to conferences and many hospitals across the country are fighting the same battles I do here. There are different approaches to the problem. We all put up posters and signage, and we are all trying to educate and empower our patients that it's okay for them to ask if our health care workers have washed their hands thoroughly. We hammer away at everyone at all our staff meetings—a broken record to many, I suppose, but it has to be done.

"I know, you didn't come here to ask me about hand washing but about those Digex gloves. Well, there's an interesting topic. Some studies show that gloves are part of the problem. They can often give health care workers a false sense of security. There have been studies showing that workers feel immune to infection and the transmission of infection when they put gloves on. But nothing could be further from the truth. To be fair, Rob Summers mentioned that Digex agreed with me on that point. And of course, I'm not implying that we shouldn't use gloves at all, but let's make sure we understand and follow the basics.

"When Rob first talked to me about the gloves, I told him I just didn't have the time to take on any new evaluations or studies. And nanotechnology—that's real cutting-edge stuff, isn't it? I don't even want to think about the cost. Luckily, that's not my department, though I can think of lots of other things around here that we could spend money on. Anyway, if Rob wanted to try a new type of glove, that's up to him. But if he was looking to incorporate these gloves into part of our IP program, then I'd have to get involved, and I was just too busy. There is rarely a time, and this is not one of them, when I'm not already working on issues that the executive has agreed are important. We set the assessment agenda and allocate time and resources, and I can't suddenly switch from that schedule every time someone comes up with another idea.

"But Rob seemed keen, so I told him if he wanted to get our CMO and CNO [chief nursing officer] on board, then we could possibly schedule a look at this technology in about six to nine months' time. He understood my time constraints and assured me he wasn't about to start championing these gloves—he just thought they may be worth trying. I said he could do whatever he liked as long as he understood that this trial was not sponsored by the IP group. He was fine with that and said he would just go ahead and let me know what the results were."

Back to Rob: "Stephanie was quite definite when I talked to her. She had no time at present to study any new technologies, and just because I liked a new type of glove, that didn't automatically make it part of CCHN's official IP program. She was adamant, and I get it. If I simply wanted to try a different glove, that was fine with her. But be careful, she said, because everyone wants to claim that their newly found magic bullet reduces infections, but she can't be involved in everything and must do what's right for our overall organization. Fair enough, I thought, though by now I'd learned a bit more about the technology Digex was using, and I was fascinated.

"However, as it happens, things came up. I got involved in a number of other initiatives, and the gloves found their way to the back burner. A couple of months later, Ted Alderson followed up with me and sent a number of interesting articles about the bioload on surgical gloves and the breakthrough aspects of the new Digex gloves. He called soon after, and I shared with him that while I could appreciate the importance of the HAI-reducing benefits of the Digex gloves, I was not the person to be talking to about infection control—that would be Stephanie Wong.

"Her name was not new to him, and he said he had called her but hadn't heard back. No surprise, as he's just one of many people trying to get on her calendar. I mildly commiserated with him, but there was no way I was going to get in her bad books by pushing for a meeting between them. Anyway, Alderson didn't seem too upset about it. It seemed to be something he'd run into before. We arranged to meet, and he offered again to set up the fourteen-day trial. I told him that while this wasn't going to be a formal trial, the ER would be happy to try the gloves and let him know what we thought. He seemed quite satisfied with that.

"One thing that does stand out is how impressed I was with the support people from Digex. They were very professional in setting up the trial. They came in and did a very polished demo—cow's udder thing again—and did product presentations to our staff, talking about their technology and encouraging people to try the gloves. They made sure they stocked enough of their gloves in various locations in the ER next to our usual gloves. Their dispensers were well designed and made pulling out gloves very easy. The informal test went very well, and most of our team said they thought they did have more 'feel' with the new gloves. I recall one person developed a rash and refused to try them again and was quite outspoken about the skin irritation she seemed to get. Alderson naturally was quite concerned but could not explain any reason for the Digex glove causing the reaction, and that situation was pretty much left unresolved.

"From the HAI standpoint, we obviously were not testing any infection-control properties. Not only did we not have the ability to do so, but that was Stephanie's domain, and I made it clear to everyone that we were simply seeing if we preferred the feel and ease of use of these gloves. At the end of the trial, most people provided their feedback on the online survey that was provided, and Digex shared the results with me: with the one exception, everyone felt the Digex gloves gave a better feel than our standard gloves.

"Alderson then seemed to be at a bit of a loss on what to do next. I think he felt he'd pretty well done all he could and that it was now up to me to really further anything. He did send me a very nicely done report summarizing the results of the test that also included pricing information—though that's certainly not an area I could even start to get into, and he must have known that. And I wasn't about to comment on the efficacy of the infection-control characteristics of the Digex gloves or champion them in any way—not my area. But I did write a short summary of the trial and emailed that along with the Digex report to Stephanie and Bret Rogers. I got a short reply from Bret and a confirmation receipt from Stephanie, but nothing from her indicating any follow-up would be forthcoming. No surprise there—she's a very busy person.

"I gave Alderson the name of the person in procurement who I assumed was responsible for purchasing these supplies, but I don't really know anybody over there. I sent them a quick email as well, simply saying that we had tried these gloves and liked the feel of them. I also sent our departmental business manager, Claire Summerfield, the summary of the test and let her know what we had looked at, just to keep her in the loop. After that, as so often happens, I simply went back to everything I have to do and cope with every day."

Peter Woods is a procurement manager at CCHN. He manages a team of four contracting specialists, and together they are responsible for purchasing what are defined as disposables. Says Peter, "It's amazing all that comes under that title—generally anything we buy in quantity, use once, and then throw out. Most of the items in this category are quite low in cost but high in volume, so we see many thousands of items and many millions of dollars pass through here every year, and most of what we buy comes from just a few of the major medical equipment suppliers.

"We obviously don't negotiate the price on every syringe and tongue depressor. How it really works is we negotiate each contract once every two or three years for a wide range of disposables from each supplier. They then get all the CCHN business for those items over that period of time. At the end of the contract period, we usually issue a new request for proposal (RFP) and see what everyone wants to bid. But contrary to what some may think, this is not a rubber-stamp, 'just redo the last contract' sort of thing, as there are changes to these contracts and to our needs fairly regularly. In those situations, we tend to go with the suppliers we already have under contract and see what they can do for us.

"Now, just so you know, these suppliers—several of whom do millions of dollars of business with us—all talk about wanting, or even having, a 'strategic relationship' with us. But I can tell you that relationship runs as deep as their pricing to us. That's not to say we would do business with just anyone. Whoever we deal with has to be able to deliver what we want, when we want it, and where we want it. If they let us down too often, we will be having some tough conversations with them and ultimately could look for another supplier. That rarely happens, though—they do too much business with us to not pay attention if we have any legitimate concerns.

"So, the sci-fi gloves. Yeah, I remember talking to them. One of their sales reps had run a trial of these fancy new surgical gloves over in ER and got my name from the head doc there. I can't imagine how this sales guy thought we were just going to start buying surgical gloves from him. I mean, we buy a load of those things along with a lot of other supplies from Comdexia, a major supplier to us and indeed to the industry. I'm not about to start breaking up a contract with a major supplier by piecemealing out separate items to just anyone. Plus, the price they wanted for those gloves was unreal. He gave me a pitch about what we would save in reduced infections, but really, if everyone wanted me to start taking these kinds of things into account, where would I be? I've seen it many times before with these salespeople trying to overreach on how valuable their stuff is. Let me give you an example.

"We buy nonslip paint for the stairways. It has some additional gritty material in it that makes it less slippery, even when it's wet. That is clearly important, not to mention the health and safety regulations. So I'm happy to spend a little more on that paint, as it clearly costs more to make—but we're talking maybe 9 or 10 percent here. But what if those paint suppliers tried to sell it for twice the price because it avoids industrial accidents and then tried to justify the price against the cost of the injuries? Nice try, but really, I am not going to waste my time on such farfetched justifications for that high a price.

"Then there's what I call the 'bandwagon benefit.' Let me explain. Here's glove boy hyping his major benefit—infection reduction—that's going to offset the price of his gloves. But he's forgetting, or ignoring, the fact that the HVAC sales guy is plugging the same benefit: how their new-and-improved filtration system is going to save us money by—you guessed it—reducing infections. Then there's a new cleaning company knocking on our door looking for our cleaning contract, and guess what the big benefit is that's going to cover the cost of their more expensive service? You're right again. Everybody jumps on the 'reduce HAI' bandwagon, all trying to justify their costs with the savings from that one beat-up benefit. Not on my watch.

"So, yeah, this guy came around and tried to sell me these high-tech gloves at a much higher price than what we pay today, trying to justify the price against the infections these gloves are going to prevent. Sorry, dude, nonstarter there. I told him even if he was to come in cheaper than what I currently pay for gloves, I'm still not going to break gloves out of our contract with Comdexia. I know what would happen. They would charge me more for other supplies, and perhaps rightfully so, as their overall business volume with us would come down. He would practically have to give me those gloves for free for me to even be interested. I don't think he was surprised, and it was left at that."

And then CCHN's world got turned upside down by an article in the Chicago papers:

> *Earlier today, the independent health care watchdog JumpToad Group, a leading advocate for transparency concerning the safety and quality of health care systems, released its annual survey rating hospitals across the nation. It must have come as an unwelcome surprise to the local hospital network CCHN that they were below the midline ratings regarding hospital-acquired infections (HAIs). The survey results showed that CCHN is below the national average in a number of areas associated with HAIs. This can't be good news for CCHN, as patients and insurers alike are encouraged to utilize the information in these surveys when choosing a provider for their medical care.*
>
> *Dr. Ron Stewart, CEO of CCHN, shared at an earlier press conference how seriously they take these results and underscored their commitment to gain a top-quartile ranking in each of the survey categories. He dwelled on how CCHN already scores very highly in many areas but admitted that they have fallen behind the curve in this one area.*

Claire Summerfield, departmental business manager, CCHN, says, "When the annual JumpToad survey results were released, it was a real shock here because we really pride ourselves on all our clinical and patient practices. But looking back, we had a few exceptional cases, including a Legionnaire's outbreak, and I guess they pushed our scores down in the area of hospital-acquired infections. As you may imagine, poor Stephanie Wong became the center of attention overnight. However, we all have a lot of confidence in her, and what eventually transpired ended up being good for her and, by departmental osmosis, good for all of us.

"It became clear that she was understaffed, so we immediately allocated extra head count for her. Our CEO, Ron Stewart, asked every department head for a list of initiatives that we could all get behind to get on top of infection control. I went back and asked my team for their input, and Rob Summers in the ER reminded me of those 'nano' gloves. We were already somewhat familiar with them, as a few of our staff had tried them and liked them, although there was some talk that they could cause a skin irritation. Anyway, I included them on my list of possible initiatives we could get behind to respond to this crisis. I probably shouldn't say it, but it's almost as important to be seen as doing something as it is to actually be doing it at times like these. That could be why the new nanotechnology used in these gloves was such a hit with everyone—it makes for great PR. So when we got together as a senior management team, each individual was given at least one initiative to handle, and I was asked to look into the Digex gloves.

"I talked some more with Rob Summers and became quite excited about what this new technology represented. Like many before me, I pretty much took the gloves we used for granted. Put them on—no bugs. But I had no idea that the surgical gloves we use every day could in fact not only harbor but also breed a significant level of pathogens. The more we looked into it, the more we all started to get a better idea of what Stephanie was always going on about, and we could appreciate her level of concern. So given the level of visibility we now had on this overall project, it was much easier and quicker to get a team together to properly evaluate the gloves.

"With any new device, we need to get quite a few people onside and even more involved in the actual testing. It's amazing how many folks come out of the woodwork and want and/or need to be involved. I focused my attention mainly on Stephanie and her team representing Infection Prevention and Control and our chief nursing officer and her group. Even with a spotlight on us (that begat a deadline), we still took a few months to evaluate the technology and what it would take to switch to these gloves. Thankfully, Stephanie now had some people on her team who could also look at this. Obviously, we weren't going to go with just the information that Digex provided to us. As good as they may be, you can't go around believing everything you read in brochures and on websites. Stephanie's people were able to track back the actual technology that Digex was using. They had the license to utilize this nanotechnology in the health care field, and we were able to find a bit more about the science in journals and from third parties who have been involved. Earlier Rob and I had also gone over the in-depth information Digex had provided, which we'd cross-referenced with what was available online from the CDC and the WHO [World Health Organization], and the more we looked, the stronger the data became."

Stephanie Wong relates, "My life changed overnight—and not comfortably—with the release of that JumpToad report. It was like having the temperature turned up to boiling for a few months there. But everyone from the CEO on down knew we had to do something about HAIs, and additional resources were provided and allocated accordingly to get the job done. Thankfully, Claire Summerfield scored some additional staff to research and evaluate various initiatives and help plan revised practices across our network.

"As for those Digex gloves, well, to this day I am not really sure about the technology. We largely ignored the marketing material from them, as you know what that can be like. A lot of the testing they had done was with a university out west—I won't say which one, as it doesn't matter. But I can tell you I didn't like the tests they used. They used the X10200-a testing approach, and I much prefer the X10300-c test analysis, so I tended to discount most of their results. I ended up looking for different test results and certification under the X10300-c standards, but there just wasn't anything available. I could certainly agree that their technology should decrease the bioload inside a glove and probably reduce, at least to some extent, the possibility of cross contamination, but I wasn't about to quantify it or agree with their numbers, and I certainly wasn't about to start singing their praises. While I'm not saying they weren't as good as reports made them out to be, would better gloves really make much of a difference? I was far more concerned about where our own HAI issues were coming from, and I didn't really think our current gloves were the problem. I think a bigger problem was the hands using them."

Back to Claire Summerfield: "We were meeting every two weeks to review our progress in several initiatives, all aimed at reducing infections.

Overall, we had twenty-six different initiatives to consider, and all seemed worthy to me. By now, I had quite a few people from across the organization involved in my own push to evaluate the Digex gloves. It's amazing when you start to look at something that seems quite simple how there are all sorts of details to consider. These new gloves would require us to install different dispensers throughout the building—not a big deal, but the maintenance folks said they were tapped out and would need more time. Thanks to the unions, even though it is only two screws to change—and let me tell you, even as mechanically challenged as I am, I could do it in five minutes—the job had to be done by our maintenance people. Then there's the entire purchasing side of the equation. If we swap out who we purchase gloves from, then we could realistically anticipate some pricing action taken on other supplies from Comdexia. Then we also had the skin irritation problem. Thankfully, for that one, we have our own allergy lab, so we asked them to look at the new technology and if there was anything that could cause a negative reaction. They took a few weeks but came back with an okay for us, though a couple of nonbelievers weren't quite as convinced.

"At this point, I was asked to put a cost analysis and business plan together. I called Digex looking for Ted Alderson but was put in touch with another salesperson, Susan Matthews. Apparently, Ted had moved on. Susan supplied some numbers for me and was eager to come in and do a fourteen-day free trial. I told her we had already done a trial, so she went off to find the details. She came back with some pricing information, and we estimated these gloves would cost us about $300,000 more a year than the gloves we were already buying. Ouch! The next thing I had to do was call Purchasing and talk to Pete Woods. And it was at this point that Purchasing virtually brought the whole process to a screeching halt. In no uncertain terms, Pete said there was no way he would ever authorize buying surgical gloves that cost us even a cent more than what we were currently paying. 'And three-hundred grand? Dream on.' Well, I figured—so much for the Digex gloves.

"However, when I reported back at our biweekly IP control meeting and shared that the Digex gloves cost $300,000 more than what we are currently paying for surgical gloves and that Purchasing was having none of it, it was pointed out that the Digex gloves shouldn't be compared to 'ordinary' gloves. If we believed they really could reduce infection, then they were not the same and shouldn't be compared as such. A fine point perhaps, and usually just wishful rationalization, but with the JumpToad report looming over everything, the board had already budgeted several million to invest in what they defined as 'superior products and protocols to help reduce infection across the organization.' Well, considering that Digex had put most of their marketing eggs in the 'reduce HAI' basket, maybe we still had a chance. So the next step was to take the business case and proposal to Rageet Singh, who heads up our Value Analysis Committee (VAC), and see what he had to say."

Rageet joins us: "FYI, just about every hospital has a Value Analysis Committee, and it's our job to review and essentially approve any new product or service someone somewhere wants to bring into the organization. The VAC team is cross functional and includes representatives from Purchasing, or what many now call Strategic Sourcing; from the clinical and administrative side of the equation; plus representatives from our major departments and areas together with nursing and Infection Prevention and Control.

"The VAC team meets every two weeks and generally reviews and reports back on about fifteen new items. And the variety of items that find their way to us is really quite remarkable. It seems like everyone on the planet has some new way we can decrease costs, increase our clinical efficacy, enhance patient satisfaction. I guess those are the hot buttons and everyone knows it. So in comes the parade of great ideas, new products, and approaches, and our job is to cut through all the noise and determine if any of these really do deliver value to our business and to our patients. And I can share with you that in most cases, additional work is often required to discover what the real costs and implications are of us moving to a new device, service, or protocol."

Back to Claire: "I prepared a detailed case to take to our VAC. I was confident we could represent what these Digex gloves could offer and make a good case to offset the increased cost. Of course, that the gloves had a better feel compared to what we use now was just a side benefit; what we were basing our main argument on was their role in the reduction of infection. Well, we didn't get too far into talking about Digex and HAI prevention before Stephanie Wong took over. She said that although there was evidence to support the new technology's ability to reduce the bioload on gloves, there was absolutely no evidence to support that they would reduce infection in our hospitals. She even quoted studies that talked about the false sense of security health care staff may get from assuming that this technology would protect them and their patients in ways it could not. In a nutshell, that was the end of the topic on the agenda, and I agreed to spend some time with Stephanie and scheduled to meet with her the following week. I know she has a tough row to hoe, especially with the focus so much in her area now, and in the end, her overall goal to reduce HAIs was more important than whose gloves we were going to use, and I'd be more than happy to help wherever I could. But I still liked those gloves."

Says Stephanie, "Claire is a very well-respected business manager, and I like working with her. She's very straightforward and open to new ideas. Claire was exploring the use of the Digex gloves across our organization. I can admit, those things still worried me. With it being new technology, I was worried that people might think they were some miracle cure for infection control. I explained this to Claire and found that she wasn't trying to champion the use of these new gloves if it didn't make sense. She is as keen as anyone around here to reduce infections for both our patients and our staff. She quickly understood where I stood and was interested in other initiatives we're pursuing to reduce infections. I shared how I would like to see more awareness around hand hygiene. I told her that although we have most people now using hand sanitizers, too many often miss the areas between their fingers and their fingertips.

"It was in talking to Claire that we had a sort of breakthrough idea. We came up with the idea of launching a new hand hygiene campaign across CCHN. We thought we could tie it into World Hand Hygiene Day in early May. We would promote all aspects of hand hygiene, and the new Digex surgical glove could be part of the campaign. Claire could see how we could turn the new glove into a constant reminder of the need to put hand hygiene at the forefront of everyone's mind. While I wasn't completely sold on that, I have to admit it was a good fit—'hand in glove,' I suppose, forgive the pun. We would put signs on all dispensers with our 1-2-3 steps to good hand hygiene. We needed a campaign name and decided to pinch a line from the CDC's own 'Clean Hands' program and call our campaign 'Clean

Hands Save.' Claire said she would make sure that was okay with the CDC and thought we might even get some help from them. Also, it had been a while now since the Digex trial in the ER, and there was no way we would ever make a complete commitment to some new device, supply, or protocol without a full trial. This would now allow us to trial the Digex gloves with all the staff, and I asked Claire to contact Digex, let them know what we were planning, and hopefully get their commitment to provide enough product for a thirty-day clinical campaign."

Back to Claire: "The meeting with Stephanie was great. I know she had some issues with simply agreeing that the Digex glove would translate into a reduction of infections. I get that. Although the glove undoubtedly reduces the pathogens, we really don't know if it's a cure-all for reducing HAIs. As we talked, though, we both agreed that there was a need for a greater focus on hand hygiene and how the Digex glove could be a part of that program. It's always going to be a tough call to say that the Digex technology is a sure thing in the war against HAIs, but when positioned as part of an overall hand hygiene campaign, I believe the whole premise became far more viable. When I called Susan Matthews at Digex, she was very cooperative and thought the tie-in with World Hand Hygiene Day was a great idea. They pushed back a bit on the idea of a thirty-day trial and tried to go for their usual fourteen-day program, but Stephanie had made it clear we needed thirty days. They somewhat grudgingly agreed, and Susan got some numbers from us for the anticipated needs for the run of the campaign and had one of her marketing people get in touch with me for further coordination. I also emailed a contact at the CDC and let them know what we were doing, and a short reply back indicated that they thought it was a great idea calling our campaign 'Clean Hands Save' and wished us all the best.

"It was back to the VAC, but now with two big differences. First, we were asking for their review and approval to launch an overall hand hygiene initiative, and second, Stephanie was now an active supporter. VAC gave us their blessing for the campaign including a trial of the Digex gloves. At this stage, I pulled in Samantha Cardle. Sam had been a senior RN who had moved into the business side of things. She helps in all sorts of areas; she's a great project manager and knows just about all the senior staff. When it comes to getting things done, she is my go-to person, because—and this is an important point—when you try to change things around here, people don't like it. I know everyone says they love change and that the medical world is forever changing, but I know most of our staff just don't like change, no matter how small.

"Who can blame them? We live in an environment here where we literally don't know what's going to come in the door at any given moment. Though it may sound a bit dramatic, it's a fact that we're in the business of saving people's lives, where often every second counts. Imagine an emergency situation in which the doctor or nurse turns around to where the supplies cart has been for the last ten years, and it's moved, or it's a different cart, or it's loaded differently. Yes, there may be a good reason for the change, but someone's life may be hanging in the balance while that person sorts it out. Sam understands this world, and she is great at thinking of everything that needs doing to minimize the negative aspects of change and how to do it with minimal disruption to everyone's routines and effectiveness. So I asked Sam to organize the Digex trial segment of the 'Clean Hands Save' campaign and to coordinate closely with Stephanie Wong."

Samantha explains, "Claire Summerfield asked me to organize the trial of these new Digex gloves and told me the trial would be part of Stephanie Wong's IP campaign for better hand hygiene. For these types of trials, we have a fairly standard approach. We pull together a committee and first determine what we are trialing, how we will conduct the trial, where we will do it, and what the criteria for success will be. It took a few weeks to get organized, but once we were ready, I called Digex.

"I called them, but when I asked for Susan Matthews, the salesperson Claire had worked with, I was told she had been reassigned, and I was forwarded to David Fox. Turns out he was a fairly new guy and was as eager to get together as was I, so we set a date. He came in all excited and ready to do a demo, offer me a special deal, and do a fourteen-day free trial. I had to settle him down and explain that I would not be doing the purchasing, I was not the decision maker, and we had already arranged a thirty-day trial under clinical conditions with Susan Matthews. This was more than a little disconcerting, as it seemed that we basically had to start over again with Digex and that not much information from the previous rep seemed to have been forwarded to young Mr. Fox. He wasn't sure at first what his manager would say, but he took notes about what we wanted to do and said he would get back to me as soon as possible. A few days later, I received an email from him saying everything was a go, and he would introduce me to their client services team, and they would work with us through the trial.

"Long story short, we conducted the thirty-day trial. Digex was very supportive. They gave us all the supplies, gloves, and dispensers we would need for the campaign. We reported back to the committee that the gloves were almost universally seen as an improvement over our usual surgical gloves. They somehow felt superior and stronger yet offered a better feel, as if they were thinner. And then Stephanie Wong took the floor."

Says Stephanie, "While I don't argue with the opinions most had about the comfort and user-friendliness of the gloves, let me point out that these or any gloves, no matter how good they may be, don't offer any real guarantees of the reduction in infection rates. I was and still am concerned about the testing standards Digex used. And let's please keep in mind that with the welfare of our patients on the line along with the reputation of CCHN, this is not the time to accept second-rate standards on any new initiatives. There are also cost considerations. It's fine to say that while the extra cost would be absorbed this year by special board funding, we know that the gloves will eventually find their way back onto Purchasing's disposables shopping list and reboot all the same issues with Pete Woods and Comdexia. Let me suggest that with the extra funding that's available, we pay more attention both literally and figuratively to several other areas of concern in our battle against HAIs.

"For instance, my group is quite able to closely monitor the four basics of infection control—disinfection and sterilization, environmental infection control, hand hygiene, and isolation precautions. But what I would also like to do is put together another group to deal with two of the other major HAI concerns: antibiotic resistance and device-associated infections. What's the latest on MRSA and MERS-CoV[3]? Can we update our sterilization equipment in those two older downtown locations? And how about, for starters, we take those slightly more expensive and labor-intensive solutions and practices we use in HDU[4] and make them standard procedure across the network?" At this point, Stephanie took a quick look around the suddenly quiet room and then asked, "Have I spent all of that $300k yet?" The tension was immediately relieved, and her very rare and dry humor was met with smiles and chuckles.

But Stephanie wasn't smiling just because of that. "Let me tell you the good news. I am very positive about the overwhelming success and the cooperation everyone provided for the 'Clean Hands Save' campaign itself. The program was a winner, and I know—as do most of you, I think—that the emphasis on frequent and thorough hand cleansing indeed *could* offer guarantees on reducing HAIs. I can see every reason to believe that this program could run continuously and could present new and refreshing impetus to further the awareness and efficacy of better hand hygiene—and at a fraction of the cost of those gloves. Let me finish by saying that I hope you don't think I'm being a dinosaur when it comes to new technology. But perhaps this technology is just a bit too new, a bit too expensive, and a bit too unproven to be a viable choice right now. Let's look at them again in a couple of years and see how they've done. And in the meantime, let's do what we know works to reduce hospital-acquired infections at CCHN."

So that was that. Sam Cardle sums up: "With the trial complete, I worked on an implementation plan for Claire for the ongoing hand hygiene program. I worked closely with one of Stephanie's people to help in the overall design of the new program. We even thought about running a contest for the name of the program, but we kept coming back to 'Clean Hands Save' and decided to use all four lines of the CDC program—Clean Hands Save, Clean Hands Care, Clean Hands Protect, and Clean Hands Count—and alternate them quarterly. We also found a supplier of prepackaged sterile cleansing towelettes that was happy to label them with our slogans and provide handy personal dispensers that could clip to a belt or pocket. We even took the program to some local schools and had the kids design posters that we had printed up for both their schools and throughout CCHN.

"It's interesting that this discussion started with Rob Summers asking me about the Digex gloves, but when all was said and done, this was far more about the hands than the gloves. What we were really looking for was an increased awareness of the importance of better hand hygiene, and while we didn't buy the gloves, we bought the program."

CHAPTER 13

CCHN CASE STUDY ANALYSIS

AS MENTIONED IN the first case study analysis, we would never suggest that a Customer Buying Journey is mapped by looking at just one organization in a single buying experience. However, for the sake of study, we'll analyze the CCHN buying journey as if it was common across the market. Once again, as we analyze this case and interpret the DNA of the Customer Buying Journey, we must focus again on the buyer. While it would be as tempting as ever to comment on the sales and marketing side of the equation, I will resist—at least for now—and stay focused on the buyer and the buying.

WHY THE JOURNEY?

I'm sure you have noticed a major difference between the DiaNascent case study and the CCHN case study. DiaNascent had no choice but to go on a buying journey to find a solution—the implementation of their new Syncron software system. They had to initiate all actions and had a clear goal of acquisition and adoption.

In case study 2, CCHN was not looking to buy nanotechnology anti-microbial gloves, and in fact, they did not need to. Not only that, but they ended up not buying the Digex gloves but instead made investments in related areas. I will examine the DNA for this particular Customer Buying Journey up to the point where CCHN decided *not to buy* the Digex gloves. In doing so, I will address the second half of the book's title and show *why they didn't*.

DNA STRAND 1: TRIGGERS & DEPENDENCIES

Let's start by blowing an easy assumption out of the water. The CCHN buying journey did not start with Dr. Rob Summers when he read the article in *HealthCare Worker Monthly*. Neither did it start when he met Digex at a tradeshow, nor even when the first Digex sales rep called on him and he agreed to do a trial. All the considerable activity that led up to, including, and following the original fourteen-day trial was purely information gathering. Rob and his colleagues were exploring a new technology and had no intent or capability to actually buy. Rob understood his role was not purchasing and that he could not represent the Infection Prevention and Control group, so regardless of how he felt about the gloves, he knew he couldn't make any commitments. Although this activity did lead to the organization being aware of Digex, there was no real buying journey yet. In fact, if it hadn't been for the JumpToad Report, Digex gloves would have remained at best on the back burner and at worst forgotten.

The JumpToad Report was the trigger for the CCHN Customer Buying Journey. CCHN's low ranking on this survey and the public attention it caused placed their focus on infection control and led to the start of a buying journey. The critical issue for Digex was that somebody in a position who was looking to help reduce hospital-acquired infections (HAIs) needed to be aware of Digex, and there was. So not all the previous sales and marketing activities were wasted—they led to the right individuals at least being aware of the Digex gloves—although it is apparent that this could have been achieved more effectively. But keep in mind one key question throughout this analysis: what was CCHN's buying journey really looking for?

DNA STRAND 2: STEPS

ILLUSTRATION 13.1. CCHN: STEPS AND BUYING ACTIVITIES

STEPS	KEY ACTIVITIES	TOUCH POINTS
1. Awareness	• read trade articles • attend trade shows • talk to potential supplier • generally educate	• perform web research • possibly engage in direct dialogue with sales/marketing

(continued)

ILLUSTRATION 13.1 (*continued*)

STEPS	KEY ACTIVITIES	TOUCH POINTS
2. Initial assess-ment	• evaluate possibilities • identify key players across organization and review with them • discover more about the possible solution(s) • search for credible background information • gain input and feedback from different players across the organization • assess alternative approaches • consider what will be required to adopt	• perform web search
3. Business case	• evaluate costs • compare costs to current expenditure • review with purchasing to understand current costs • evaluate where funds could come from	• obtain pricing information from sales
4. Committee approvals	• prepare committee presentation • review with members of committee • present case to committee • work to gain further information required by committee • coordinate with committee members	
5. Clinical trial	• determine nature of trial • coordinate trial and summary of findings • coordinate with multiple players on trial • summarize finding of trial	• gain support for clinical trial
6. Final review	• coordinate with multiple players on business case and clinical trial results • assess priorities and alternative uses of resources • allocate funds and gain budget approvals	

In contrast to case study 1, little meaningful interaction occurred between the buyer and the supplier—a lot of activity, but not many touch points. CCHN decided to conduct their own research into the technology and largely ignored all of Digex's marketing materials and studies. In fact, key player Stephanie Wong of Infection Prevention and Control proactively dismissed the information from Digex almost to the point of skeptical distrust, which did not bode well for Digex. CCHN only had to rely on Digex for pricing information and to support the clinical trial, so this buying journey largely progressed without much influence from the supplier, Digex.

As mentioned, much of the activity with ER doc Rob Summers at the early stages occurred before the buying journey was actually triggered. It would be tempting to list a trial as an activity under step 1 of the buying journey. However, the first fourteen-day trial was incidental to the Customer Buying Journey. It was not a formal clinical trial sponsored by CCHN and did not have the support of key player Stephanie Wong. That first trial in the ER played no significant role in the buying journey other than to remind key players of the antimicrobial gloves when the negative JumpToad Report brought about a heightened interest in infection control.

DNA STRAND 3: KEY PLAYERS

Rob Summers, our ER doctor who figures heavily at the start of the case study, turns out to be only marginally involved in the actual Customer Buying Journey. His efforts led to his manager, Claire Summerfield, becoming aware of Digex, but she was the one who ended up being the provisional champion for the possible acquisition of Digex gloves. Rob was never the champion and clearly stated it was not his role to evaluate the gloves from a cost or infection prevention perspective, nor could he make any commitments on behalf of the organization. It was also quite clear that he had other things to worry about than new gloves. He was purely looking at the offering from an interest point of view—taking them for a test drive, so to speak. We can't ignore his role in the overall Customer Buying Journey, as his actions led to an awareness of the offering across the organization, but other than that, he played no role in the ensuing buying journey. Clearly, Claire Summerfield championed the potential acquisition of the Digex gloves across the organization, although it is important to remember that her support of the gloves evolved into a somewhat secondary position with the emerging Clean Hands campaign.

Stephanie Wong was the key player. Digex essentially positioned their gloves as a way to reduce infections, which placed it squarely within Stephanie's domain for the go/no-go decision. Interestingly, without this attribute, the glove issue would simply have moved to purchasing, where Pete

Woods was certainly not going to entertain buying gloves outside of his contract with Comdexia.

When Claire started to consider the possible switch to Digex gloves, many other people started to show an interest. In her own words, "It's amazing how many folks come out of the woodwork and want and/or need to be involved." Quite possibly, if any or all of these interested parties were allowed to become involved in the actual acquisition process, it could have eventually slowed down or even stopped the overall buying journey. However, as the JumpToad Report regarding the HAI problem at CCHN triggered everything, this became Stephanie Wong's journey, and her singular and steadfast vision kept outside interest and interference to a minimum. This is just as well, as we are left to wonder if anyone would have had the tenacity and motivation to corral these various players and keep forward motion throughout this particular Customer Buying Journey.

Although the CEO was highly involved in the overall response to the negative press regarding CCHN's HAI rating and was clearly the overall sponsor for the initiatives that would respond to the challenge caused by the survey, he was not directly involved in the Digex assessment. Would it have made a difference if he had been? We can only guess it would not have. Stephanie Wong mentions that she sometimes has potential suppliers passed down to her from the CEO, but as she states, that doesn't provide them any priority or favors. The CEO obviously put her in place to do the job and empowers her to do so. He would be unlikely to start making decisions to overrule her or bypass her position or processes. Similarly, the chief nursing officer and chief medical officer are aware of Digex but are not actively involved in the buying journey. As was stated by the various characters in the case study, they were never short of hopeful suppliers knocking on their door with great *value propositions*, just as they were never short of things to do in their days' work. The summary of the key players is shown in illustration 13.2

DNA STRAND 4: BUYING STYLE

In the 4Q Buying Style model, the vertical axis determines that the buyers at the lower end of the scale already know exactly what *product* they want, while the buyers at the top of the scale perceive that they need help to provide a *solution*. Second, the horizontal axis in the 4Q model determines

ILLUSTRATION 13.2. CCHN: KEY PLAYERS BY STEP

STEPS	ER HEAD DOCTOR ROB SUMMERS	BUSINESS MANAGER CLAIRE SUMMERFIELD	PURCHASING PETER WOODS	INFECTION PREVENTION STEPHANIE WONG	CHIEF NURSING OFFICER	CHIEF MEDICAL OFFICER BRET ROGERS	PROGRAM MANAGER SAMANTHA CARDLE	CEO RON STEWART	VALUE ANALYSIS COMMITTEE (VAC) RAGEET SINGH ET AL.
1. Awareness	LEAD	Minor	Minor	Minor	Minor	Minor			
2. Initial assessment		LEAD		KEY	Minor				
3. Business case		LEAD	Some	Some					
4. Committee approvals		LEAD		KEY					Major
5. Clinical trial		Major		Major			LEAD		
6. Final review		LEAD		KEY			Major		

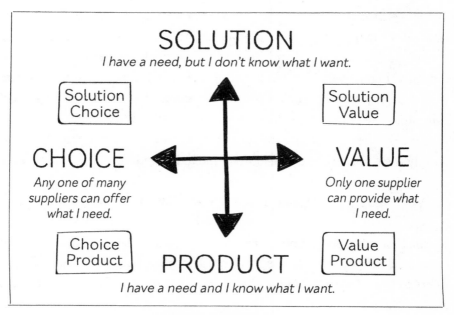

ILLUSTRATION 13.3. 4Q model

that the buyers on the left side believe that they have a *choice* of suppliers, while the buyers on the right side perceive a single supplier as being unique in the *value* they offer.

In the case of the CCHN Customer Buying Journey, the buyer believed they knew what they wanted. If they had approached suppliers and asked them to help with the HAI problem, that would have implied they were buying in the top half of the 4Q model. This was not the case, as they never thought they needed any assistance in knowing what to buy. That isn't to say that they would not have benefited from asking certain suppliers for their recommendations and help, but this is not their buying style.

In the horizontal axis of the 4Q model, a very interesting anomaly exists between the two key players. Through the earlier stages of the Customer Buying Journey, Claire Summerfield was considering acquiring and utilizing the Digex gloves. She was therefore buying on the right-hand side of the 4Q model, as Digex was the only possible supplier for these nano-based antimicrobial gloves. However, Stephanie Wong was never completely convinced that buying these gloves was part of the solution to the HAI challenge. She thought many alternatives existed and many suppliers could help. Her buying style was therefore in the left-hand *choice* segment of the 4Q model. This is a very important point. If they were looking to buy antimicrobial gloves, it would have been a right-hand *value* option in the 4Q model, but when they were looking for solutions to their HAI challenge, it became a left-hand side *choice* buying style. When Stephanie convinced Claire that they should be looking for a hand hygiene program and not simply the gloves, the buying journey moved completely to the *choice* side of the 4Q model.

Pete Woods in purchasing made a comment about how they buy their disposables: Every few years, they put out a request for proposal (RFP) and search for the best supplier—definitely a bottom-left *choice/product* buying style. But then he shares that as the hospitals' needs change, they go to existing suppliers to see what they can do. Thus the buying style shifts to bottom-right *product/value* once they have selected a major supplier. They view the fact that they already have a contract and business relationship with that supplier as valuable and unique. Therefore, instead of shopping around for various suppliers, as would be the case on the left-hand side of the 4Q model, they move to the right-hand side and favor the incumbent. If it hadn't been for Stephanie Wong changing what they were buying, Claire may have reached the end of the buying journey staying on the right-hand side of the equation, and CCHN may have ended up buying from Digex as the only provider of antimicrobial gloves.

DNA STRAND 5: VALUE DRIVERS

The overwhelming *value driver* throughout the Customer Buying Journey was responding to the JumpToad survey scores by tackling, and being seen to be tackling, the HAI infection challenge. Illustration 13.5

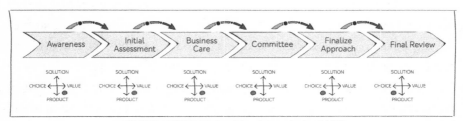

ILLUSTRATION 13.4. 4Q buying style for CCHN

ILLUSTRATION 13.5. CCHN: VALUE DRIVERS BY STEP

STEPS	ER DOCTOR ROB SUMMERS	BUSINESS MANAGER CLAIRE SUMMERFIELD	PURCHASING PETER WOODS	INFECTION PREVENTION STEPHANIE WONG	PROGRAM MANAGER SAMANTHA CARDLE	CEO RON STEWART	VAC RAGEET SINGH ET AL.
1. Awareness	• education • reduction of infection		• reduction of costs • protecting current contracts	• implementing current programs • educating others on infection control			
2. Initial assessment		• responding to the survey results • efficacy of the glove		• overall infection control • efficacy of the glove		• responding to the HAI survey results	
3. Business case		• responding to the survey results	• cost containment	• overall infection control			
4. Committee approvals		• responding to the survey results • efficacy of the glove		• overall infection control • overall hand hygiene			• efficacy of the glove • costs • overall support
5. Clinical trial		• responding to the survey results • efficacy of the glove • ease of adoption		• overall infection control • efficacy of the glove • overall hand hygiene	• efficacy of the glove • ease of adoption		

summarizes the value drivers of the key players at each step of the buying journey.

Rob Summers, the first person to get involved with Digex, was motivated to learn more about a new product offering, but he was also aware of the need to control infection, and Digex's claims to minimize pathogens on surgical gloves would have been a motivator for him to learn more.

The JumpToad Report was responsible for many things happening across CCHN with a focus on HAI reduction. This was the trigger for the buying journey Claire Summerfield championed. Her value drivers were responding to the survey results and promoting the efficacy of the Digex glove in reducing HAIs. However, later in the buying journey, she was also motivated by the ease of adoption and the switch from using the incumbent product to the new Digex gloves.

Stephanie Wong has somewhat different value drivers. Her world has been, and continues to be, all about the reduction of infection across the hospital network. She originally wanted to stay the course and not simply react to every new idea that came along that claimed to help with infection control. Although she is somewhat motivated to understand the efficacy of the glove, she is far more motivated by overall hand hygiene, and this becomes her value driver as they move through the Customer Buying Journey.

Claire's project manager, Samantha Cardle, was brought in late to the project, but her value drivers were the efficacy of the glove together with a focus on the implementation and adoption of the Digex glove.

DNA STRAND 6: BUYING CONCERNS

At the early stage of the Customer Buying Journey, the *buying concerns* would have been the overall process, which was not at all apparent in terms of the Digex gloves given their existing budgets and obligations to Comdexia. No one from the organization who was involved at that point had the authority to make any commitments. Also, Infection Prevention and Control, along with Purchasing, would have actively blocked any attempt to move forward with a possible acquisition. There was also no way to justify the additional expenditure on the Digex gloves. But as the buying journey

ILLUSTRATION 13.6. CCHN BUYING CONCERNS BY STEP

PROCESS	PRIORITY	INDIVIDUAL	ORGANIZATIONAL	ALTERNATIVES	BUSINESS	IMPLICATIONS	FIT	CHANGE
1. Awareness								
2. Initial assessment								
3. Business case								
4. Committee approvals								
5. Clinical trial								

KEY

- A buying concern that would likely stop the buying journey
- A buying concern that could slow down and possibly stop the buying journey
- Not a significant concern

moved through the later steps, you will see the following buying concerns materialize, as shown in illustration 13.6.

1. PROCESS

Process remains a buying concern, as no process exists for acquiring these antimicrobial gloves. CCHN buys gloves as a small component of an overall contract with a major supplier. Digex is essentially introducing a new product category, and one that the existing processes at CCHN cannot easily accommodate.

2. PRIORITY

Given the JumpToad survey results, the HAI reduction gains a lot of attention across CCHN; therefore, the priority given to the possible purchase of the Digex gloves increases dramatically. However, as alternative approaches to the overall topic of hand hygiene start to emerge, the priority given to acquiring Digex gloves decreases.

3. INDIVIDUAL

Through most of the Customer Buying Journey, there is a clear champion: Claire Summerfield, who is motivated to move forward. This motivation drops when the notion of switching to a hand hygiene program takes over the original focus on acquiring the Digex gloves

4. ORGANIZATIONAL

Various players across the organization had concerns about the efficacy of the Digex gloves. These concerns mainly came from Infection Prevention and Control. Stephanie Wong was never convinced of the efficacy of the gloves and never had the information she believed she needed to lend her support to the gloves' role in reducing infections. She stated she was not a fan of the testing procedure Digex used and preferred an alternative testing approach. Although she was never the lead person for owning the buying journey, she was highly influential through most of the steps and was responsible for the change in focus from acquiring the Digex gloves to launching a hand hygiene program that ultimately would not include the new gloves. She was clearly not onside and also not an early adopter of new and thus unproven technologies.

5. ALTERNATIVES

Although no alternatives to the Digex glove exist, there are many alternatives to the reduction of infections. At one time, the organization was evaluating twenty-six possible initiatives to reduce infection. Further, as the focus moved to hand hygiene, many alternatives to antimicrobial gloves offered a reduction in potential infection. We also hear a recurring theme from the characters at CCHN: they are never short of great ideas to help them in their operation and business.

6. BUSINESS

This started as a buying concern and was never resolved. The fact that the Digex glove would cost some $300k more was never justified. For a while, CCHN thought they could meet this cost by allocating additional board-sponsored funds to respond to the HAI challenge, but then they realized this would be an ongoing cost.

7. IMPLICATIONS

Several implications arise during the course of this buying journey. Purchasing pointed out the potential impact on the existing contract with Comdexia. A reduction in their business volume caused by purchasing gloves from Digex could then lead to pricing action and CCHN having to pay more for other supplies. Infection Prevention and Control was concerned that the gloves would give health care workers a false sense of security, a misperception that could increase with the adoption of the high-tech nano-based Digex gloves. As the buying journey moved toward thinking about implementation, it became apparent that the glove dispensers would need changing. That was not as easy as it may have appeared due to the backlog of work in maintenance.

8. FIT

Although it is likely safe to assume that Rob Summers embraces new technology, it becomes apparent that Stephanie Wong is not an early adopter.

It's interesting to reflect on her position at the VAC meeting when she positioned the Digex gloves as a new technology and unproven, and it may be prudent to look at them again in a couple of years. She followed up by stating, "Let's do what we know works." This seems to be the sentiment that carried the day, so we would suggest that the "fit" of a new technology into her area of this organization represented a very real buying concern.

9. CHANGE

The change that would be required from the gloves CCHN uses today to the Digex gloves came up several times. CCHN is sensitive to changes in operations, as they see they could impact patient safety. Although not rated as a "red flag" buying concern (i.e., one that could potentially derail the overall journey), it appears as if the change associated with switching to the Digex glove is a pervasive concern.

SUMMARY

This case study reflects a typical buying journey: it's not simple, it's not straightforward, it involves multiple players, it involves many activities, and it involves looking at many alternative approaches, prioritizing, reprioritizing, and carefully evaluating the implications of the decisions. If anything, this case study is actually simpler than what we see in real life. If you read the story and thought I was deliberately adding twists and turns you wouldn't see in real life, I can assure you that is not the case.

When we talk to buyers, their stories sound very much like this case study. Their journeys are rarely straight lines where someone on high instructs the organization what to do and what to acquire. Even when buyers are faced with undeniably great opportunities to add value to their organizations, they don't always buy. It is very easy to start presuming what a customer *should* think, or *should* do, or *should* buy, but this is a dangerous approach based all too often on myth, pretzel logic, or wishful thinking. I can promise you we will always focus on how customers *actually behave*.

Because buyers don't appear to act logically, they don't act as you may expect. But time and time again, they do act in a predictable manner. It was this observation that unlocked the mystery for me. If you can determine how a buyer is going to behave, what their motivations and concerns are, and how they make their decisions, then you have taken the first steps toward a far more effective, repeatable, and scalable approach to successful revenue generation.

PART 2
DEVELOPING THE MARKET ENGAGEMENT STRATEGY

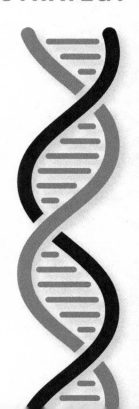

CHAPTER 14

WHAT TO DO ABOUT IT

REVENUE GENERATION TOO often relies on the assumption that potential customers will make their buying decisions based simply on the value that an offering will deliver to them or their organization—a decision devoid of both emotion and the far wider context of the actual world in which they operate. The fact that most buyers don't buy in this way often gives the appearance of illogical buying behavior or, worse still, the supplier's failure to communicate the value of their potential offering. But when suppliers gain a deeper understanding of the world in which they sell, along with the emotional aspects of a buying decision, buyers' behavior is logical, predictable, and very human.

In part 1 of this book, I shared how my company's research resulted in our identifying and developing the six DNA strands of the Customer Buying Journey, which then allowed us to accurately map how customers buy and why they don't. Among other things, we found that the buying journey is quite logical and, most importantly, *predictable*. Once that DNA is decoded, you will see that people or organizations within a specific market, when faced with a particular offering, will buy in a remarkably similar way. Our research also enabled us to further define that a similar manner of buying can actually define a discrete market. And an interesting adjunct to that thinking prompted another discovery: two identical offerings bought in dissimilar ways denote *two distinct markets*.

TURNING THE TABLE

In part 1, I urged you to focus your attention only on how people and organizations buy. This is always one of the hardest things I have to do when working with clients—keeping that focus as opposed to how the supplier would like them to buy or indeed how the supplier wants to sell to them. But let's reverse the view now and look at how suppliers go to market.

Let me remind you up front that this is about the very purpose of business: how to create a customer. It's about everything across the organization that results in getting someone, somewhere to buy and doing so in a predictable, manageable, and scalable fashion. Because how often are you surprised as revenue growth or market share seems to stall? How often are forecasts not achieved? How frustrating is it to see success in some areas or by some people versus areas or people that are not so successful and wonder why? In my experience, far too often. Although I would be the first to say that sales and marketing will probably never be a perfect system—the likes of which we regularly see in manufacturing and logistics with the adoption of Six Sigma and similar approaches—there is no reason why sellers should suffer through the upsets, anomalies, and general unpredictability that seem all too common in today's world of revenue generation.

Before looking at how the supplier can develop and implement a business strategy that will result in predictable, manageable, and scalable approaches to creating customers, here's what I have found in many organizations today.

LET'S GET REAL

Hopefully I have already laid to rest the fallacy that getting a customer to buy is all about gaining their understanding of an offering and their belief in its value to them and their organization and that only a fool would not buy such a beneficial offering. From this viewpoint, the world seems to be full of fools who are not buying. Yet this fallacy is still the basis on which most of the corporate sales and marketing activities and initiatives seem to lie. To really understand the folly of this thinking, let's first look at five chronological stages of a typical purchase—of how customers actually buy.

EFFORT TO BUY

For the sake of this illustration, I should stress that this is not an *actual* buying journey; rather, it is what I would call a macro and a generic buying journey for the purposes of illustrating a timeline of the effort expended within such a journey. When performing this exercise for any client, I always use their own market's actual Customer Buying Journey and its associated DNA. However, this gives a good indication of what goes through the minds of most customers during their purchase processes (see illustration 14.1). Given this macro buying journey, let's look at the amount of effort or energy required by the customer at each of these steps to successfully keep things moving along from awareness of an offering to adoption of that offering.

Today's marketing can be a powerful and ubiquitous machine, but too often the focus is placed purely on generating awareness and interest but little else. So looking at illustration 14.1, it's easy to see that very little effort is required on the part of a potential customer to develop *awareness* of a new offering. Of course, this idea is at odds when you consider what it takes for a selling company to make a prospective customer aware of their offering, and I'll come to that. For the moment, let's continue thinking about this from the customer's point of view.

For the prospective customer to gain *interest*—strong interest—it does take more, but not a huge degree, of effort. It may take them quite some time to come around, but when they do, they will probably do additional research to fully understand and evaluate the offering. They will likely consider some alternative approaches and perhaps quantify the value it will bring to them and/or their organization. At some point, they will start believing that this offering is worthy of serious consideration, and they will move from interest to commitment.

Commitment is the point where somebody understands and believes in the offering enough to become its "champion," to widely promote the offering across the organization. And if you look at illustration 14.2, commitment is a mountain to climb. When we talk to people about their buying

ILLUSTRATION 14.1. A MACRO BUYING JOURNEY

STAGE	DESCRIPTION
1. Awareness	Becomes aware of a new offering
2. Interest	Seeks more information, understands and evaluate the offering in terms of its potential application, utility, and value
3. Commitment	Gains the organizational review, input, and okay to proceed with an acquisition
4. Acquisition	Enters into sourcing, negotiation, and contracting to acquire the offering
5. Adoption	Adopts the offering that may be one time or over time and hopefully derives the benefit and value associated with its adoption

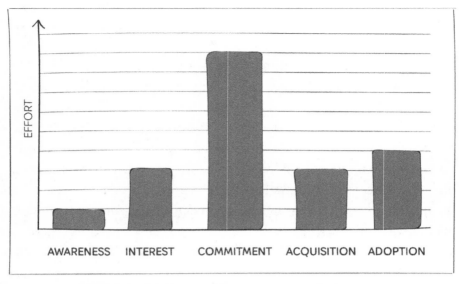

ILLUSTRATION 14.2. Buying effort across a macro buying journey

journeys, this is when we hear the deep sighs, when they share with us all they had to do, the obstacles they faced, and the people they had to get onside to secure organizational commitment.

When mapping the DNA of the Customer Buying Journey, at this stage—when an individual or group is sufficiently convinced that they both understand an offering and believe in its value—several things almost invariably happen:

- an exponential increase in the amount of activity required to successfully move forward
- the involvement of multiple players
- growing complexity and lack of alignment of the motivation to move forward with the acquisition
- a significant increase in the number and type of *buying concerns*, including (and compare these with the nine categories identified as possible buying concerns earlier in the book)
  - different agendas introduced by different players
  - many other initiatives positioned as higher priorities
  - potential lack of clarity regarding the overall buying and funding process

- concerns about the implications that may arise for acquiring and adopting the offering
- far greater detail required on the investment and its potential return
- fit of the possible acquisition to the culture of the organization
- reluctance to embrace any change necessary to adopt the offering

These result in a significant amount of work for someone. At the same time, he will undoubtedly have other things to do and very likely not enough time in the day to do them. Unless this person is highly attached to the notion of acquiring this new offering, more than likely he will run out of momentum and motivation to keep going. This is why more than 50 percent (often far higher) of buying journeys simply stall out at this step.

For those who make it over Commitment Mountain in the Customer Buying Journey, it's on to *acquisition*. Acquisition potentially involves an RFP (request for proposal) process, detailed evaluation, and/or configuration of the offering, perhaps a trial, and it certainly ends up with negotiation and contracting.

After acquisition comes *adoption*, which can range from simply turning on a switch to a much more complex series of activities, including commissioning, building, deploying, integrating, training, testing, and many other activities associated with implementation. It might be a one-time occurrence, or it could continue over a long period of time. It is through adoption, however, that the customer finally realizes their reward. That reward could be turning on a new power plant that will save tens of millions of dollars a year, or it may be the scent and prestige of driving a new Mercedes around town. The payback can come in many ways, and hopefully it provides everything the customer was expecting as they traversed the ups and downs of their buying journey.

EFFORT TO SELL

Let's flip around and look at what the typical sales and marketing organization does during the Customer Buying Journey. Illustration 14.3 adds the typical degree of effort and attention given to each of these five buying journey steps.

Not surprisingly, and quite understandably, we see companies, especially marketing organizations, make a huge investment in developing potential customers' *awareness* of the offering. This is in marked contrast to the effort the customer puts in at this step, but that's to be expected. At the

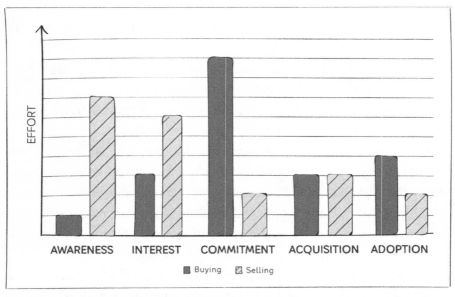

ILLUSTRATION 14.3. Buying and selling effort across a macro buying journey

interest stage, we see a typical and very busy sales force dedicating a significant percentage of their time to ensuring that potential customers understand the offering and clearly see and believe in the value of that offering. Selling activities will include providing demonstrations, conducting needs analysis, configuring, designing solutions, and undertaking ROI (return on investment) analyses. This is the ground of consultative selling in many ways, with an overall objective of understanding what a customer needs or wants and then gaining a sincere interest or belief in a proposed approach.

But here is where the tables turn, and you'll see a startling major inversion of effort. The amount of time and effort invested by sales and marketing in activities aligned to the *commitment* step of the macro buying journey abruptly falls away. When their customers are faced with the greatest amount of work, sales and marketing tend to remain a step behind in a continual loop of reinforcing the already proven value of the offering. This paradox goes right back to the fallacy I have already pointed out—the thinking that if only the customer "gets it," they will buy. If they aren't buying, it must be because they either don't understand the offering or don't believe in its value.

This is the exact position that led to the epiphany I spoke of in the prologue. In the vast majority of cases, the customers do get it; they believe in the value. And they have moved on to the next stage of their buying journey—*commitment*—where they get mired down with all the friction that can cause the journey to falter, to slow down, and so many times, to stop. This is where most Customer Buying Journeys wither and die. And where is the salesperson in this process? Too many times, she is still hammering away in the belief that she has yet to get the customer's understanding of the offering's value.

I find myself again needing to come to the defense of the somewhat put-upon salespeople here. They are only responding to the age-old logic that people will buy something if it is of value to them. Everyone around them reinforces this axiom on a continual basis. Traditional sales training reinforces this and devoutly transcribes it in their internally focused, dog-eared sales processes. Salespeople are doing everything they think is right. But in today's world of third-generation buying, they are falling sadly short of the mark.

We often hear from optimistic sales folks at this stage in the journey that they indeed have a champion—someone inside who's carrying the ball, making things happen for them. Surely that champion is in the best position to do whatever it takes to get the organization onside. And surely that champion is armed with a good business analysis that shows the value to the organization of the potential acquisition—and, well, you know the rest . . . who wouldn't buy?

But for the moment, let's get back to the remainder of the corresponding sales effort. In illustration 14.3, you can see that the effort and energy salespeople invest at the *acquisition* stage matches that of the customer. Here the salesperson is busy finalizing the proposal, pricing, terms, and conditions. As the customer moves into *adoption*, our research found a high degree of variability in terms of the energy invested by sales. Sometimes the salesperson almost acts as a project manager and is highly involved with implementation, and at other times, the salesperson quickly moves on to other activities.

THE OPPORTUNITY

You have the opportunity to solve the inversion of selling energy between the buying journey stages of *interest* and *commitment*, but this is only possible if you, the seller, understand and map out what really goes on during each stage of that journey. This is where all our research into the DNA of the Customer Buying Journey pays off for you. Finally, you will know what is really happening throughout the buying journey. For a particular offering in a specific market, you will know that buyers buy in remarkably similar ways, and you will know what is going to happen in the commitment stage:

- who will take what roles and what their motivations and concerns will be
- what activities are likely to happen
- what buying concerns are likely to come up
- what the buying style is and how it may change

Interestingly enough, you will often know these things better than most customers themselves will. When you think about it, that's not unexpected. As a supplier, you hope to go through, or at least to closely watch others go through, this process multiple times, whereas a particular customer may only go through it once. Imagine the resource you can become to the champion if you can predict that person's needs and work with him or her from interest to commitment to acquisition and successful adoption.

THE NEW ROLE OF SALES AND MARKETING

The new role of sales and marketing is to become not explainers and persuaders of the offering but knowledgeable managers of the entire Customer Buying Journey. The focus must move from simply gaining an awareness of and a belief in the offering to supporting and managing the customer through each step of the journey, from an internally focused sales approach to the external reality of how customers actually buy. Of course, none of this is possible without the framework of decoding the specific Customer Buying Journey in part 1. Armed with a deep understanding of how customers buy and why they don't, you can now wholly develop new and effective approaches to creating a customer—approaches that are predictable, manageable, and scalable.

The new role of sales and marketing is to manage the entire Customer Buying Journey.

In part 2 of this book, I will share with you how to craft your overall Market Engagement Strategy—the approach to implementing an optimal customer engagement approach based on how the customer actually buys: the world of Outside-In Revenue Generation.

CHAPTER 15

CRAFTING THE MARKET ENGAGEMENT STRATEGY

WITH FEW EXCEPTIONS, any organization that has sustained success can articulate its processes, approaches, and operating standards as to how they design and manufacture their product and how they deliver their services to customers. They can fluently discuss and describe their logistics, their hiring practices, and the way they account for their finances. They can quickly bring new employees up to speed and easily observe how things are done and what is important to the organization. They have carefully thought through all these areas and have meaningfully acted on them. Yet talk to many people across any organization, including the executive, about how they create customers, and too often all you'll hear is a series of ill-defined and nonspecific ideas—some very fuzzy thinking.

In most organizations, each individual salesperson is left to deal with the actual task of creating customers in his or her own way. You now know the root cause of this predicament—being left alone to make a sale happen armed only with the inherent belief that the offering they are presenting to their market is of such value that only a fool wouldn't buy it.

Having spent the last twenty-plus years talking to thousands of people across hundreds of companies, one thing is consistently apparent: in any successful enterprise, the employees are highly enthusiastic about their offering They believe! And that is only natural. Imagine what it would be like to work for a company where you thought your offering was second rate, or at best no better than anyone else's. People want to believe, and they do believe, that they have an offering that delivers clear value to their potential customers. And they may well be right—in fact, they often are. However, three misconceptions remain constant:

1. They significantly overestimate the value of their own offerings to their customers.
2. They significantly underestimate, or are even blind to, the barriers to someone actually acquiring and successfully adopting their offering.
3. They believe (especially given 1 and 2 above) that to get a customer to buy, all they have to do is get a potential customer to understand the offering and verify the return on investment (ROI).

These three misguided beliefs have led to a dire lack of appreciation for just how important the customer creation process is. However, this is not to say that a lot of these people aren't performing many sensible actions. Most know you have to speak to the right person, link the offering to what he really cares about, and handle objections or hesitations. But the basic formula remains the same. The variable in the equation becomes the somewhat mythical sales skills that the salesperson brings to each situation. Hire the salesperson with the "right stuff"—the one who can call high, sell consultatively, handle objections, close the deal—and you are largely there.

This thinking has compromised many organizations. Start-ups, once they finish selling to friends and family, fail to gain market traction. Industry giants miss revenue forecasts. Well-established companies can't penetrate new markets or respond to changing market conditions. All are running afoul of the tough, serious business of creating a customer—all due to these three misconceptions.

STRATEGY

Over the years, it has become patently apparent to me that many companies lack and desperately need a well-crafted Market Engagement Strategy. Now, *strategy* may be one of the most overused words in the business lexicon, so let's take a good look at what we're really going after here. *Strategy* is defined as "a careful plan or method for achieving a particular goal."[1] In this case, the goal is to create customers and do so in as predictable, manageable, and scalable manner as possible. In my mind, the word *careful* in the definition implies the immediate loss of those three blind mice listed above. Anyone trying to define a careful plan or method for creating customers in today's G3 buying world needs to walk into the process with eyes wide open. The very foundation of creating such a strategy relies on these three elements:

1. Understanding exactly how a potential customer will view the value of the offering in light of everything else they face
2. Understanding everything a potential customer must deal with to not only acquire the offering but also successfully adopt it
3. Bypassing the fallacy of the assumptive sale by keeping all "show-and-tell" sales activities in their place and working within the reality of how customers actually buy

Careful readers will have noted that these three elements are diametrically opposed to the three misconceptions, so it's no wonder so many companies lack a careful plan or method for creating customers. It's no wonder I hear so many senior executives and CEOs share that they simply want their sales force to get in front of the decision maker, position the offering properly, and close the deal. You also may have noted how the three tenets for crafting a successful strategy map directly to the DNA of the Customer Buying Journey. Armed with the knowledge of the six strands of the DNA described in part 1, you can now craft a successful strategy based on the external reality of how customers buy and why they don't versus the internally driven notions of positioning the product and its benefits to the marketplace. This is the very core of the concept I have defined as Outside-In Revenue Generation.

Organizations that lack a careful, strategic plan for creating customers are exposed to the vicissitudes of the marketplace. They rely solely on the ability of individual salespeople to work it out largely by trial, error, and sheer luck, all resulting in massive waste across the enterprise. Though some combinations of these factors may be successful for a short-term and occasionally longer period of time, in reality, this is a high-risk, expensive approach. While some organizations can afford this, unfortunately, most don't gain the success they deserve in their chosen marketplaces. I see it weekly: companies that have given care and attention to all other facets of their business go about the job of creating a customer with a marked lack of effective strategy, because they don't have a carefully crafted, all-encompassing Market Engagement Strategy based on the three guidelines listed above.

Many organizations defend their actions by showing me the processes and methods they use for training and supporting their sales force and sharing their marketing campaigns and the ways in which they manage their sales pipelines. They might use the latest in sales techniques and methodologies. I have even heard some say they don't have time for strategy in today's fast-moving world—that today's business environment is all about getting out there now and trying things.

Well, I totally agree that the world won't stop while you take the time to develop a plan, and I totally agree with the notion of always learning from what you are doing. However, I simply cannot subscribe to or even understand the idea that anyone would commit significant money, time, and effort to experimenting in the marketplace rather than taking a few weeks to gather knowledge of how their customers really buy, or why they don't, and then craft and align those findings to an effective Market Engagement Strategy.

But before I delve into the nuts and bolts of all this, let's look at the big-picture view of what we are trying to achieve.

CHANGING THE COURSE OF EVENTS

Before embarking on crafting the Market Engagement Strategy, let me make a fundamental point. All this focus on understanding how the customer buys does not suggest that you have to market and sell in exactly that fashion. The last thing I would ever suggest is to just react to how customers buy and simply cater to their needs along the way. In fact, the very reason you need to invest in any sales or marketing is to change the course of events. The singular objective for sales and marketing must be to positively impact the market, resulting in the customer doing something they otherwise would not have done—to change the course of events in one or more of four, and only four, ways.

The Sales and Marketing Imperatives
1. *Initiate.* To get a customer to enter into a buying journey that they otherwise would not have done.

2. *Complete.* To increase the probability of the customer successfully completing that buying journey through the acquisition and adoption of your offering.
3. *Expedite.* To increase the speed at which they move through their buying journey.
4. *Augment.* To increase the amount they will spend in acquiring your offering.

These are my four horsemen: the Sales and Marketing Imperatives. I have faced many people who believe there are other reasons to invest in sales and marketing, but I have never been proven wrong that everything comes back to one or more of these four imperatives.

As you start to think about the Market Engagement Strategy, it brings an extraordinary level of focus to the equation to consider that *this is what it is really all about*. And as you develop that strategy, it will become apparent what you have to change to achieve one or more of these four imperatives. At the very least, I hope you will alleviate *buying concerns*, as these are the most critical influences on how the market otherwise behaves and impacts both the speed of the buying journey and the probability of completion. As you explore each aspect of crafting the Market Engagement Strategy, you will see more examples of how you can assess the time, cost, and difficulty of changing how your customers buy.

CRAFTING THE MARKET ENGAGEMENT STRATEGY

Over the next few chapters, I will share the five goals of developing an effective strategy with an understanding of the target market's Customer Buying Journey DNA. Using the 4Q Buying Style model, I will first look at the impact of how the target market makes decisions. I start there for reasons that will soon become clear, as the buying style of the market likely has the most significant impact on your overall Market Engagement Strategy, and perhaps even beyond.

I have already defined *strategy* as having a plan to achieve a goal, so let's define exactly what your goals should be when engaging in the market to create customers:

Goal 1. *To harmonize your selling approach with how the market is buying or change how the market buys to how you want to sell.* The overall approach to how you sell and position yourself in the market must synchronize with the customer's buying style. Failure to do so will result in significant waste and loss.

Goal 2. *To initiate or engage in a Customer Buying Journey.* You need to either start a customer on a buying journey or effectively engage with customers already on a buying journey.

Goal 3. *To ensure the customer has adequate motivation to invest in the buying journey and ultimately in the acquisition and adoption of the offering.* Once you are engaged with a customer in a buying journey, you must ensure that the Customer Buying Journey *value drivers* are recognized and deployed to provide adequate motivation for the customer to continue to invest in the buying journey and ultimately acquire and adopt the offering.

Goal 4. *To ensure you remain engaged in the buying journey.* You must stay engaged with the customer and do everything possible to ensure that the customer continues to move positively through the buying journey.

Goal 5. *To reduce friction across the Customer Buying Journey.* Nine different categories of buying concerns (see chapter 9, "The Nine Faces of Buying Concerns") can cause a buying journey to slow down or stop. Your strategy must include a component to ensure that the Customer Buying Journey is as friction-free as possible.

ILLUSTRATION 15.1. MARKET ENGAGEMENT STRATEGY GOALS WITH THE SALES AND MARKETING IMPERATIVES

IMPERATIVES → MARKET ENGAGEMENT STRATEGY GOALS	INITIATE	COMPLETE	EXPEDITE	AUGMENT
1. Harmonize approach		*		
2. Initiate/engage	*			
3. Adequate motivation		*	*	*
4. Positive progress		*	*	
5. Friction-free		*	*	

These, then, are the five Market Engagement Strategy goals. Illustration 15.1 provides a look at how these five components interact with the Sales and Marketing Imperatives.

We are now ready to explore these Market Engagement Strategy goals in detail.

TAKEAWAYS

⇒ Most businesses adhere to the fallacy that if a prospective customer understands their offering and believes it will deliver value, then that customer will logically buy. This in turn leads to the toxic notion that the only revenue generation strategy required is to make the market aware of the offering and its benefits.

⇒ Businesses must invest in a Market Engagement Strategy to determine how they will create and keep customers in a consistent and predictable manner.

⇒ The new role for sales and marketing is to manage and positively impact the Customer Buying Journey. There are only four ways in which to do this—the Sales and Marketing Imperatives:

1. *Initiate.* To engage or trigger a Customer Buying Journey.
2. *Complete.* To increase the probability of successful completion of a buying journey.
3. *Expedite.* To increase the speed of the buying journey.
4. *Augment.* To increase the spend the buyer will make as a result of their buying journey.

⇒ An effective Market Engagement Strategy must be based on a deep understanding of the specific market's Customer Buying Journey.

⇒ There are five goals of the Market Engagement Strategy, which are explored in each of the next five chapters.

CHAPTER 16

GOAL 1: HARMONIZING TO THE BUYING STYLE

THE 4Q MODEL FOR THE MARKET'S BUYING STYLE

THE IMPORTANCE OF understanding the target market's buying style cannot be overemphasized. Of the six strands in the DNA of the Customer Buying Journey, it is the starting point for understanding and crafting a successful Market Engagement Strategy. It establishes an absolute foundation and a robust cornerstone for successful revenue generation. I will repeat something I said earlier—that it is *what I now know to be arguably the most powerful means of analyzing and thus discovering, how people buy*. It unlocks vital aspects of the behavior and motivations affecting the Customer Buying Journey, and its significance will become apparent as I dig deeper into its theory and application.

Let's briefly review the 4Q Buying Style model (illustration 16.1) and take a quick look at each quadrant.

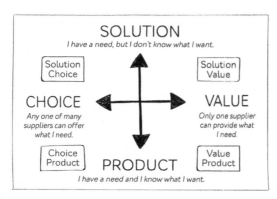

ILLUSTRATION 16.1. 4Q model quadrants

BOTTOM LEFT: CHOICE/PRODUCT, "SORT AND SELECT"

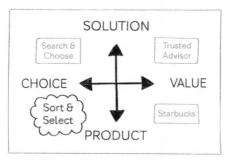

ILLUSTRATION 16.2. 4Q: Sort and Select

In this quadrant, the buyer perceives that they have a choice of provider and that they know exactly what they want. They can therefore sort through their various options and select the provider that can offer them the best price, availability, or fit to what they want. Unless for some reason their buying style changes, if faced with the same buying journey again, they would resort to the same Sort and Select approach. We often call this style of buying RFP Land, and this is also where Commodity lives, though not to suggest that all offerings herein are commodities.

TOP LEFT: CHOICE/SOLUTION, "SEARCH AND CHOOSE"

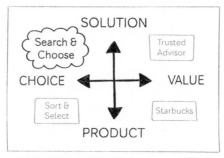

ILLUSTRATION 16.3. 4Q: Search and Choose

Within this quadrant, the buyer believes they have a choice of a potential supplier, but they know they need assistance in determining what they should be buying. They will search through the various potential suppliers and choose one based on how they perceive that supplier can help, and they often make that choice based on availability and their perception of how well the supplier's expertise will enable them to understand and recommend what is required.

TOP RIGHT: VALUE/SOLUTION, "TRUSTED ADVISOR"

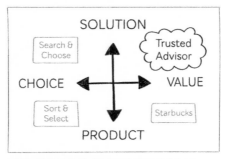

ILLUSTRATION 16.4. 4Q: Trusted Advisor

Although massively clichéd and often used incorrectly, the term *Trusted Advisor* does fit the top-right quadrant. This is where the buyer believes they need assistance to determine what they need to acquire, and they turn to the same person or organization time and time again to provide that assistance.

BOTTOM RIGHT: VALUE/PRODUCT, "STARBUCKS"

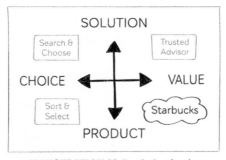

ILLUSTRATION 16.5. 4Q: Starbucks

In this quadrant, the buyer knows exactly what they want, they know where they will buy it, and they do not require assistance. While not everyone will buy coffee (or anything else) this way, those who do make up the bottom right quadrant. And to the good folks at Starbucks, well done.

Knowing and understanding the buying style of the market, you can now start crafting an effective Market Engagement Strategy. Like all good plans, there are rules, but again, like all good plans, those rules are good ones, and they work. Read on.

RULES OF ENGAGEMENT

RULE 1: THERE ARE NO GOOD OR BAD QUADRANTS

People tend to think that one of the 4Q quadrants represents a better way of doing business than the others, but this is not true: there are many examples of successful companies doing good business in any one of these quadrants.

Many of our clients in the high-tech industry perceive they have to be a *Trusted Advisor* to their customers, and the very notion of doing business any other way is strange and almost repugnant to them. I understand that, but I can also put forward a strong argument showing that selling in that manner has a very high cost associated with it. Even more importantly, as you'll shortly see, it is not often up to the supplier to choose the style of relationship they want with their customers. Many companies have been successful over the long term by simply having the best price, connecting with many buyers, and making it easy for them to buy. There's nothing wrong with that; it's just a different way to conduct business and can be extremely profitable. However, as rule 2 will show, there is very definitely a right way and a wrong way to go to market.

RULE 2: YOU MUST GO TO MARKET THE SAME WAY THE CUSTOMER IS BUYING

This is often a tough one to swallow. Often it means letting go of preconceived or just plain ill-conceived ideas and perceptions about your organization's place in the market. But unless you go to market in the same 4Q quadrant where the customer is buying, your chances of selling aren't very good. Keep in mind that the supplier doesn't really get to choose—the buyer decides the buying style. Later, I'll discuss how you can change someone's natural buying style, but for the moment, you have to sell how the market is buying.

The Vertical Solution/Product Axis

The bottom two quadrants—Sort and Select and Starbucks—represent buyers who know what they want. They don't see any need for assistance to determine what they need to acquire. Many indicators bring about this situation. They might have expertise in the area—perhaps they have acquired these types of offerings many times in the past—or maybe they are from the school of Strategic Sourcing, where they see it as their job to determine what needs to be acquired. These product buyers are going to be interested in the *ease in which they can get the information they need*.

A salesperson can launch into their best consultative "solution selling" skills, but this is likely to frustrate this buyer, who will likely view the salesperson as a barrier between them and what they want. And beware the fallacy of solution selling. This concept has crept into the lexicon of sales and marketing, and although it is a very effective approach in certain situations, it only works when the customer is actually buying in one of the *top two quadrants* of the 4Q model: Search and Choose or Trusted Advisor.

Imagine you're driving to work the morning after a late night out that included a fiery curry resulting in wicked heartburn. You make a slight detour to your local pharmacy for some quick relief, but when you pop into the store, you're confronted with an obvious expert who wants to engage you in an in-depth analysis of your situation, possible causes, and solutions. Please, just Tums and a bottle of water! This is how a 4Q product buyer feels when they run into a 4Q solution-style supplier.

Talk to any salesperson who tries to use this style of selling with knowledgeable individuals in Purchasing or with IT people about end-user applications. These buyers see it as their job to fully understand what is required. They are 4Q product buyers all the way, and they simply want the seller to answer a few questions or respond to an RFP. They neither want nor need a solution seller trying to tell them what the seller thinks is required. Sure, they might benefit from the advice and guidance of that salesperson, but they perceive that they know what they need and don't need any help. Nothing is wrong with consultative selling; it's just ineffective when not matched to how the customer is buying.

Inversely, the top two quadrants—Search and Choose and Trusted Advisor—represent solution buyers looking for assistance. This is not the time or place to just drop off a catalog of part numbers, a price list, and a business card. There's work to be done here. The buyer wants someone who demonstrates a level of expertise in the topic—someone who takes the time to work with them, understand their situation, consult with them over alternatives, and recommend what it is they should be buying.

The Horizontal Choice/Value Axis

On the right-hand side, "Starbucks" and "Trusted Advisor," are buyers who value something about a certain offering or supplier that they see as both unique and valuable. If a salesperson approaches them and simply starts talking about discounts and better pricing, they are likely to be frustrated. The opposite is also true—buyers on the left-hand "Sort and Select" and "Search and Choose" side perceive an overall equality among potential suppliers, so when salespeople try to position their offerings as unique, these buyers will likely not believe them or will simply dismiss them as "typical" salespeople.

We work with thousands of salespeople from multiple industries and companies, and when we share this thinking, we usually see the smoke clearing; they start to see how and why they have wasted so much time with certain buyers. Whichever 4Q quadrant they tend to sell in, they will have many stories of how they have spent so much energy getting caught up with buyers that simply don't seem to follow the rules, buyers that didn't match up against the well-documented stages of their sales process. They didn't know it at the time, but they were coming up against buyers with a different buying style representing a separate and discrete market. They weren't out of their minds; they were just out of their quadrants.

For example, individuals who buy cars are not a market. However, single people in their thirties who have an income over a certain respectable level, are image conscious and drive more than ten thousand miles a year—now, that may be a market. But what happens if someone who ticks all of the above boxes except the "image" bit walks into an Audi showroom? He starts a conversation with the salesperson, telling her he has always driven a Toyota and is looking for a new car. He's heard that the Audi is quite a car, but he's compared it to his favorite Toyota and found that the Toyota is less expensive to buy, depreciates less, and is cheaper to maintain—and these things matter to him. The Audi salesperson now faces a buyer from a different market than the quadrant in which she operates. The right response is not to discount the Audi or offer cheap service. The right response is to see if she can shift the buying style. And if she can't, she should offer him directions to the nearest Toyota dealership. This brings us to the third rule of engagement.

RULE 3: YOU CAN SHIFT THE BUYING STYLE

At this stage, some of you may be saying you wouldn't be happy selling to customers in the way that they want to buy. Perhaps you believe your offering has the chance to stand alone in a sea of commoditized offerings, or perhaps you see an opportunity to mass-market an offering where a major player has dominated the space. That may be okay, and you might be able to shift the buying style of a particular buyer or even an entire market. However, notice I used the word *might*, and I also must note that in doing so, you would be creating an entirely new market, and perhaps eroding others.

Shifting the Buying Style from Value to Choice

In this case, you are dealing with a buyer, or a market, that repeatedly buys the same offering or repeatedly buys from the same supplier. The buyer perceives they are gaining something uniquely valuable to them, and they can only get that value from that particular offering or that particular supplier. So if you want to shift this buying style, you must do one of two things: You must demonstrate either that what the buyer values (their DNA *value driver*) is not actually valuable or that it is not unique to that offering or supplier. Of course, the implication is that you can provide it just as well.

We see the latter of the two—demonstrating that what the buyer values is not unique to that offering or supplier—much more often; it is far easier to prove parity than to erode a value driver. In fact, that is the natural course of events, as markets do tend to commoditize. But winning this point is not as easy as it may seem. Buyers have a strong tendency to stay with what they know and to continue to do what they have always done. It's called the "status quo bias," and it is one of the hardest things to address, let alone dislodge. In our research, when analyzing any Customer Buying Journey DNA, we often found that status quo was one of the most significant value drivers, and to move a buyer away from that is one of the most intractable *buying concerns*.

To shift a buyer from value to choice, first you must convince the buyer that you can offer the same as what the buyer values in either the offering or supplier or both. But it's not enough to achieve parity; you also need to provide further value to cause the shift to happen and address the buying concerns inherent in that switch. How many sales and marketing organizations actually build that into their strategies? Not many. Too many blindly hope that the benefit of what they are proposing will urge a prospective customer to jump across all those hurdles.

To illustrate this point, consider a medical device company we worked with. They were bringing to market a new device for a particular type of wound treatment. The market was significant and was dominated by a single provider. The incumbent provider's technology was somewhat dated, and potential customers almost universally viewed their pricing model as not only expensive but onerous. However, the market had little choice and had adopted their technology as the standard of care in this particular area. When health care providers—hospitals, doctors, nurses—needed this equipment, they overwhelmingly turned to this provider. Although there were a number of small suppliers, the majority of buyers did not shop around; they simply did what they had always done. It was Starbucks in the 4Q model; the buyers knew what they wanted (product) and they knew where to get it (value).

Our client had a technology that was clinically proven equal or superior to the incumbent supplier with a far simpler pricing model and genuine savings of 15 percent to 20 percent. In the 4Q model, they were trying to shift the buying style from value to choice. Did the market switch? No, it did not. The market continued to do what it had always done. The *perceived risk* of changing from the technology they knew, the supplier they knew—the status quo—was greater than any real cost savings they could gain. With everything else that was going on in these buyers' worlds, it just wasn't worth the effort.

Now think of the big fish—the franchises. Starbucks has more than twenty-three thousand locations in the world each selling five hundred to seven hundred cups of coffee a day. Starbucks confidently sells to those millions of buyers who believe they are being offered something unique that they value. That's what brings people into Starbucks over any other shop that offers coffee.

McDonald's envisioned an opportunity to take coffee drinkers away from Starbucks and get them to line up at McDonald's instead. If they could pull it off, it would be a neat strategy to boost sales, and McDonald's was proud of their ability to not only flip burgers but also brew a fine cup of coffee. To back this up, they took a leaf out of the old Coke/Pepsi blind taste-test challenge. They believed that a majority would prefer McDonald's coffee over straight Starbucks coffee in such a challenge and duly launched a significant marketing campaign to communicate this preference to the masses.

In essence, McDonald's was trying to destroy the uniqueness buyers were attaching to Starbucks and demonstrate that they could brew a better cup of coffee themselves. Did it work? No, not really. Why? Well, the coffee was okay, but it was the experience that let McDonald's down. People don't just go to Starbucks because they perceive that the coffee is the best in the world or that they provide more combinations of coffee possibilities ever thought humanly possible. They go for the Starbucks experience (and possibly because it isn't McDonald's).

Let's take a look at a highly successful example. Back in the 1980s, any business buying a personal computer would do what they always did: they would turn to one of the big computer companies that they always bought from, and often that was IBM. After all, they had relied on IBM since the dawn of the mainframe to supply them with computing power. For quite a few years, organizations were happy to pay a premium over "commodity" providers such as Dell and Compaq in order to buy IBM. This market was buying on value, as they perceived that *real* computers must come from a *real* computer company. They perceived that their provider would offer them a business computer that was reliable and came with the level of service and support they were used to.

But in the late 1980s, Dell and Compaq got business buyers to see that there was no real difference between the traditional computer company offerings and their own. They didn't win by suggesting that their computers were superior; they didn't win by becoming the new IBM; they won by destroying the perceived value being attached to the traditional computer company's offerings. They won by shifting how the market bought from the right-hand side of the 4Q (value) to the left-hand side (choice). With their success came the commodity era of buying PCs in the business world by features, service, and price.

Given that we define a market as buyers who buy in similar ways, what happened in the late 1980s was the emergence of a new market. The old, traditional market operated on the perception of the quality, service, support, and perhaps also the relationship the buyer had with a traditional computer provider such as IBM. The new market, created by the shift in buying style, was for buyers who did not perceive any inherent value in buying PCs from traditional suppliers. The new market perceived and believed that they had a choice and could buy from any one of several suppliers.

Shifting the Buying Style from Choice to Value

Now let's turn the tables and look at the inverse: What if you need to shift buyers from perceiving they have choice and can shop at any of a number of potential suppliers to attaching a value to you or your offering that they see as unique and that causes them to only consider buying that particular offering from you. This is what Starbucks did when they introduced their "West Coast Coffee Lounges." Up to this point, buyers, including myself, simply dropped into any deli or coffee shop to get coffee. Sure, we may have had a preference, but that was largely a matter of convenience. Starbucks did not enter the market as just another coffee shop, nor did they portray their coffee as either cheaper or superior. They offered a different experience. They created a new market giving people something unique to the Starbucks brand and that buyers obviously valued. Now, not everyone shifted their buying style. Many people went on getting their coffee as they always had. But no one can argue that Starbucks has created a new market, shifting multitudes of buyers a year from the left-hand (choice) to the right-hand side (value) of the 4Q model.

Earlier, I mentioned price. People usually associate price with commodity and therefore see it as part of the left-hand side (choice) of the 4Q. Part of that reasoning is correct: when the buyer had a choice, the decision of who to buy from would often come down to price. But price *itself* can be the value that moves buyers from the left to the right (value) of the 4Q. You can best see this in supermarkets, with their claims to have *every-day, all-day low pricing*. Some supermarkets achieve this brand positioning in the minds of their buyers. Many people in the United States shop at Costco, as they perceive they offer the best prices. Costco has shifted many buyers from left to right with the offer of being unique among their equals in providing lower prices. Their buyers value low pricing and see Costco as unique in their ability to offer such value. And here's the kicker—the vast majority of those customers rarely comparison shop; they head straight to Costco. Here you can see how pricing—or at least the perception of low prices—is the *value* a certain market of buyers associates with the Costco brand.

These examples speak to shifting the buying style of a market or, more accurately, shifting the buying style of a group of buyers in one particular market to a different market. Let's now look at how you can use the same approach on an individual buyer. We normally associate shifting the buying style of a group of buyers with a marketing effort and shifting the buying style of an individual buyer with a sales activity.

To shift the buying style of an individual buyer left to right, from choice to value, the same theory holds. All you have to do (said somewhat tongue-in-cheek) is generate a perception in the mind of the buyer that they should be valuing something they previously had not. In the language of the Customer Buying Journey DNA, you need to get the buyer to introduce a new value driver into their buying journey. Now, if you are successful at doing that and, in the mind of the buyer, only you can deliver on that value driver, then you will have shifted their buying style.

In the first case study (chapter 10), you saw how one supplier, Orion Technologies, was able to shift DiaNascent (DGI) from choice to value. (Interestingly, they also shifted DGI from product to solution, which I'll look at a little later.) DiaNascent believed they knew exactly what they needed—resources to globally implement their new software system—and that several suppliers could do this. It's almost a textbook example of the choice/product, "Sort and Select" lower left of 4Q. But in their interaction with Orion Tech, their beliefs changed. Orion was able to introduce two new value drivers into DGI's buying journey: management change issues and end-user training. Not only did they introduce these new value drivers, but they also convinced DGI that Orion was unique in being able to deliver them. As a result, DGI boldly went back to their Finance people for more money to pay for this newfound value.

Here's another situation I was closely involved in. We were working with a company I'll call ABC Pumps that sold large, complex pumps to the construction industry. They didn't manufacture these pumps but were a distributor of many leading brands, implying that they were selling exactly the same pumps as their competitors. You may well think that this is therefore a commoditized market, and to win business, ABC Pumps would have nowhere to go aside from price and availability. You can imagine general contractors and project managers simply calling around for price and availability information, and whoever has the pump in stock at the right price wins the business. Well, that is certainly a market—a market typified by being in the bottom left of 4Q (Sort and Select) with a clear buying style of product and choice: "I know what I want, and I have a choice of suppliers. Let's get an RFP out."

However, this is not the market they sold to. They were able to work with contractors to provide not only a pump but all the most likely fixtures and accessories required for installation. They also had a very clever logistical system that enabled them to deliver pumps and accessories on a highly reliable, just-in-time basis. Not just that, but they were able to get additional parts on to a job site extremely quickly when an installation ran into trouble. They had become very adept at meeting with prospective customers and getting them to add a value driver into the buying journey in a market where the value drivers had typically been availability and price. And their salespeople successfully got their potential customers to consider the ancillary project costs of either waiting for parts or searching for components that had been delivered off schedule.

They were successful in establishing those factors as value drivers—factors that a potential customer *perceived as important*—so then they only had to illustrate how they were unique in their ability to satisfy that new value driver. Once again, you see the emergence of a new market: contractors who value just-in-time delivery. Not everyone will shift to this new market; some buyers believe their current suppliers do a "good enough" job, and they don't see much added value in just-in-time delivery.

The common thread that runs through each of these examples is that the suppliers—Starbucks, Costco, Orion Technologies, and ABC Pumps—know the market in which they operate, and they operate in that market only. Starbucks didn't get caught up in McDonald's "taste and switch" or start flipping burgers. Costco's internal "comparison shoppers" ensure that their pricing is kept extremely competitive yet profitable. Orion Technologies, while seeming to swim in the RFP, Sort and Select quadrant, introduced unique and genuine value drivers to their client's buying journey, notwithstanding having the highest price. And ABC Pumps showed a remarkable knowledge of their market by adding innovative logistics and dependable just-in-time delivery that provided very real and unique value to their offerings. And most importantly, buyers perceived these values as *unique* to these four suppliers.

Shifting from Solution to Product

Shifting the buying style from the top (solution) to the bottom (product) of 4Q can be quite a natural transition. It means moving the buyer from a perception that they need the assistance of the supplier to provide a solution to a perception that they know precisely the product they need. As I shared when I first introduced the 4Q model in part 1, the natural "gravity" of the market usually shifts buyers in this direction as they gain more knowledge about the particular offering. When personal computers were first introduced in the days before the internet, a buyer would rarely think they knew how to configure and select the PC they required. They were solution-style buyers that sought the assistance of a supplier, usually a salesperson, to assist them in determining what they needed. Most people buying a computer today have more than enough knowledge to know exactly what they want and have therefore shifted to becoming product buyers.

Let's redefine exactly what differentiates a solution buyer from a product buyer. The solution buyer must display the following traits:

1. A belief that they lack the time/expertise/knowledge to determine what's needed
2. A perception that a supplier has the expertise and knowledge to determine what's needed
3. A belief that the supplier will make a fair and trustworthy recommendation

All three conditions generally have to be true. A bit of an anomaly, though, is if the buyer perceives they can't trust the recommendation of a potential supplier; if the need is great enough, they may still move forward with the acquisition, but they will most likely feel forced into buying in a compromised process, and next time around, they will either search for another supplier they perceive they can trust or educate themselves so that they shift their own buying style to one of product and are thus no longer reliant upon the recommendations of a supplier. Yes, this does indeed represent a way to shift the buying style, but it's one the buyer is adopting based on their negative perception of the recommendations coming from suppliers. It happens, but it is hardly something with which to build a dependable strategy. So that notwithstanding, it's reasonable to assume that you can cause a shift from solution to product by removing any one of the three conditions above. Let's look at conditions 1 and 2, which are usually sequential—that is, lack of knowledge leads to talking with an expert or lack of time leads to delegating the acquisition.

If you can demonstrate to the buyer that it is not time consuming or is fairly easy to understand what they require, then you can shift their buying style. Again, the internet provides multiple examples of this style of shift. Several years ago, I recall looking to buy a new camera. In the past, I would have walked into my local camera store, which I had visited on several occasions over the years, and talked with one of their sales assistants. I would have judged whether this particular individual knew what he was talking about and was making what I perceived as a bias-free recommendation in my own best interests, then I likely would have gone with his advice.

But not anymore, because the three conditions mentioned above are no longer true—any of them. Because I have slipped the bonds of assistance dependency and can now just go online and click into one of many automated configuration matrices available to the camera buyer. I answer questions about my budget, usage, preferences, and so on, all of which produces a series of recommendations along with extensive user rankings, pricing, and reviews. I'm essentially buying the same product, but I am no longer buying in a solution style. Like so many others, I have switched in these instances to being a product buyer. And once condition #1 is no longer valid—in that I can now determine for myself what it required—conditions #2 and #3 are irrelevant.

But let's be careful, because here is yet another fallacy I have seen many people fall into when it comes to *consultative* or *solution* selling. If the salesperson is simply educating the buyer, thereby enabling them to buy in the product half of Q4, that salesperson is neither consulting nor selling a solution. She is simply educating her prospective customer—she is a walking, talking brochure, if you will—and enabling that prospect to become a product-style buyer on their own. This may be a successful strategy or tactic, but it is usually helpful to understand what is really happening and why it might lead to either success or a lack of it.

Shifting from Product to Solution

Lastly, you could shift the buyer from thinking they know what they need to feeling they need the assistance of a supplier/advisor to determine what they need. In some ways, this is one of the most difficult shifts to make in the buying style, as it goes against the natural gravity of how markets tend to mature and is somewhat like telling the buyer that they don't know what they are doing. Obviously, the best tactic would not be overtly telling them so. Also, in accordance with my own theory, the buying style must be determined prior to selling to the buyer, so this is a difficult one.

If a buyer is starting their buying journey thinking they know what they need to buy, then to shift that buying style, you must cause *all three of the above conditions to be true* in their mind. Shifting the buying style from the prospective customer perceiving that they are able to make the decision about what is best for them, to surrendering that decision to a supplier can be quite tricky, or indeed impossible. Try telling an IT consultant that you know better than he does about what software application to use. It's his job to know. He might also see a representative of a certain supplier as being biased, and he's probably right.

However, in certain cases and at certain times, you can shift buying style from the bottom of the 4Q (product) to the top (solution). How? Usually by asking insightful questions that get the buyer to see something in a different light—questions that get them thinking differently, that bring new insight into the equation, that broaden the scope of what they were thinking, and that lead to them thinking that their own expertise and knowledge may be insufficient to make the decision regarding what they need. Here are a couple of examples.

We had a client that sold complex computer systems complete with software, service, and support. They were often faced with product-style buyers who believed they knew exactly what they wanted—and probably did, up to a certain point. However, one question would usually get them to think a little differently. That question was, "What thoughts have you given to training the users?" Some buyers could answer that easily, as they had a comprehensive plan in place. However, in this particular market at that particular time, many of these buyers had focused far more on the technology than on the usage. Salespeople could then follow up by stating that 78 percent of all technology implementations fail due to a lack of user training. Now, if the prospective customer responds, "Good point, we hadn't really thought of that yet," the buying style may well be shifting—more so if the customer then acknowledges that they lack the expertise to train their users and that the supplier has that expertise and the customer trusts their recommendations.

You saw a similar scenario with Orion Technologies in the first case study. They took the same end-user training questions and added some very pertinent queries into DiaNascent's (DGI) plans (or lack thereof) for the inevitable change management issues that would follow in the wake of acquisition and implementation. This strategy immediately separated Orion from the other two short-listers even though Orion had the highest price. Orion also resisted DGI's attempt at breaking the solution up into two segments by showing DGI that to do so would severely compromise Orion's custom-made end-user training videos. All this was done so professionally that in the critical Finalize Approach stage of DGI's Customer Buying Journey, Orion had not only shifted DGI from left to right—choice to value—but also edged them up to the top to solution. In doing so, Orion came very close to Trusted Advisor status with DiaNascent.

A Market Is Born

Let's consider how a significant part of an entire market may shift and form a new market. This is most common when new or changed offerings enter the marketplace. When this happens, organizations whose expertise may be outdated are confronted with something new and different, the expertise in which they now lack. One example could be new or changed regulatory requirements. Take the example of employment law. Perhaps HR people inside companies were quite happy buying payroll services and insurance based on their own knowledge and expertise in the area, so they were product-style buyers. Along comes a series of new tax regulations, compounded by associated penalties for improper implementation. Now those same folks who were buying services in a product style now see that they no longer have the knowledge and expertise to know what is best for their organizations. They must now seek suppliers to advise them. A shift has happened in their buying style from the bottom (product) to the top (solution) of the 4Q.

In some cases, companies may cause this same level of disruption in an industry by introducing totally new categories of offerings with new and different capabilities. Buyers may then realize that they no longer have the knowledge and expertise to determine what they need and may default to seeking the advice and guidance of a supplier. Again, exercise care in these situations not to mistake educating a buyer so they can again buy in a product style for actually shifting the buying style to one of solution.

Let's take the same example of the introduction of new government regulations. Up to that point, the buyers believed they had the necessary knowledge and expertise to make their buying decisions. Along come the new complex regulations, together with associated penalties. Two things may happen. Current suppliers of these products may run a series of webinars to alert their customers to the complexity and risk associated with the new conditions, in which case these buyers may move from product to solution and rely on their suppliers to help them make the right acquisitions. On the other hand, some suppliers may offer webinars that educate buyers so they now understand what they need to do. In this case, they remain product buyers. This is not to suggest that there is no value in doing this; perhaps the supplier may be seen as the only one that provides this critical information to their buyers, and in so doing, they might move a buyer from the left (choice) to the right (value)—and that's likely a great thing to do. But don't get confused about what is happening here: the buyer is being educated and is still buying in a product fashion.

To summarize, the buying style of an individual or a market component may shift from one style to another. In shifting the buying style, you are either creating or adding to a different market. When the buying style shifts, such buyers move from one discrete market to another. You must shift the buying style prior to selling to them in a new way—that is, the buyer has to be buying in the buying style in which you are selling, even if they only just arrived there and got there because of your own actions.

RULE 4: PICK ONE

This is the big one—the game changer. When I talk about this topic, I typically get the most raised eyebrows and discomfort in the room:

> *To be successful, the supplier must pick only one quadrant in which to operate; you cannot build a successful brand in more than one of the four quadrants.*

Whoa! I hear you say. *But we have buyers in more than one quadrant!* That may be true, but if you do, you are not as successful as you could and should be. Greater success will come to you by picking one quadrant and one quadrant only. Over the years, clients have challenged us on this rule more than

ILLUSTRATION 16.6. OPTIMIZING FOR SUCCESS IN EACH OF THE QUADRANTS

CHOICE/PRODUCT "SORT AND SELECT"	VALUE/PRODUCT "STARBUCKS"	CHOICE/SOLUTION "SELECT AND CHOOSE"	VALUE/SOLUTION "TRUSTED ADVISOR"
• low operating costs • highly competitive pricing • distribution and logistics • marketing to be in the mind of the buyer at the point of decision • bringing to market competitive products • availability to customers • provision of choice and high utility	• promotion of an attribute of the brand that delivers value to the customer in an area that can be protected from other entrants into the marketplace • continuous reinforcement of the value that is inherent in the brand • operational excellence in the brand promise	• continuous marketing to the chosen market to reinforce expertise • high availability to prospective customers • competitive pricing • customer service and support	• investment in customer relationships • provision of high-quality expertise • high touch in all customer dealings

anything else. But across the globe and across multiple industries, *no one has ever provided an example of a single brand that has sustained success in serving more than one quadrant.*

Let's explore why this is. I have previously listed what the buyer is focusing on in each of the four quadrants. Now let's reverse the situation and look at what you, as a potential supplier to a market, must focus on to be successful in serving the market in that particular quadrant.

Illustration 16.6 shows that the specific qualities necessary for sustained success in each specific quadrant differ substantially from the other three quadrants. Walmart is successful in providing low prices to bottom-quadrant (product) buyers by keeping overhead low, squeezing suppliers to provide low wholesale costing, and skipping high-touch service. The leading consulting companies are successful at attracting and retaining top-right (Trusted Advisor) solution buyers by investing in their client relationships and providing what the customer perceives as an expertise and knowledge they could not function without.

The biggest point here is that rule 4 implies—or actually, let's be frank, it insists—that your entire business must be aligned and optimized to the quadrant in which you choose to operate. Not only that, but the whole culture of your operation—not just sales and marketing—must also reflect the specific values associated with that particular quadrant. Trying to operate across markets in different quadrants will result in brand confusion and an inability to build an image of who you are and what you offer in the minds of prospective customers. This is how far-reaching the development of a truly effective Market Engagement Strategy is—to be effective, *the supplier must pick only one quadrant in which to operate.*

Let's return to a word I have used very deliberately when presenting these arguments. That word is *brand*, and I posit that no brand can operate across more than one quadrant. A company can get around this maxim, and several have, by splitting into different organizational units, each with their own brand.

For instance, most people know that Toyota owns both Toyota and Lexus. However, these brands operate very differently. You don't buy a Lexus where you buy a Toyota, and you don't take a Lexus for service where you take a Toyota. Most significantly, you don't have the same experience or expectations with these two operations. As discussed, people who buy cars are certainly not a single market. Toyota realized this when they launched Lexus and separated it from their usual operations and business.

Lexus has built an enviable brand around luxury and service. People who buy a Lexus are not the same market as those who buy a Toyota. Oddly enough, although the same individuals may actually buy a Toyota and a Lexus, I am willing to bet that when they describe the two buying and owning experiences, they use very different language for each. When you buy a Lexus, you expect and get a higher level of service. No waiting in lines behind a service counter for the Lexus owner—you have your own service manager waiting for you with the keys to a loaner vehicle while your Lexus is being serviced. People don't get, or expect, that same level of service when they take their Toyotas in for service—nor will they ever, because Toyota profits would fall precipitously if they offered all Toyota drivers the same level of care and attention afforded to Lexus owners. So not only are the brands very different, but the operations in each of the two divisions are very different; each is optimized around the quadrant in which they are operating.

We worked with a consulting company that provided business services with a high level of expertise in contracting to organizations seeking help in that area. They prided themselves on their expertise. They carefully hired their consultants and invested in their continual training. They could also demand a high daily rate for the provision of such expertise. However, as they expanded their business, they encountered many selling situations that put them up against lower-end providers—what they termed (not kindly but perhaps somewhat realistically) "body shops." They responded to many RFPs but often lost to these other firms based on price. They suggested it would be hard for them to break even at the rates these other firms were accepting.

What they were dealing with, of course, was two markets—one in the bottom right of the 4Q (Starbucks) and one in the bottom left (Sort and Select). One market believes they have a choice in the marketplace based on price and availability. The other market is happy to pay for a highly experienced resource with true and deep expertise. Through our research, we were able to prove our theory and show that two different markets were in play here. We were also able to show our client that by pursuing the clientele of the lower-left "body shop" business, they were dangerously close to compromising their original brand, which was associated with the provision of high-level expertise. The solution to their challenge was to do the Toyota-Lexus thing: they started a separate but wholly owned subsidiary to go after the lower-end contracting business. All those competitive opportunities in which the price was a big factor went to the subsidiary while they focused on the provision of high-end expertise in their "home" quadrant. The two separate organizations could then optimize and run differently, each around its chosen quadrant in the 4Q model. In this case, it was a happy ending, and not only were both organizations successful, but the lower-left quadrant turned out to be a great feeder for the lower-right consulting company.

FOCUS

Let me reinforce this concept of focus and picking one quadrant only. I'll also explain why this is, and always has been, a tough sell to many companies, including many of our own clients. I have noted that two things must happen for a supplier to fully comply with this rule: first, you must determine and commit to which 4Q quadrant you are going to sell to, and second, your organization must fully optimize its business operations and culture around the factors that will enable success in that one quadrant. All this will be necessary to avoid compromising the ability to build a strong brand and the associated revenue growth.

Our clients often find it incredibly difficult to accept this level of focus. It appears as if their sales organizations run under the mantra "There's no such thing as a bad opportunity" while their executives go for an "anything to anybody" approach, all in the name of revenue growth. This is folly. I have seen time and time again how the mistaken, short-term strategy of pursuing markets with buying styles in different quadrants leads to wasted resources, effort, and diminished results.

In addition, it's not easy to adopt this level of focus. If you want to see it in action, look to the successful businesses and brands. The challenge is to let go of poor opportunities. For example, if you are going to market with a premium service, there is no issue with a strategy that seeks to change a buyer who is clearly on the choice (left-hand) side of the 4Q to perceive your offering as unique and valuable and not simply compare you to other more commoditized offerings. However, when the strategy fails and the buyer does not switch, they belong to a different market, and you should abandon the hunt. Failure to do so simply pulls you into that left-hand side of the quadrant, where all that matters is price, availability, and perhaps some particular features. You are essentially commoditizing yourself. It's equally difficult to abandon an opportunity when the buyer changes their buying style during the buying journey.

Any attempt to span different quadrants will result internally in compromised business operations and externally in brand confusion. So endeth the lesson.

RULE 5: UNDERSTAND THE MARKET OPPORTUNITY

The final rule of engagement can have as profound an impact on a business as rule 4 can. In rule 4, you saw the need to pick one quadrant of the 4Q model in which to operate, and you should make that choice with a clear understanding of how your customers buy and by examining where your greatest opportunity lies. However, in choosing or focusing on one quadrant in which to operate and thereby harmonizing with how the market buys, you might need to change what you are offering to the market.

Again, let's turn to Alliance Medical, an early player in the field of medical equipment reprocessing. Alliance takes used medical devices, reprocesses them using FDA-approved procedures, and then returns the devices to the hospital for a 40 percent discount compared to the purchase of an identical new device, thereby offering value and a nice reduction in toxic waste. However, the market wasn't buying. Alliance was selling what they saw as a straightforward service. The market, however, saw multiple issues in adopting any reprocessed device. How do inventory systems recognize such devices and restock them? How are devices identified and prepared for shipment? What are the liability issues? How are the staff trained to select these devices? Is there a need to ask for patient permission to utilize reprocessed devices? The list went on and on, and then throw in our old nemesis status quo.

Thinking of this relative to the 4Q model, the market lacked the expertise, knowledge, and time to work out how to embrace this new service. They saw the benefits but lacked the will to get there. The solution was for Alliance to offer not just a reprocessing service but also the expertise to assist the hospital in implementing reprocessing. Alliance needed to change their brand from that of a provider of reprocessed devices to an expert in the successful implementation of reprocessing throughout the hospital. In other words, Alliance needed to move up the 4Q model by offering a complete package of consulting services for a solution buyer, a buyer that could see the value but needed help accessing it. Did it work? Yes, outstandingly so. They saw revenue growth accelerate as customers viewed them as not just a provider but experts in the implementation of reprocessing.

TAKEAWAYS

⇒ Every business must select one of the four quadrants of the 4Q Buying Style model in which to focus their operation and offering(s).

⇒ In order to address that single quadrant successfully, the business must optimize their efforts around the specific factors pertaining to that quadrant. In most cases these factors are mutually exclusive.

⇒ Customers that buy in quadrants other than the supplier's chosen quadrant represent a different market and should not be addressed in the same manner or with the same offering; doing so will result in a compromise to the brand and ultimately the business.

⇒ There are no inherently good or bad quadrants, but a business must either sell the way that the market is buying or change the way the market buys to the chosen quadrant.

CHAPTER 17

GOAL 2: INTO THE CUSTOMER BUYING JOURNEY

TRIGGER OR ENGAGE?

I LIVE IN SONOMA County in Northern California just outside Santa Rosa, essentially in the middle of the Sonoma/Napa wine country. Over the last few years, however, this area has been lucky enough to also become a center for brewing and the fast-rising craft beer industry. Downtown Santa Rosa is now home to a microbrewery, and not just any brew pub, but the famous Russian River Brewery. They brew an IPA known as Pliny the Younger, which is consistently rated as one of the top ten beers in the world. When "the Younger" becomes available, the line outside the brewery stretches for blocks. Folks actually start lining up the night before, waiting for the doors to open the next morning. Whenever I pass that brewery downtown, I always think how great it must be to have a business where your customers line up outside your door, money in hand, waiting to buy your offering. All you have to do is open the doors and satisfy the demand.

Of course, few businesses have this luxury, and even fewer started this way. Not even Russian River Brewery started this way, as I do recall before the word got out that there wasn't always a line outside. Like most selling entities, they had to do a lot more than just open the doors to trigger a Customer Buying Journey, so it's no surprise that this is indeed a key component of any Market Engagement Strategy: how do you either *trigger* a buyer to enter into a Customer Buying Journey or *engage* a buyer already going down that path?

In part 1, you saw what could trigger a buying journey and the possible dependencies for such a journey to come to successful fruition. Now you want to consider, as part of the strategy, the most effective way to make this happen. In this chapter, I will examine this process more closely and review several fatal flaws I've seen time and time again.

Let's start by determining the mode of Customer Buying Journey you are either triggering or engaging in.

SUBSTITUTION, AUGMENTATION, DISRUPTION

SUBSTITUTION

Substitution is when a customer is already buying a certain product or service, but for some reason, they seek to change their supplier. This change may be triggered by either dissatisfaction with the current supplier or offering or awareness of a better alternative. That alternative may be cheaper, or perhaps it comes with better service, guarantees, or delivery commitments. Essentially, the customer is substituting, or being asked to substitute, one supplier for another. This can often be a simple and fairly fast buying journey, as the customer knows what he needs, knows how to utilize the offering, and has a process for acquisition and little change is likely required.

When the customer triggers such a buying journey, there is usually little friction, and the buying journey can be short and simple. However, several barriers can appear when a potential new supplier endeavors to trigger a substitution-style buying journey. The first, which I see repeatedly, is simply the customer's desire to stay with the status quo. Even when faced with cheaper and superior offerings, customers often don't have time to evaluate an alternative and often perceive a risk with changing things. This presents a classic change management challenge: people "cling" to what they know and what feels comfortable. When decoding the buying journey DNA, this situation should reveal itself with either a *value driver* of "status quo" and/or a *buying concern* of "change."

I have also seen many situations where suppliers believe they are simply asking customers to substitute their offering for their current one, but the customers don't see it that way. We have seen this multiple times with our clients that sell to the health care market. The supplier believes they have an offering superior to the one in everyday use—and in many ways, they do. They think it will be a simple substitution, but when we talk to their potential buyers, a different story emerges. For example, from the customers' perspective, the adoption of that new offering implies that physicians use a different form to order a test. It might require a change in workflow and perhaps even training. To the supplier, this seems trivial; to the customers, these are major buying concerns (in the categories of implications and change in our DNA analysis).

AUGMENTATION

With augmentation, the buying journey is triggered by an offer of something the customer already acquires that is augmented with new functionality or additional features. If the customers themselves trigger this style of buying journey, it can, in a similar way to substitution, be in response to either dissatisfaction with their current acquisition or awareness of additional functionality, utility, or service they value. For example, consider a customer that has always acquired computers and technology supplies from a local provider that is now offering training services. Perhaps they will continue to acquire technology from this supplier, but the offering will be augmented by the training services. This could again be a simple and straightforward buying journey. However, complications may arise if they already have a training provider or, at the other end of the scale, see no value in the additional cost of training when they perceive that adequate training is available online for free thanks to YouTube. Once again, this situation should be revealed when decoding the buying journey DNA in terms of either the value drivers or the buying concerns.

DISRUPTION

Disruption, the third mode of Customer Buying Journey. occurs when the acquisition of the offering disrupts the organization's day-to-day operations. This happens when the customer decides to or is being asked to look at something new and different from what they currently do. So many suppliers think their offering represents a substitution or an augmentation mode of buying journey, yet the customer views it as a disruption. This doesn't mean the offering is bad or negative, but it does mean the customer is likely to go through the stages of their buying journey with several *key players* who have different motivators and buying concerns.

Illustration 17.1 summarizes the three modes of the Customer Buying Journey.

ILLUSTRATION 17.1. THE THREE BUYING MODES

MODE	DESCRIPTION	NATURE OF THE CUSTOMER BUYING JOURNEY	CHALLENGES
Substitution	Switching from one product or supplier to another for the same offering	Often a simpler Customer Buying Journey	Status quo bias The full implications of the switch, and any change that it may imply, can offer more resistance than expected
Augmentation	Continuing to acquire an offering but with an additional feature, attribute, or function; could be from the same or a different supplier	Can be a simpler Customer Buying Journey if the proposal is made by the current supplier Can be a more complex Customer Buying Journey if a switch in supplier is required	Even a simple augmentation to a currently acquired offering can share all the elements of a disruptive Customer Buying Journey
Disruption	Acquiring something new to the organization	Almost certainly a far more complex Customer Buying Journey	All the challenges associated with a full Customer Buying Journey

THE FIRST DECISION: TRIGGER OR ENGAGE?

One of the most fundamental questions to ask yourself is this: where in a Customer Buying Journey does a potential supplier engage? Do they endeavor to trigger a buying journey that otherwise may not have happened (or at least not at that time), or do they plan to engage at some point after the customer has already entered into their buying journey?

There is no single right answer. It depends on first fully understanding the Customer Buying Journey DNA of your target market and then selecting and initiating the appropriate approach. Determining the relative costs and attractiveness of these two alternatives is one of the most important elements of the strategic process. Your choice also heavily depends on the relevant buying style and the way you've chosen to engage in the 4Q model.

You could choose to trigger a buying journey and perhaps in doing so cause the buyer to see you as the only game in town, thus making their decision on the right-hand value side of the 4Q model. Or you might choose to let the customer enter their buying journey and as they close in on the decision to purchase, you could move to capture the buyer's mind with the right offering at the right price. Again, no single approach is wrong, but you can make the correct approach for each situation only with a full understanding of how customers buy and why they don't.

I recall an amusing and very telling example of the question of when and how to engage in a Customer Buying Journey that clearly makes the point that there is no single correct answer. So bear with me as we go back through the mists of time to the days of the mainframe computer. IBM was the premium supplier of serious computers and computing equipment to large corporations. It would be hard to pick a better example of industry leadership and market domination than IBM in the late twentieth century. If you were a corporate buyer looking for computing power and services, you always had to consider Big Blue. Now, at that time, there was an interesting company, for those who may recall, called Amdahl. Arguably the vanguard of computer clone technology and marketing, Amdahl basically sold IBM-equivalent hardware at a much-reduced price. Many corporations picked up on the fiscal opportunity it represented, and a not insignificant portion of the market bypassed IBM to buy the Amdahl equivalent. These buyers had moved to the left-hand side of the 4Q model and believed they had a choice. IBM did all they could to show their unique value, and indeed many buyers stayed on the right-hand side of the 4Q model and continued to acquire all their computing goods from IBM.

I was sitting in a corporate boardroom at Amdahl discussing their overall Market Engagement Strategy. Several senior executives suggested that they needed to be involved earlier in the buying journey and "sell high" in order to gain more influence in the overall buying process. It so happened that one of their senior sales managers was in the room listening to these executives talk about their belief that they should be engaging earlier and at an executive level. He listened to the argument for a while and then interrupted to say that his sales force would not have a clue how to do that and certainly wouldn't have the patience to do it. He shared with the collected dignitaries exactly how they sold, had sold for many years, and had been extremely successful. He minced no words.

He said, "Let IBM do all the clever and expensive stuff. Let IBM wine and dine the executives at their conferences in fancy places. Let them work with all the people involved in any million-plus-dollar purchase. Let them work out all the budgets and justify the expenditure. Let them do all the configurations and simulations to propose exactly what is needed."

He then shared that his sales team knew all the purchasing managers and data center managers many levels down from the executive team and far away from the decision makers. And just when they sought a final quote and pricing details from IBM, Amdahl got their contacts to fax over what they were looking for. Shortly thereafter, a competitive quote from Amdahl arrived that offered the equivalent hardware for a substantially lower price. He explained that his people knew all the questions customers were likely to raise about buying hardware from a source other than IBM, and most importantly, they knew how to handle each objection.

There you have it: Amdahl was waiting to engage in the Customer Buying Journey essentially at the point of acquisition. IBM was carrying the cost of educating, supporting, and in many cases triggering the entire Customer Buying Journey, and it often took more than a year to fulfill the order. Amdahl swooped in late in the buying journey with a significantly reduced cost of sale and a cycle time often measured in weeks. This strategy served Amdahl well, as they enjoyed almost two decades of success. Of course, IBM was also successful, but you can see that these two companies had two very different strategies for triggering or engaging in a Customer Buying Journey.

If your strategy is to trigger a buying journey, then, if successful, you will be involved with the customer from the outset of their buying journey. On the other hand, if you choose to engage later in the buying journey, as Amdahl did, then you have a number of factors to consider that may have a significant bearing on your decision of whether to trigger the Customer Buying Journey or engage along the way.

First is the factor of time. Almost universally, business folks want to speed up their sales process. I am always amused by this ambition, as the salesperson rarely has control over the speed of the process. Rather, it is the customer and the buying process that needs to be the center of your attention and your focus in trying to speed things up. One great way of creating a shorter sales cycle is to engage later in the buying journey. Amdahl's sales cycle was a lot shorter than IBM's, although the Customer Buying Journey's time stayed relatively the same. It was just a case of engaging later in that buying journey.

So why not come in at the end of the buying journey every time and enjoy the benefit of a short engagement? Not only is it a short engagement, but it is often significantly cheaper, and the probability of the customer actually buying something is fairly high. Well, this can be a very valid and successful Market Engagement Strategy. However, let's look at the argument for the longer and often far more expensive strategy of engaging much earlier in the Customer Buying Journey or actually triggering it. The single reason for earlier engagement is simply the degree of control and the ability to influence the buying journey. When you engage late in the buying journey, the customer has usually determined their need, their budget, and how they are going to acquire and either adopt or use the offering. They also often know who they are going to buy from. The degrees of freedom, as it were, to influence that customer are vastly more limited later in the buying journey. Oddly enough, this can end up hurting the customer. They might make their decision of what to buy based on limited information or without all the knowledge. However, they are well into their buying journey and are likely deeply invested in the approach they have chosen. They may have presented this approach to others, likely have many key players onside and budgets approved, and perhaps have implementation plans finalized. It would take a lot to upset this apple cart.

Early engagement on the Customer Buying Journey, including actually triggering it, usually offers a far greater ability to work with the customer (some would say "consult") and help them understand their needs and options. It enables the seller to provide value significantly beyond the product and service being offered. In providing this level of support to the customer, you can influence, or "shape," what the customer thinks they need and how they will approach their overall buying journey.

If you consider the 4Q model, it is far easier to move a buyer into a different quadrant when you engage earlier in the buying journey. This is true no matter in which quadrant the customer may start their buying journey or no matter which quadrant you may influence them to move to. I examined the strategies for changing the buying style—that is, changing the quadrant in which the customer is buying—in the previous chapter. The successful deployment of these strategies is largely dependent on early engagement in the buying journey.

To emphasize this extremely important point, I recall a discussion I had with the global VP of sales for a multibillion-dollar software company. I was in his office and had asked him if he had one wish for how his sales force might behave differently. In response, he drew the diagram in illustration 17.2 on his whiteboard.

The x-axis and horizontal line represent the time through the buying journey. He explained that when his company engaged with a potential customer early in their buying journey, as shown by opportunity #1, they had a great deal of latitude. They could help the customer understand their needs and the different options and possibilities that they might have. The company could provide their wealth of knowledge about the application and the use of their software to help the customer solve their business challenge.

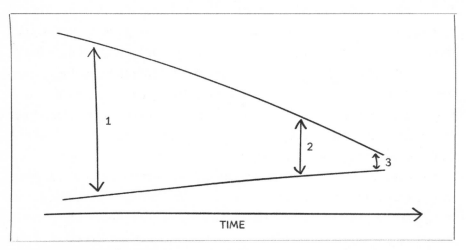

ILLUSTRATION 17.2. Whiteboard sketch: Degrees of freedom across the buying journey

In so doing, they are likely to either move the customer's buying style to the top right quadrant of value-solution or at the very least reinforce that buying style if the customer was already there. With opportunity #2 on the whiteboard, he shared that by this time in the buying journey, budgets are usually set and the overall approach agreed to, and thus his company had far less "room" to help and perhaps influence the customer's position. By the time they got to opportunity #3, the customer knew exactly what they wanted and what they had to spend, and there were few degrees of freedom to influence the buying journey. In many situations, this may result in the customer actually not getting the best solution for their needs. You can also see that by the time the customer gets to the place in the buying journey represented by opportunity #3, they are likely buying in a bottom quadrant of the 4Q model, either commodity or product. If the customer has not been working with a particular supplier, then there is a strong likelihood that they will issue a request for proposal (RFP), and the winner will be the supplier who can best meet the defined needs at the lower cost.

After drawing and explaining this diagram, the VP of sales answered the question I posed: "If there was one thing you wished your sales force would do differently, what would it be?" "That's simple," he replied. "Take all the energy and focus we place on trying to close opportunities in position 3 and move that to opportunities at position 1 in the buying journey. If we did that, then we wouldn't have all the problems we experience when we engage later in the buying journey." It's interesting to note that the horizontal funnel shape is not a depiction of the usual (and incorrect) sales funnel shape. Rather, it represents the closing in of the degrees of freedom to work with the customer. Ironically, this early engagement in the buying journey would likely have the effect of shortening the buying journey as a result of the expertise and help that could be offered to prospective customers through their buying journey, although the length of time that the salespeople were engaged with the customers would still be significantly longer than if they came in late to the game.

Illustration 17.3 summarizes the various factors related to when you engage in the overall Customer Buying Journey.

A final word on the decision and impact of where you engage in the market's Customer Buying Journey: many of our clients think they will

ILLUSTRATION 17.3. EARLIER VERSUS LATER ENGAGEMENT IN THE BUYING JOURNEY

	EARLIER ENGAGEMENT	LATER ENGAGEMENT
Time	Longer	Shorter
Cost	Higher	Lower
Ability to shape, including changing the buying style	High possibility	Low possibility
Probability of the customer buying (at least something)	Lower	Higher
Ability to change the buying style	Higher	Lower

trigger or engage early in their market's buying journeys. I always caution that they should temper their aspirational desires with reality. If you are selling a complex offering or one that could be considered a large-ticket item, you can't imagine that you will trigger a buying journey and enjoy a short sales cycle. It simply doesn't happen that way, no matter how compelling and valuable you think your offering may be (see our old nemesis Fallacy #1 below).

So let's start by looking at the challenges associated with actually triggering a Customer Buying Journey and the challenges that apply when engaging in a buying journey after the customer, or perhaps another supplier, has already initiated the buying journey.

FALLACY #1

As you've already learned, customers will rarely buy something solely based on its value to them and/or their organization, even if they understand and believe in that inherent value. While seeming illogical, I have shared what our research has revealed, that such behavior is not only logical but, just as important, predictable.

This brings us back to Fallacy #1: suppliers think they will trigger a buying journey by turning up and proving to a potential customer that their offering will translate into value. If only it were that simple!

Compounding this fallacy is the idea that if the supplier kicks over enough rocks, they may eventually find someone who will enter and successfully complete a Customer Buying Journey. Sadly, this only reinforces the belief that this approach works and all the supplier needs to do is hire more boots and kick over more rocks. This invariably leads to ever-increasing investments in sales and marketing with ever diminishing returns. A great offering regardless of how well presented is so rarely a buying trigger that it must be discounted as such. It is only by studying the full DNA for each Customer Buying Journey that you will fully realize that this high-level belief is fraught with danger.

NEVER THE RIGHT TIME

Another reason the "turn up with a great offer" approach rarely works is simply because it's never the right time. If the offer solves a major and urgent problem for the prospective customer, I am willing to bet that the customer wasn't sitting around waiting for you to show up and solve it for them. Organizations faced with an urgent business challenge or opportunity will likely solve or take advantage of it in a timely fashion and move on. You would have to be there at exactly the right moment to be considered a solution to their problem. And yes, if you try enough times, you may occasionally get lucky and find yourself in that situation, but not often enough that you should consider it a healthy and scalable Market Engagement Strategy.

Conversely, you could turn up with a substantial and worthwhile offer that solves a legitimate problem, but the customer has yet to do anything about it. It is then very likely that the problem—in the customer's mind—is not urgent (or budgeted), and therefore nothing is going to happen at that time. In today's world, if something is urgent, the organization likely deals with it promptly, while initiatives on the wish list too often wither and die.

Another school of thought subscribes to the theory that a supplier can highlight an opportunity or a solution to a problem that the prospective customer was not aware of. However, it is highly unlikely that an outsider can turn up with intimate knowledge of a problem or opportunity that demands immediate attention and investment and that the customer was unaware of the problem and not already investigating possible paths of action. I should be clear that someone could indeed turn up and highlight a new opportunity or solution of value to a prospective customer. However, a Customer Buying Journey—if indeed triggered—will be subject to the same DNA protocols described in part 1. And so we loop back to Fallacy #1: the prospective customer is not going to invest purely because the supplier's offering can generate value for them, even when they believe that value to be true.

EDUCATING OR ENTERTAINING VERSUS TRIGGERING OR ENGAGING

Another major challenge associated with triggering a Customer Buying Journey is the confusion between truly starting a buying journey and simply educating and/or entertaining someone. Interestingly enough, I was thinking of ending that sentence with *a prospect* but changed it to *someone*, as this individual is rarely a prospect. While this person will take your time and even prove to be a good listener to your pitch, he rarely has any intention of buying. Auto salespeople call such people "tire kickers," but that term may be too simplistic to cover the dynamics of what may be happening.

When marketing or selling something new and interesting, you will have no shortage of people who will show keen interest. They will let you educate and entertain them, but they aren't buyers for all the reasons you can see by understanding the full buying journey DNA. Think back to the company I referred to in part 1, with the stunning 3D display and demos that consistently entertained and impressed. Consider some laggards, as defined in the traditional marketing maturation curve, who can be especially good at "looking" with no intention of buying. I call them "reluctant laggards," and as they never want to be seen as such, so they keep abreast of the latest developments. When challenged by their management or colleagues, they can always say that they checked out the new stuff but, for whatever reason, decided it wasn't the right fit at that time.

WHEN DOES THE JOURNEY REALLY START?

I have given a lot of thought to this notion of when a Customer Buying Journey actually starts. It's like window-shopping. Most glance in the windows with no intention ever buying—like when I pass a Ferrari showroom. I love those cars, but am I ever likely to buy a Ferrari? Not likely. So when does window-shopping turn into a true Customer Buying Journey?

It is the point in time—anything from a subtle nudge to a knock on the head—when someone starts to seriously consider *the possibility of acquisition*. The moment that person starts to think how she would use it, where it would fit, how it could be funded, and who would have to be involved in making it happen. Going back to automobile sales, any rep will tell you that once a customer starts discussing colors, the rep knows the buying journey is well on its way. That's the moment when curiosity and interest turn into a possible Customer Buying Journey. Such a journey might not result in acquisition or might result in acquisition later, but that's when the journey *starts*. So how do you know or find out when that moment happens or indeed what causes that moment to happen?

We were working with a high-technology company with a very interesting virtual reality offering. The demo was extremely powerful, and normally people would be lining up to experience the technology for themselves. Their sales force dedicated a lot of time to entertaining and educating the market without a correspondingly high number of buyers. After our research, our first step was to get their sales force in front of the most likely buyers. We equipped them with one question—one that could either trigger a buying journey or illustrate that the individual was not a prospect. That question was, "How would you see your organization using this technology?" That one question would lead to some thinking and hopefully to the prospect sharing how he could see this technology being used within his organization. Thus a Customer Buying Journey could be triggered. A blank response, or "I'm not sure," or "I can't see that happening for a while" would usually imply that no buying journey was going to be triggered as a result of that interaction. The point is, asking someone to envision how he or she would use that offering was what it took to potentially start the buying journey in that particular case. Without that question, the interaction was not much more than an education and/or entertainment session.

TRIGGERING WITHOUT DEPENDENCIES

Now that you've considered when a Customer Buying Journey actually starts, let's look at the next fatal flaw: when somebody somewhere inside an organization starts a buying journey but something on which the successful conclusion of that buying journey depends is not in place. We call these *dependencies*. An easy one to consider is the funds necessary to acquire the potential goods and services. Maybe someone starts the buying journey without full knowledge of all the costs, or perhaps that person is a little naïve. As a result of moving through the journey, the costs become apparent and the buying journey is abandoned due to either an inability to find or an unwillingness to spend the required funds. Funding is a simple dependency, but there are many others. We worked with a company that was selling a pharmaceutical robot. As it happens, the robot required both a certain amount of space and a robust location that could manage its weight and provide a vibration-free platform for this sensitive equipment. No matter how excited a buyer might become about the benefits of this robot, it was a clear dependency that the buyer must have suitable real estate available for its installation.

The successful completion of the Customer Buying Journey may rely on many variables. These dependencies are those that do not change from situation to situation and that can be predetermined. In the robot example, the size of the pharmacy, the funds to invest, and the real estate to install were dependencies. I want to stress that someone enthusiastic enough may have triggered a buying journey, but unless these dependencies were in place, that buying journey would not end in the successful acquisition and adoption of this robot.

TAKEAWAYS

⇒ The Market Engagement Strategy should consider the mode of the Customer Buying Journey as either substitution, augmentation, or disruption for the customer.

⇒ The Market Engagement Strategy should determine if the supplier is going to endeavor to trigger the Customer Buying Journey or engage in a journey that has been triggered by some other event.

⇒ If the supplier opts to trigger a buying journey, then it must be clear what causes that buying journey to start as opposed to simply educating or entertaining a nonbuyer.

⇒ If the supplier opts to engage in a Customer Buying Journey that has already been triggered, then they must be clear about how and when they will engage in that buying journey.

⇒ For the supplier to engage successfully, the Customer Buying Journey not only needs to be triggered, but any and all dependencies need to either be in place or be enabled during the course of that journey.

CHAPTER 18

GOAL 3: ENSURING ADEQUATE MOTIVATION

N PART I, I looked at the fifth strand of the Customer Buying Journey DNA, the *value drivers*—what customers believe they will gain as a result of acquisition. Value drivers provide the motivation for the buying journey, the reason to keep going, and ultimately the reason to acquire and adopt a new offering. Let's look at the situation from the supplier's point of view by taking those value drivers—what the buyer wants and expects—and translating them into *value propositions*, or how the supplier perceives and defines the benefits of their offerings.

When engaging in, or triggering a Customer Buying Journey, it is clearly beneficial to you to ensure that what you are selling, and indeed how you are selling, aligns with what the customer is hoping to get from the acquisition. This really is very simple logic—some may say obvious—yet I repeatedly see a significant lack of alignment between what a supplier states they are offering and what a buyer is really looking and hoping for.

Take any company offering a new and improved way to conduct a particular procedure. As good as it may be, many of their prospects are not looking for new and improved ways to do things; they are just fine with what they are doing. What they would like is an easier life. Perhaps they are stressed about everything they have to do in a day, the growing demands on their time, the ever-decreasing resources that are available to help them. It's never hard to find those who don't want change, who don't want something new to learn, who don't want more hassle.

You may be surprised to learn that even with this lack of alignment, buyers still may buy. These situations come to light when we ask buyers why they bought and the reasons they share are not the same reasons the supplier thinks inspired the purchase. In these situations, the buyers have looked beyond the sales and marketing messages—the value propositions, as it were—and have found their own reasons to buy.

Large corporations spend a lot of money on messaging. As a result, there are many marketing taglines out there, and some are spot on. Yes, you can have it your way at Burger King, and diamonds are indeed forever. But I wonder how many people actually rent a car from Avis because they think the company tries harder or how many buy their insurance from State Farm believing the company is like a good neighbor? And I won't even mention flying the friendly skies.

Getting away from retail and into the intensely competitive world of business-to-business sales and marketing, we find many products sporting a lengthy list of "features and benefits," all purporting to solve innumerable day-to-day problems. They emphasize value propositions that all too often are of little or no value to their prospects while ignoring the areas that really are of value. In some extreme cases, we have even seen companies stress value propositions that represent *negative* value to their potential buyers, in effect representing reasons *not* to buy. Although this may seem incredibly stupid—and it is—it happens. From marketing departments investing in messages that do not align with the buyer's motivations to salespeople pitching benefits that aren't benefits at all, we continuously see this mismatch between the supplier's value propositions and the buyer's value drivers.

If you still find it hard to believe that such a lack of alignment exists, just think about what you buy. In particular, look at why you buy it—in both a personal and business sense—and see if the sales and marketing claims match your own motivations. In some ways, it shouldn't be surprising. Each and every company—and more to the point, all the people who make up that company—wants to believe, and believes passionately, in the value of their offering. So people in companies create these value propositions that expound the virtues of their offering. But how aligned are they with what will really cause someone to buy—not simply be interested, but actually commit and acquire the offering?

I'll present this statement of the obvious as a revelation: *Value is only valuable if it is so in the mind of the buyer.* I could also bring in the notion here that value isn't always a tangible thing. Many buyers value things that don't cause additional work or don't change what they do. Simplicity and the status quo are often very significant value drivers. This leads to an important consideration of organizational value versus individual value.

ORGANIZATIONAL VERSUS INDIVIDUAL VALUE

You can consider value as organizational and individual. Let's start with the old maxim that "organizations fund and people buy." Organizations, institutions, companies, associations, or whatever collective term you want to use cannot in themselves buy anything. It is only through the people that work for, and on behalf of, those organizations that things actually happen. It's people who buy. People have their own motivations, and those motivations will hugely impact their value drivers. Something that may undoubtedly be good for the organization may not be good for the person engaged in the Customer Buying Journey. It may sound heretical to state it, but people do not always make the decision that is best for the organization. Yet, for the most part, suppliers shape their value propositions to appeal to the organization, not the person making the decision.

For example, we worked with a company in the business of print production. Their work ranged from small print jobs up to the production of scientific papers and journals that demanded high-quality printing, binding, and production. One of their long-term customers was a department of a large university located in the western United States. The person they dealt with was under ever-increasing pressure to reduce costs, and although this person and the university were more than happy with the service and support they were receiving from our client, they put their business out to bid. They found a company in New Jersey that offered to undertake the print work for slightly less money. Our client created quite a spreadsheet to show them that if they included the shipping costs of the materials, the New Jersey–based competitor would actually be more expensive. What do you think happened? The university went with the New Jersey company, as shipping costs were out of a different budget that did not come under their control.

Is this selfish and/or stupid behavior? At first look, it would seem so. But in defense of the buyer in this situation, she was given a bonus to cut costs in her department. So in this situation, you have a buyer making a decision and being financially rewarded for it, which helps the individual but hurts the overall organization.

This happens more than you would think. When looking to engage in a market, you cannot be successful by promoting a value proposition that appeals to the organization while ignoring the motivations—the value drivers—of the individuals managing the buying journey.

By decoding a particular market's buying DNA and understanding the value drivers, how do you ensure that your value propositions align to the target market's value drivers? In some ways, this is almost the Holy Grail. How do you ensure that you are selling something that people want to buy?

Our process for assessing value propositions, and perhaps even rethinking those propositions, is quite straightforward but usually highly revealing. We have our clients, people from the sales and marketing side of their organizations, write down each of their potential value propositions on a two-inch sticky note, one value per sticky. We are often surprised by how many there are. It's almost as if the concept is to overwhelm potential buyers with reasons to acquire the offering. This leads to another important finding from our research, which we call . . .

GIVE ME ONE GOOD REASON

When we talk to buyers about why they bought something and why they selected a particular supplier or product, they very rarely share a long list with us. Usually they share just one or maybe two reasons. This is interesting, as we often have the opportunity to ask the supplier why they think that customer, or customers in general, selected them over the competition. From their point of view, there are five or more reasons. Just imagine the amount of effort they could save and the focus they could bring to the equation if they really understood what one value driver would make a difference to their customers.

I watched a documentary about an African tribe living in one of the poorest countries on the planet. This particular tribe exists for much of the year as foragers, but they are also hunters. Once a year, they engage in their hunt. There is much planning, and it can last for weeks. They carefully consider what kind of animal they are going to bring down, where they will hunt, and how. They rehearse the hunt with dozens of the tribe involved in locating, herding, and then shooting the animal. The kill then will nourish them for several months. Why, you may ask, do they only do this once a year? The answer is that they can only afford one bullet a year.

I sometimes think that many suppliers would be better off thinking like that tribe. Too many behave as if there is no shortage of bullets, with their sales and marketing folks spraying their value propositions everywhere hoping that one will hit the target. But even then, the scattergun approach usually fails, as our research has found that even if one of the value propositions *does* hit the target, the volley of other bullets usually annuls its effect because the buyer just tunes out all the noise. Instead, you must carefully understand the quarry and the lay of the land and know exactly how you can match your value proposition to your target market's value driver.

ALIGNING VALUE PROPOSITIONS TO VALUE DRIVERS

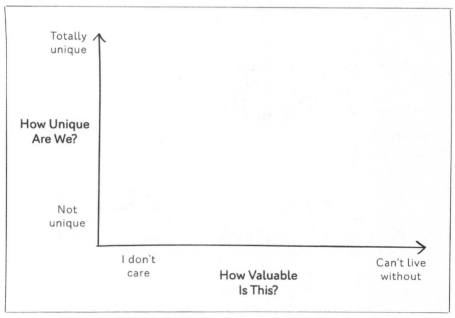

ILLUSTRATION 18.1. Plotting the relative strength of value propositions

As I mentioned, we start our process by asking our clients to write down each of their value propositions on a sticky note. We then ask them to stick their notes on a chart with a single vertical axis and a single horizontal axis. The horizontal axis is the degree to which their target buyer would value this, from a zero of "I don't care" to a high of "I can't live without it." The vertical axis is the degree—again, in the mind of the buyer—to which the buyer would perceive that the client is unique in their ability to offer this (illustration 18.1). As they select exactly where to place each sticky note on the chart, we often have to refer to and remind them of the work we did in decoding the Customer Buying Journey DNA. We aren't asking how much our client (the supplier) should value something or how unique they are in providing something; we are asking these questions in relation to the minds of their buyers. This is usually a tough exercise for clients, as they start to see that many of their value propositions look less like valid benefits and more like what we call *claims to fame*.

Once everyone believes they have their value propositions appropriately placed on the chart, we start to categorize them and align them to the target market's value drivers. You can look at groups of value propositions as in illustration 18.2. Let's look at each in turn.

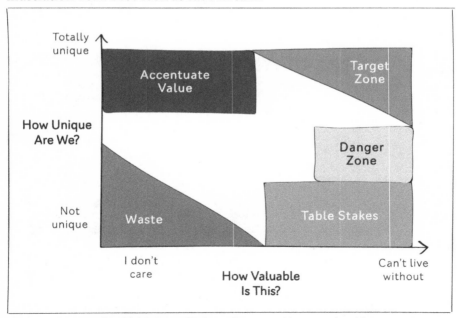

ILLUSTRATION 18.2. Aligning value propositions to value drivers

TABLE STAKES

Table stakes are value propositions the buyer does indeed value. These would be among the buyer's value drivers, but he doesn't see the supplier as unique in their ability to provide them. The supplier must provide them, but they are clearly not going to differentiate the supplier from others in the market. These are not the value propositions the supplier wants to headline, but they should always make sure that the buyer knows they are there.

WASTE

Waste describes value propositions the buyer neither values nor sees the supplier as unique in providing. Spending time in these areas is simply . . . a waste. If our African tribe above could afford more ammunition, in this case, they would be spraying bullets around for no reason whatsoever aside from trying to make themselves feel that they are doing something.

TARGET ZONE

The *Target ZONE* covers the buyer's primary value drivers and where he perceives the supplier's ability to satisfy those drivers as unique. If the supplier did only have one bullet, this is where they would want to shoot. They also would not want any noise of other bullets to distract from this one. Unfortunately, the target zone is far harder to find than most would like to admit. It is difficult to hit the target of what the buyer truly values and at the same time be seen as unique in the ability to do so. Linking to the work we have covered in the 4Q Buying Style, this is value land on the right-hand side of the 4Q. Few companies own these quadrants, but those that do and can protect their proprietary fiefdom, however tenuously, enjoy the luxury of customers perceiving that they alone can satisfy those values. But always be cautious; this is neither an easy nor inexpensive territory to capture and protect.

DANGER ZONE

Danger zone value propositions are aligned with the buyer's value drivers, but in the mind of the buyer, the supplier may not be unique in their ability to provide. As the supplier emphasizes these aspects of their offering, they may be both helping their competitors and also moving themselves into more of a commodity role and wandering over to the left side of the 4Q

Buying Style model. As they promote the benefits of some aspect of their offering that others also may be able to provide, they are underscoring for the buyer that he may have choice. The danger here is obvious: the supplier is investing—indeed, wasting—a lot of time and effort while simultaneously moving the buyer from value over to choice, thereby eroding any uniqueness the supplier had been hoping to demonstrate.

ACCENTUATE VALUE

Perhaps the most interesting area of the value map, *accentuate value* represents aspects of the offering the buyer sees as unique to the supplier but at the same time not aligned with his own value drivers. In other words, the buyer doesn't really care about it. Take, for example, a global supplier with the ability to provide consistent, quality service around the world. If the buyer is strictly based in the UK, why should he care about global delivery and service even if the supplier is the only one in their class able to offer it?

However, these value propositions may offer the supplier the ability to change what the buyer values. They may be able to get the buyer to change his value drivers so that they align with the supplier's value propositions. Here they are changing what the buyer values, which is why we call this segment accentuate value.

Recall ABC Pumps, the water pump distributor that changed how buyers in their market bought. Previously, buyers had only valued price and availability. But ABC Pumps was able to do two things: they highlighted the expense and nuisance of downtime on construction sites waiting for ancillary parts, and they were able to demonstrate their ability to make those parts available in a timely and effective manner. They changed what many of their buyers valued by accelerating the value of the service they could provide by eliminating the most common cause of downtime on the job site. Sure, some buyers may only value price and availability and are not concerned with the possibility of downtime, or perhaps some have other processes in place to eliminate the potential problem. But these buyers represent a different market. Yes, they are buyers of water pumps, but they are not the target market ABC Pumps was going after. They were not the quarry this particular bullet was aimed at.

TAKEAWAYS

⇒ The supplier must align its value propositions to the value drivers of the target market.

⇒ The Market Engagement Strategy should ensure that
- the supplier stresses value propositions that the buyer will perceive them as both highly valuable and unique in the ability to offer this value
- the buyer is aware that the supplier can deliver the attributes of value that they see as important but are not viewed as unique to your business (i.e., the table stakes)
- the supplier tries to change what the buyer values so that they will then see that the unique attributes of the offering are indeed valuable to them

⇒ The Market Engagement Strategy should seek to narrow the focus to just a few salient value propositions, as buyers tend to buy due to one or two compelling reasons and not as a result of a long list of benefits.

CHAPTER 19

GOAL 4: STAYING ENGAGED AND ENSURING POSITIVE PROGRESS

THE FOURTH GOAL of the Market Engagement Strategy is twofold: to stay engaged in the Customer Buying Journey and to ensure positive movement throughout the buying journey. Let's start by considering each of these two different but related aspects of this goal individually.

It is perhaps needless to say, yet critical, that with the overall goal of positively influencing the Customer Buying Journey (the sole objective of sales and marketing), you must be fully engaged—riding alongside the customer, as it were—to have any chance of actually influencing anything. As I'm sure you won't be surprised to hear, it is my inherent belief that lack of engagement in the Customer Buying Journey lies at the very heart of significant sales and marketing investments going awry with the inevitable fallout of disappointing revenue results. I have seen how it takes far more than gaining awareness, far more than developing interest, and far more than confirming belief in an offering to get a customer to buy.

Why? Because, as discussed in chapter 14, the bulk of the work required of the buyer in a normal buying process actually comes after awareness and interest have been achieved. Illustration 19.1 shows the typical G2 buying journey, comparing mismatched efforts between buyer and seller.

As you can see, the aim of the vast majority of today's sales and marketing investments and activities are about getting to the point of gaining interest and not what happens next. And as you can also see, the vast majority of the buyers' efforts take place after this point, from interest on.

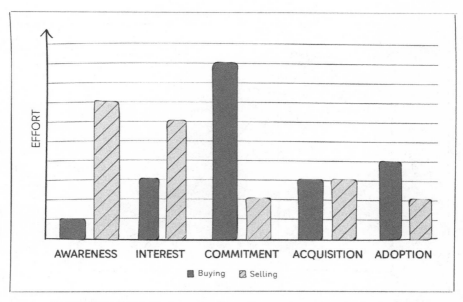

ILLUSTRATION 19.1. Buying and selling effort across a macro buying journey

This is the whole reason why, in Outside-In Revenue Generation, the focus is on managing the entire Customer Buying Journey, which by definition implies staying fully engaged throughout that journey.

Here's what happens when a supplier fails to get stay engaged. Let's assume, for the sake of this example, that the supplier indeed has a *key player*, a "champion," who is sincerely interested in the offering and believes the acquisition and adoption of that offering would result in undeniable value to the organization.

Illustration 19.2 shows what I call the half-life of the unmanaged Customer Buying Journey. The champion starts out with a surplus of energy, excited by what the offering could mean to the organization. But no matter how excited he may be, the first step down the curve reminds our champ of just how much is on his daily to-do list, and few individuals today work in a world where they have a lot of spare time on their hands. Then if that wasn't enough to slow down his momentum, he thinks of everything he has to do in order to move forward with acquisition and adoption.

Remember, most salespeople think their work ends when they get the order; they've done their job, the bell rings, and they get paid. But this reveals a serious misalignment of selling goals versus buying goals, because

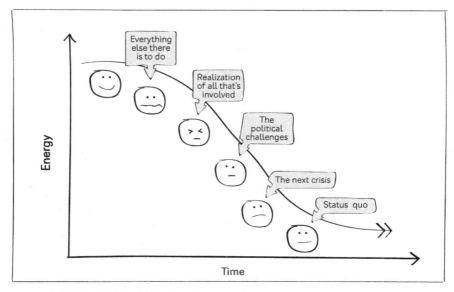

ILLUSTRATION 19.2. The half-life of an unmanaged Customer Buying Journey

the customer doesn't see things this way at all. Placing the order and the acquiring the offering are rarely the only milestones they focus on, and these are certainly never, *never* the end goals. The only way customers realize the hoped-for benefits of their investment is in the usage. Naturally, the customers' focus is on everything that has to happen for them to successfully gain adoption. This is when the second dose of reality hits: our champion starts to see how much has to happen to not only acquire the offering but adopt it and put it into practice within his organization. Once again, his energy and motivation drop and along with it the likely advancement of this Customer Buying Journey.

If our champion still has enough energy to keep going, he starts to encounter the politics of his organization. And if he wasn't aware of it before, he finds innumerable interested parties. To quote Claire Summerfield from the CCHN case study, "It's amazing how many folks come out of the woodwork and want and/or need to be involved." In the old days of more autocratic top-down leadership, this team empowerment may well have been minimized due to the organization simply implementing what came down from above; this still occurs to some extent, but it is a diminishing factor and certainly not one the supplier can count on to grease the skids of their efforts.

Once again, if any energy is left in the buying journey at this stage, our champion simply gets caught up in the numerous crises that seem to crop up weekly, if not more frequently. His thoughts of actually moving forward with the acquisition move to the back burner. Of course, it might help if one of the crises works in the supplier's favor, as it did in case study 2, when the results of a major survey were published and the hospital had a PR crisis to solve in the area of infection control.

But hope is not a strategy, and you certainly have better uses of your time than waiting for a crisis to come along to renew energy in the buying journey. I'll take it when it happens, but I wouldn't put the fortunes of the business at risk by hoping that it will. With the lack of any crisis to spur on the journey, *status quo* is likely to take over, and any life left in that Customer Buying Journey flickers and fades away.

To avoid this half-life syndrome, you must craft a Market Engagement Strategy that avoids these pitfalls. You must stay actively engaged in the Customer Buying Journey well past the point in which the casual observer, or traditional sales rep, might think "sold," and ensure that it moves positively and successfully forward. This, of course, is exactly how we have redefined sales and marketing.

It is no longer sufficient to simply create awareness, interest, and show value; the supplier has to manage the entire Customer Buying Journey.

In order to achieve this goal, you must consider five elements as part of an effective Market Engagement Strategy. These five are written not in order of priority but in an order where they can be considered in a logical and practical manner.

1. Potentially restructure the Customer Buying Journey
2. Know where the customer is in their buying journey
3. Act as the pilot throughout the buying journey
4. Add value at each stage of the Customer Buying Journey
5. Address all the key players at each stage of their buying journey

Let's look at each one in detail.

1. POTENTIALLY RESTRUCTURE THE CUSTOMER BUYING JOURNEY

Let's start with what may seem an illogical and perhaps most challenging element to achieve: to change the natural course of a particular buying journey. As implausible as it sounds, it can be an extremely powerful element of the Market Engagement Strategy. I have made the point before that although you must place your focus externally on the Customer Buying Journey, this doesn't imply that you must simply react to whatever a prospective customer might want or wherever they might go. The ability to change the natural course of the buying journey depends somewhat on how well defined that journey is. I say *somewhat* because it is entirely possible to change a very well-entrenched buying journey; however, in that case, more effort and time are usually required to do so. So let's first turn to an example where a buying journey is not well defined.

When bringing a new offering to the market, especially a new category of offering, there is often a lack of a well-defined buying journey. As you saw in case study 2, the buyer, CCHN, did not have a well-defined buying journey for acquiring and adopting those nanotech surgical gloves. In these situations, a lack of a defined buying journey is both a blessing and a curse. The downside is that no one quite knows how to move forward. Sure, there is a purchase process, but I have long made the distinction between a purchase process and a Customer Buying Journey. Due to a lack of direction and/or experience, it is very easy for the buying journey to fitfully stop and start and get totally bogged down. Various players may get involved and many activities may happen, but the buying journey can be a long and winding road. In this type of situation, the last thing you should be doing in your Market Engagement Strategy is trying to follow those meanderings. Instead, this would be an ideal opportunity to map out an optimal buying journey and then move the customer through it.

For example, maybe the customer would eventually get around to doing a trial, and possibly more than one. Many times we see potential customers conduct a trial only to realize that not all the right people were involved, or they failed to consider certain aspects that they should have included in the trial. Perhaps then the supplier's Market Engagement Strategy would be to bring the trial forward in the overall buying journey and help their prospective customer manage an effective trial process. We have also seen customers rush to do a demo or trial right away, so the effective Market Engagement Strategy might be to push the trial or demo to a time when you can conduct it with the right people and the correct overall objective. Perhaps the Market Engagement Strategy is to help the customer define the criteria for the success of such a trial and make sure the trial is conducted under the right conditions.

Now let's look at a case with a well-defined Customer Buying Journey and how it may be beneficial to change it. I'll turn to a real-life example of a stationery company that sold, among many other things, envelopes. Now, many companies have a well-defined process for purchasing such office supplies. A certain US airline was no exception; they asked for competitive bids for envelopes and gave their business to the cheapest supplier. In accordance with our 4Q Buying Style model, they were definitely a bottom-left (Sort and Select) style of buyer.

However, this stationery company was expert at changing the status quo thanks to a cleverly crafted Market Engagement Strategy. They managed to gain the agreement of this airline to study their use of envelopes. At the end of that study, they were able to go back to the airline and astound them with a few facts they had discovered. First, they discovered that their second largest application of envelopes was sending out the monthly newsletters and air-mile statements to their frequent flyers, an important market for the airline. They were also able to show that the open rate—that is, the percentage of recipients who actually opened those envelopes—was well below the industry standard. Not only that, but they found that of those who did open the envelopes, a much smaller percentage than the industry standard would actually respond to the enclosed special offers.

They then went on to show the airline that by designing a custom envelope and working with their IT and marketing departments, they could fold the newsletters and offers in a different way and make them more compelling for people to both open and respond to. By using industry data, they shared that this redesign of the envelope and its use could end up putting several million dollars of additional profit on the airline's annual bottom line. That airline now buys envelopes in a very different way. They now have a top-right (Trusted Advisor) relationship with that one supplier. This is a nice example of how a key component of the Market Engagement Strategy for that company was to change the established Customer Buying Journey.

Before leaving this very important topic of changing the Customer Buying Journey, let me once again make the point there is no one-size-fits-all answer. No optimal buying journey or particular approach fits all situations.

2. KNOW WHERE THE CUSTOMER IS IN THEIR BUYING JOURNEY

If your overall goal is to stay engaged in the Customer Buying Journey and in so doing be able to ensure that the buying journey moves positively forward, it is important to know where that particular customer is in their buying journey. This is a key point in Outside-In Revenue Generation: a total focus is placed on the customer's location in their particular buying journey. Remember, the customer sets the pace, so if you want to understand how they're doing, you have to understand two things:

1. Is the customer even in a buying journey?
2. If they are, where are they are in that buying journey?

The challenge is that many times, the customers are unlikely to share that they are at a certain stage in their buying journey and are moving on to the next stage. They are often unlikely to even be able to recognize their own Customer Buying Journey. But whether they know it or not, you can always map, and therefore predict, where they are in their particular buying journey.

When mapping the overall Customer Buying Journey, note the key activities associated with each stage of that buying journey. You can then isolate specific activities or outcomes associated with each stage. In most cases, you should strive to identify two or three things that you can observe or test to confirm that the customer has completed a specific stage in their buying journey. In process language, such things are called *exit criteria* or sometimes *stage gates*. Successfully identifying these elements depends heavily on how well you have decoded the DNA and mapped that particular Customer Buying Journey. If done carefully, here are some examples of possible exit criteria:

- time dedicated to exploring how the offering would work in their operation

- trial completed successfully
- implementation plan completed and reviewed
- budget assigned
- CEO or another significant executive in agreement
- funding approach agreed upon by committee members
- department head agrees with recommendation
- detailed analysis complete
- business case signed off
- alternatives identified and evaluated

Each of these exit criteria should be binary—either they have happened or they have not. By identifying these for any particular prospective customer, you can then tick the boxes. You can then reasonably judge, for example, whether all the exit criteria for stage 1 of the specific buying journey are complete; if they are, then that customer has completed stage 1. Note that all these exit criteria are defined by and relate only to the Customer Buying Journey. These elements have nothing to do with any activities or outcomes associated with a supplier's sales and marketing activities, such as "proposal delivered" or "demo done."

Undoubtedly, one the most important aspects of these exit criteria is to determine if the prospective customer is even on a buying journey. I call these the *stage-zero exit criteria*—the stage before which the customer has actually entered into a buying journey. This is a useful concept I will revisit later. It is important to recognize that you could engage with a prospective customer prior to the buying journey for the sole purpose of triggering a Customer Buying Journey. By having these stage-zero exit criteria defined, you can clearly and objectively know you have been successful in triggering a buying journey and that the customer is likely now at stage 1.

3. ACT AS THE PILOT THROUGHOUT THE CUSTOMER BUYING JOURNEY

In harbors all over the world, large ships entering those waters take on board a pilot. These pilots may not have expertise in the particular ship, and they're rarely familiar or concerned with the cargo, but they do have an intimate knowledge of their harbor. They then pilot the vessel through the shipping lanes and assure the ship is successfully tied up at the right dock. If you turn to the definition of this activity, you will find words such as *navigate, guide,* and *maneuver.* This serves as an excellent metaphor for the role of a potential supplier, and indeed the sales professional, in assisting a prospective customer through the stages of a buying journey. The pilot is not the captain of the ship; that lofty personage—that is, the customer—remains at the controls. But the pilot—in this case, you, the knowledgeable supplier—can help navigate, guide, and maneuver.

Once again, the extent of your ability to act in that fashion is somewhat, but not totally, determined by how well defined that Customer Buying Journey may be. Again, let's place our focus on the end-to-end buying journey, not just the purchase process. Many prospective customers will actually welcome someone working with them to prepare for and guide them on what needs to happen as they move through the overall stages of their buying journey. While I don't recommend this in all cases, I have seen a very successful approach where the salesperson actually shares the "road map" of the buying journey with her prospects. This can work very well when an organization is looking to acquire and adopt something new and innovative. For a salesperson to actually share what needs to happen, who needs to be involved, and the optimal way in which to truly evaluate the offering and successfully adopt it can be a powerful component of a highly effective Market Engagement Strategy. You saw a good example of this in our first case study, where Orion Tech took a proactive role in guiding DiaNascent through their buying journey. It was also obvious that a great deal of market credibility was required on the supplier's side to facilitate this approach without irritating or seeming condescending to the customer in any way. Even then, there were some awkward moments, so it is not a method for everyone.

On the flip side, it may be that you need to guide your prospective customer through the twists and turns of a much more convoluted and/or less well-mapped buying journey. Now, I must admit that this idea of acting as a pilot can be a dangerous thing in the hands of the wrong person. Some salespeople, ever brimming with optimism and relying on hope, could navigate their customers right onto the rocks. For example, if you look at case study 2, it's safe to assume that if the DNA of the Customer Buying Journey for the antimicrobial surgical gloves had been fully decoded and the buying journey mapped, it would have been eminently clear that the head of

Infection Prevention and Control for the hospital, Stephanie Wong, had to be involved. However, the first salesperson thought their "champion" was the ER doctor, Rob Summers, who did the first trial and really loved the product, so the Infection Prevention and Control person didn't need to be involved. Rather than shepherding the buying journey to include this individual, this salesperson bypassed her and ended up running the ship onto the metaphorical rocks. But if salespeople know there are rocks out there, it's a no-brainer to maneuver around them.

4. ADD VALUE AT EACH STAGE OF THE CUSTOMER BUYING JOURNEY

The only way for you to stay positively engaged in a Customer Buying Journey is for the prospective customer to see you as adding value. The manner in which you do this has to reflect what the customer is doing, what they need or want, or what they are concerned about. And so it follows that you must have fully mapped that particular Customer Buying Journey to determine how to add real and credible value to each stage of that buying journey.

So few traditional selling methodologies concern themselves with the dimension of time. They don't consider that a prospective customer is going to move through certain stages, over time, in the buying journey. And the time is variable—it could be in the lower end of the scale of minutes or hours, though it is more likely to be days or weeks, and at the higher end, it could even be months or indeed years. But as the customer moves through these stages over time, many things can change:

- their knowledge about a particular need or offering
- their knowledge about their own requirements
- their knowledge about their own organization
- their understanding of how a new offering could be used
- their concerns about how a new offering may be adopted
- their concerns about certain implications of selecting one approach over another

The list goes on, and of course it reflects what you discover when you decode the DNA and map a particular Customer Buying Journey. Now, as these things change and evolve, what the customer perceives they need from a prospective supplier—and indeed what a prospective supplier can offer—changes and can change quite dramatically. Think back to our first case study, where DiaNascent's *value drivers* started with a straightforward software installation but evolved to encompassing end-user adoption and training. And the eventual supplier, Orion Tech, was able—due mostly to their own stimulus—to fully synchronize with the needs of their customer.

In order to allow you to stay fully engaged in the buying journey, a successful Market Engagement Strategy has to determine what you can offer to a prospective customer that they would perceive as valuable and relevant. This will only be possible after you have fully decoded and reviewed the DNA of that particular market's Customer Buying Journey. Examples of value and relevance include the following:

- detailed information about the offering and its successful adoption
- pricing details and funding alternatives
- introductions to others like them that can act as a source of information and validation
- advice on how to navigate their internal processes and organization
- information from credible sources that can help with the knowledge that they may need
- templates and examples of business cases, implementation plans, workflow, or whatever else they may require that is new to them
- support in overcoming barriers or concerns
- assistance with change management concerns involved with the adoption of the offering
- examples of how others have successfully adopted the offering

Once again, the list can go on. But supplier beware: the customer *must* see any provision of value as relevant and valuable to them at the current stage of their particular buying journey, because a very significant aspect of any such value is that the customer can't view such advice or information as being so overly biased that it can't be trusted.

We have never talked to any customer who respected their salesperson who also did not see that individual as biased. For a salesperson to be totally independent and act as a true and impartial consultant just doesn't happen, and indeed, it should not happen. That doesn't imply that salesperson's customers don't trust her or that she does not have her customers' best interests at heart. Both of those things should happen. But it would be naïve for any customer to believe that the salesperson and other contacts they have at a potential supplier, together with any marketing collateral, do not at the very least present their own offerings in a favorable light. For this reason, you must take extra care when considering exactly what a prospective customer will value and consider relevant.

A successful Market Engagement Strategy has to consider how to deliver and acknowledge relevant value at each stage of the Customer Buying Journey and to determine the optimal method and moment at which to present that value to the customer.

5. ADDRESS ALL THE KEY PLAYERS AT EACH STAGE OF THEIR BUYING JOURNEY

Customer Buying Journeys do not move themselves forward. The only thing that moves a buying journey forward is people—people who get involved and who, by their actions, dispositions, power, and influence, determine if a buying journey moves forward, slows, or just stops. Therefore, when considering the elements of a Market Engagement Strategy where the goal is to stay engaged and ensure positive movement throughout the buying journey, addressing all the relevant key players at each stage of that journey is clearly a critical component.

Most Customer Buying Journeys involve more than one key player. The notion of the single decision maker is, as I have shared before, a thing of the past. As the customer moves through the stages of their particular buying journey, different roles across the organization will become involved. This is all part of the DNA you map as you decode the buying journey of that particular market. Your Market Engagement Strategy has to ensure that you are addressing each of these key players at the relevant stages of the overall buying journey and in the right way. Failure to do so can almost guarantee that the Customer Buying Journey will slow or stop. It is often a good strategy to bring these players in early. Instead of waiting for them to get involved and come up to speed, which often can slow down the buying journey.

Once again, it may be ever so tempting to believe that there is a "champion" and that this individual will, as the name suggests, fight his way through all the barriers, twists, and dragons to emerge victorious. But this is rarely the way customers behave. Recall the half-life I talked about earlier. Even the most motivated champions will usually lose energy with all that has to happen to move forward on a particular buying journey. And as with many of the components of successful revenue generation in today's market, there are no shortcuts. You simply have to ensure that you address all the key players in the right way at the right time. You might think certain key players won't be involved, but we have found, time and time again, that they will, and invariably the one that gets marginalized—think Stephanie Wong at CCHN—becomes or always was a major player.

In case study 2, in hindsight it would have been a good component of the Digex Market Engagement Strategy to proactively bring Stephanie Wong in from the get-go, affording her the chance to ensure that she understood the offering and—probably more importantly for her—to get the chance to discover where Digex was coming from. Yes, maybe everything would have stopped dead, perhaps for months, but at least Digex would have known what was happening and could have put themselves in a position to control things to some extent. This is far preferable to things happening without your knowledge or not knowing that things are not progressing as quickly as had been hoped. Worse still is to never realize things are not progressing and to continue to invest time and resources with little hope of the journey moving forward.

TAKEAWAYS

⇒ The Market Engagement Strategy must focus on how the supplier will stay engaged with and remain relevant to the buyer throughout the course of the Customer Buying Journey.

⇒ The strategy should encompass how the supplier will maintain positive progress through the buying journey.

⇒ The Market Engagement Strategy must ensure that the customer is supported through each of stage of their buying journey.

⇒ In some cases, it is feasible and beneficial to change the course of the Customer Buying Journey.

CHAPTER 20

GOAL 5: OVERCOMING FRICTION IN THE CUSTOMER BUYING JOURNEY

THE LAST OF the five components of an effective Market Engagement Strategy is critical for success but is likely the most overlooked component of managing the Customer Buying Journey. I define *success* here as the ability to engage with the market in a repeatable and scalable manner that maximizes revenue.

I often hear managers and executives say that they want to speed up their sales cycle. It's a worthy aspirational goal, but of course it's impossible to attain. You can't speed up the selling because the customer and their buying journey sets the pace, not the selling. A better way to put it is that they would like to speed up the *buying process*. Is this splitting hairs? I don't think so. Saying those words—that you want to speed up the buying process—forces you to focus externally, which is the key. Undoubtedly, it will be more intimidating, as you are implying that you want to speed up a process that lies outside your organization and seemingly outside your control. It sounds more difficult, and indeed, it is often difficult. Yet that is exactly how we are redefining sales and marketing: to positively influence the Customer Buying Journey.

In so doing, there can be few things more important than to keep the momentum going by reducing friction within the buying journey. If the journey begins to get mired down, the fear is that it will get stuck and then abandoned as the customer shifts focus to other important things. I have already talked about the half-life syndrome, where the ever-growing reality of jam-packed daily to-do lists and frequent crises, not to mention the customer's ever-increasing knowledge of all that will be required to actually acquire and adopt a new offering—can sideline any new initiative.

Let's start with understanding why this proves so difficult for many organizations.

BARRIERS TO A FRICTIONLESS CUSTOMER BUYING JOURNEY

FALLING FOR FALLACY #1

Back to Fallacy #1: the idea that if the customer believes in the value in the offering and the benefit they will gain as a result of acquiring and adopting the offering, then they will surely buy. I trust I've enlightened you on how I feel about this.

OVERESTIMATING THE VALUE OF THE OFFERING

Often running concurrently with Fallacy #1 is the overestimation of the value that you believe the customer will see in your offering. Hopefully, I have blown away this faulty logic as well.

UNDERESTIMATING WHAT IS REQUIRED

Sellers also underestimate all that has to happen across the Customer Buying Journey, including and compounded by a lack of attention to overcoming friction caused by *buying concerns*.

BEING BLIND TO FRICTION

Most of the companies we work with are either blind to their market's buying concerns or trivialize them. Here's a quick example. We worked with a company selling a new medical device that would be used widely in a hospital. There was little doubt of the benefits associated with its use. However, in adopting it, a hospital would be required to train all the users and potential users. Our client considered this a trivial matter well worth the effort. However, for their prospective customers, it was a deal breaker. The thought of an additional twenty minutes of training for so many of their staff—with everything else that was going on in their world— deterred them.

BEING BLINDED BY OPTIMISM

Entrepreneurs and salespeople—indeed, anyone responsible for generating revenue directly from customers—must be optimistic. They face so many challenges in an average day that surely if they were anything but optimistic, it would be hard for them to get out of bed in the morning. However, when crafting a Market Engagement Strategy, there is little place for optimism. Rather, a healthy dose of reality and a deep understanding of what it will really take for a customer to move through their entire buying journey will save a lot of time, energy, and disappointment down the road.

DON'T BUILD THE STRATEGY ON THE "OUTLIERS"

Sometimes you will get lucky. If you turn over enough rocks, yes, something good will be under one of them. If you are in the right place at the right time, good things can indeed happen. But you have to understand what led to that success. If you kick over a hundred rocks to find the one with the quarter under it, don't build a strategy that relies on turning over three more rocks to get a dollar. I know, this seems like obvious stuff, but I have seen the equivalent of this thinking used time and time again to forecast revenue. Just because all the "friends and family" bought in during the early days of a new offering doesn't mean the rest of the market will embrace the offering in the same enthusiastic way.

GATEWAYS TO A FRICTIONLESS CUSTOMER BUYING JOURNEY

Now let's turn to the critical success factors. Although some of these are naturally the opposite of the challenges listed above, it's worth taking a moment to reflect on each one. Also note that once again there is no one-size-fits-all solution to making any buying journey friction-free. You have to start with a complete understanding of the particular Customer Buying Journey and then carefully determine how you can solve or mitigate each buying concern.

KNOWING WHERE THE FRICTION POINTS ARE

When looking at the components of the buying journey DNA, it is the buying concerns that cause friction. These concerns can slow down or stop the buying journey, just as the dry spots between sliding surfaces cause friction.

By decoding the particular buying journey, you know exactly where these friction points are and indeed what causes them.

RESEQUENCING THE CUSTOMER BUYING JOURNEY

When I discussed the fourth element of the Market Engagement Strategy—staying engaged and ensuring positive progress—I shared the concept of deliberately changing the sequence of certain activities in the Customer Buying Journey. By crafting a strategy that predictably leads to the customer engaging in a different series of buying activities, you can overcome some of the buying concerns that would otherwise introduce friction, making for a powerful strategy.

For example, before any trial or proof of concept is undertaken, you can ensure the prospective customer has defined their success criteria. This can mitigate some of the buying concerns that may come up later in the process. Without this exercise, far too often a trial is undertaken and only when it is underway or complete does the customer fully consider the actual benefits and how they related to their needs or lack of same.

BRINGING THE HURDLES FORWARD

Now here is a tough one and, to many, a counterintuitive approach to take: to actually acknowledge and then bring up problems earlier in the Customer Buying Journey. If you know the customer might have funding issues, don't wait until you hit that barrier. Raise issues early when you have the time and flexibility to deal with them. In case study 2 with the antimicrobial surgical gloves, Digex should have known that when they led with the benefit of reducing infection, they had to involve the person responsible for Infection Prevention and Control. It may have been a plan to wait or hope that that person didn't get involved, or maybe they thought they could overwhelm that person with so many others voting for these innovative gloves, but that would not be a very good plan. A much better strategy would have been to bring that key individual into the process earlier. The worst case is that you find out up front that the sale is a no-go and save precious time and resources. The best case is that by bringing in that *key player* earlier, you convey that you have the customer's real interests at heart.

THE NINE FACES OF BUYING CONCERNS
Remember these?

BUYING CONCERNS

1. Process	6. Business
2. Priority	7. Implications
3. Individual	8. Fit
4. Organizational	9. Change
5. Alternatives	

You are now crafting the Market Engagement Strategy, a strategy you can use in a predictable and repeatable manner. This is a very important point to make because sometimes when we discuss buying concerns with our clients, they erroneously think of them simply as customer objections that a good salesperson should overcome in their selling approach. This is not the case. Buying concerns are very real anxieties, fears, and issues that are likely to come up across the journey. The majority of customers will face them when acquiring and adopting a given offering within a specific market. This is probably not a complete list of all the possible concerns customers may have, and conversely, there is overlap for sure. But what I want to address at this juncture are the buying concerns that I believe are common to a particular market.

Here's why you need to know and understand them. It is by understanding them—pinpointing exactly what and where the friction is in the end-to-end buying journey and then developing a Market Engagement Strategy to alleviate that friction—that you can target the right market with the right approach and the right offering. Let's look at the buying concerns, and I'll offer some thoughts as to how an effective Market Engagement Strategy can deal with them.

1. PROCESS
Having a defined and appropriate process for acquiring and adopting the offering.

You must craft the Market Engagement Strategy to clearly navigate your market's overall acquisition and adoption processes or, if there is no process, help define one. A number of flavors of buying concerns are linked to the challenge of the market's likely acquisition process. One we come across in many situations is simply the time and complexity of the purchase process.

The purchase process is only one step in the overall Customer Buying Journey, but it is clearly an important step. And there will be time and complexity at other steps of the overall buying journey as well, such as trials, proof of concept, committee approvals, and funding processes, to name but a few.

When the customer lacks a well-defined process for acquiring and adopting the offering—or when the process the customer uses is not one you consider "appropriate" to your offerings—a good strategy is to try to create such a process. In case study 2, the hospital had a process for the acquisition of surgical gloves as a commodity item. However, the supplier, Digex, was endeavoring to position their antimicrobial surgical gloves as significantly impacting the reduction of hospital-acquired infections. Therefore, their success was dependent on their ability to influence the buying journey to bypass the hospital's normal commodity purchase process. They would have to overcome this buying concern and engage with their prospective customers to define and initiate a different buying journey for their new gloves.

2. PRIORITY

The priority the customer attaches to the acquisition and adoption of this offering.

One of the reasons customers delay or refuse to acquire what seem to be undeniably beneficial offerings is that they simply have other priorities at the time. It may be hard to understand why someone is refusing to invest $12 to make $20, but if they are tapped out in other areas, they will. They may not have the time or resources to evaluate the offer, or they may not have the time or resources to adopt it.

Your Market Engagement Strategy should ensure that you are targeting a market in which your offering would likely match their priorities or where you can change their priorities to gain that match. An interesting conundrum is associated with this. Over the last few years, most organizations have learned what is important to their customers. Basic sales and marketing techniques today encompass positioning the offering with high-level and compelling benefits. Now just about any offering is positioned to "decrease costs," "increase productivity," "increase competitiveness," or fulfill some other lofty goal.

Take a look at this ad (illustration 20.1) that appeared in a series of national magazines and try to guess what is being sold. Give up? There it is: we have all learned to show how we can impact the customer's highest

ILLUSTRATION 20.1. A great claim of . . . ?

priority goals—or at least what we think are their highest priorities goals. But we have two challenges, which this ad demonstrates.

To start with, everyone is essentially saying the same thing, so buyers generally tune it all out. Second, are organizations sitting and waiting for you to come along to help them boost their productivity and lower their costs? Not if they are successful organizations with living, breathing leaders. No, they have set their priorities and are well into implementation.

And maybe a third challenge is that the supplier massively increases their competition. By positioning that you can boost productivity and lower costs, you are now competing with just about everyone.

Your Market Engagement Strategy must go well beyond the obvious and the superficial. You might need a tighter definition of the target market, and you need to step away from the notion of wanting it all. The strategy is to target organizations in which the offering is likely to be a high priority for them. You can also explore how you may be able to "attach" what you are offering to one of your prospects' high priorities.

A great question to ask yourself when crafting the Market Engagement Strategy in this area is, "What would happen if my prospective customer did not acquire and adopt my offering?" Clearly, if the customer won't face a significant consequence or it is something they can easily put off, then I think you know what will probably happen: not much.

Remember, if you don't know why your offering should be a clear priority for a prospective customer, especially in light of everything that is going on in their world, don't expect them to know.

3. INDIVIDUAL
The profile of the main buyer(s).

This is about the actual people involved in any buying journey: the primary contacts or the roles or persons you hope to fully engage with. You should craft your Market Engagement Strategy to engage with the right roles in the right way at the right time. This is highly dependent on the other components of the Market Engagement Strategy, such as if you are trying to trigger a buying journey or engage in one that has already started. It is dependent on who the key players tend to be across the particular buying journey and who you can realistically engage with. An interesting component of this part of the strategy is that the key roles usually change through the stages of the Customer Buying Journey.

In crafting the Market Engagement Strategy, look at the key players at each stage of the buying journey and determine how you will engage with each. I have already covered the myth of the single decision maker and the thinking that the key is to get in front of the executive. Another risky assumption is that an internal champion will do a lot of the selling. Yes, that person may have great access to her own organization, and yes, she may be passionate about the offering, but that does not necessarily mean she will be an effective or dependable "inside" salesperson.

4. ORGANIZATIONAL
The different players that may get involved and the politics they may impose on the Customer Buying Journey.

This is where the work you did in mapping the DNA strand of key players really comes into play. Your Market Engagement Strategy has to carefully consider what roles get involved at what times in the overall Customer Buying Journey. It has to consider each role's buying style, *value drivers,* and buying concerns. And then there's all the politics, which can have far-reaching implications. Very rarely does a singular *value proposition* and approach appeal to all the various roles that will play a part in the buying journey, so this is not the time to develop a long list of value propositions as a sort of "catch-all" approach. Two reasons stop this from being effective.

First, a long list of value propositions is about the same as having none. They simply all blend together, and a prospective customer is left without a firm imprint of what the supplier stands for and can offer. Second, you may find that a value proposition that appeals to one of the roles does not ring the bell for some of the others. Perhaps some of the key players are excited about embracing new and innovative approaches, buy others in the organization are far more risk adverse and concerned with proven capabilities.

The old notion of calling high and finding the decision maker has been replaced with a far more complex equation that more resembles a political campaign where the various influences have to be individually understood, mapped, and then addressed. In a similar way, the Market Engagement Strategy should ensure that the supplier is addressing the various roles with the right message, in the right manner, and at the right time. If that sounds like more work, it probably is, but our overall goal here is to create a customer, and this is what it takes in today's world.

5. ALTERNATIVES

The alternatives the customer may consider—not just competitive alternatives but any other claimants for their time, money, and resources.

Once again, there's a distinction between selling techniques and the overall Market Engagement Strategy. A good salesperson will always strive to understand what alternatives his prospective customer is considering and be able to position favorably against them. That remains a key selling approach. But with the Market Engagement Strategy, you are crafting an approach to overcome the alternatives the target market is likely to be concerned with. You then need an overall strategic approach to position against those alternatives rather than let each individual salesperson try to work it out. Even more importantly, after considering the alternatives, you may even change how you are going to market, which market you will target, and indeed what your offering is. You might even be in a situation where the customer loves and believes in the offering but opts to invest their time and resources in something else. In that case, it's not actually a competitive alternative, but it's an alternative option for their time and money.

Returning to case study 2, it wouldn't be a stretch to assume that other hospitals Digex was trying to sell to had an interest in a hand-cleansing program. If this was the case, perhaps Digex could position themselves not as leading with their antimicrobial gloves but in helping hospitals put effective hand-cleansing practices in place, an important part of which is their new infection-reducing gloves. They would then engage with prospective customers by offering to perform a survey of their existing hand-cleansing practices and benchmark them against other hospitals. And instead of losing the sale, as Digex did in the case study, they could lead with the alternative of a hand-cleansing program and reposition to engage along those lines.

Before leaving the topic of alternatives, I must point out that the alternative we see customers opt for the most is to do nothing. This must be identified when mapping the buying journey, such as either "status quo" as a value driver or "change" as a buying concern, or perhaps both. The Market Engagement Strategy must embrace this as a legitimate alternative, and there must be an approach to ensure that a prospective customer is compelled to take the leap and not simply opt to do nothing.

As ever, you can see that the only way to develop an effective Market Engagement Strategy is to gain a deep understanding of the Customer Buying Journey. You have to understand the alternatives the target market faces, what else they may be doing or looking to invest in, and then craft a strategy that places your offering in the most favorable light against those alternatives.

6. BUSINESS
The business and/or financial aspects of acquisition and adoption.

Of the nine buying concerns, this is the one we see most organizations get on top of. Most suppliers can arm their prospective customers with a detailed business case and can share a comprehensive return on investment (ROI) analysis. But reality bites, as it's another matter to assume that those prospects believe everything contained in them, because in most of the cases we have studied, they do not. These ROIs usually fall short of the line in two ways.

For starters, too many suppliers assume that everything is downhill with a tailwind. Customers usually pick up on this—that the underlying assumptions are highly favorable to the supplier's business case and may not accurately represent the world the customer actually lives in. It's like the "multiple benefits" issue. Think back to Pete Woods, the CCHN procurement manager in case study 2 when he said, "It's what I call the bandwagon benefit. Here's glove-guy hyping his major benefit—infection reduction—that's going to offset the price of his gloves. But he's forgetting, or ignoring, the fact that the HVAC sales guy is plugging the same benefit; how their new and improved filtration system is going to save us money by—you guessed it—reducing infections. And then there's a new cleaning company knocking on our door looking for our cleaning contract, and guess what the big benefit is that's going to cover the cost of their more expensive service? You're right again. Everybody jumps on the 'reduce-infection' bandwagon; all trying to justify their costs with that one set of savings from that one beat-up benefit." We see it all the time, when every ROI analysis builds in all the costs the customers are going to save, but—like success—each cost-benefit has many mothers.

Second, and trickier, is that these ROIs do not build in all the variables and costs the customer will see. Examples of these missing elements can include the following:

- costs associated with adoption, training, and associated lost opportunity costs
- costs associated with the other things the customer may have to do or acquire to successfully adopt the offering (see "Implications" below)
- costs and disruptions associated with switching from current suppliers, practices, or approaches
- accounting for depreciation, tax, or other areas either missing or not accounted for in the same way the customer would

The optimal way to develop the business case is in a totally collaborative fashion with the customer. They are part of the process, their accounting practices are used, and all their thinking is built into the business case. For the Customer Buying Journey to successfully move forward, the business case, however arrived at, must convincingly indicate and bolster the perception that the value gained will exceed the overall cost.

The Silent Killers

The final three buying concerns—implications, fit, and change—are the silent killers of so many Customer Buying Journeys. Unlike the business concern, suppliers generally don't handle these in such a forthright manner. Many either trivialize the impact these can have on the buying journey or are simply blind to them. This myopia is reinforced because customers rarely share these concerns with their suppliers. In light of the benefits associated with adopting the offering, the customer may think it seems trivial to mention that a simple change, for example, is stopping them from moving forward. We all know by now that change is good and that we thrive on change. Nobody likes to hear people say they are just fine with the status quo and they don't want to change, no matter how small that change. So instead, customers say things like, "It's not quite the right time," "It's not in this year's budget," "We have a lot going on at the moment," or "The price seems high." These are all essentially smoke screens disguising probably one or more of the following:

- There are elements and/or aspects of buying and, even more importantly, adoption that they can't or don't want to fund, manage, or handle (implications).
- It isn't really the sort of thing they do (fit).
- Things are fine the way they are (change).

So yes, these can be and are silent killers, but they're still just three more buying concerns. And once again, your objective is to craft an overall Market Engagement Strategy that places you in the best position, engaging the most attractive market(s), with the optimal offering and approach.

7. IMPLICATIONS

The implications of moving forward with acquisition and adoption.

In mapping the Customer Buying Journey of your target market, you have developed a clear understanding of how a prospective customer would view the implications of acquiring and adopting a certain offering.

These implications are often many and far-reaching, and until they are resolved, the customer is unlikely to move forward in their buying journey. The effective Market Engagement Strategy should seek ways to minimize or manage the implications for prospective customers. Once again, it's a case of understanding each of the implications and dealing with them.

An easy example of this is what providers of new equipment do to mitigate the implication of further and unknown costs after acquisition due to breakdowns: they offer a warranty, thus eliminating the implication. How about those selling technology who offer free training to mitigate the implications of how the buyer will use the new technology? Another of my favorites comes from the insurance industry: When switching from one broker to another, one big implication in many buyers' minds is that they would have to "fire" their existing broker. Many of these relationships go back years and may even involve social relationships and connections. In many ways, this can be the number-one buying concern and source of friction in the buying journey. The strategy to overcome this implication is to help the buyer find the right language and rationale to share with their existing broker as to why they are going with someone new. Some brokers will even compose the email for their new client to send to their existing broker.

As further examples, if you are selling capital equipment, there is an implication that the customer will require financing. Offering lease terms or partnering with a financial company can mitigate that concern. If that capital equipment is complex machinery, then an implication may be that it needs careful installation and then training of staff to utilize it. Again, offering those services to the customer or partnering with someone who can will help mitigate these concerns.

Think back to Alliance Medical, the company that was an early entrant into the market for reprocessing medical devices that had historically been designated as "single-use" items only. Their market believed in the concept of reprocessing and the money they would save. It seemed like a slam-dunk, yet when we talked to the prospective customers, we found the list of implications they saw if they went with the service:

- dealing with insurance exposure for physicians
- getting the computer systems to restock devices

- training staff in selecting reprocessing devices
- communicating with patients
- ensuring the devices were selected for reprocessing
- handling and shipping

Alliance Medical was able to alleviate these concerns by changing who they were and what they offered. Instead of simply providing a reprocessing service, they became experts at helping hospitals transition to reprocessing programs. As a result, the major buying concerns disappeared and revenue growth followed.

8. FIT

How a potential acquisition aligns with how and what that company would usually buy.

Fit is often one of the most difficult buying concerns to overcome. In some ways, if the offering is not a "fit" for your market, you may well be in the wrong market. This comes down to market definition. Take, for example, restaurants buying food supplies. If a particular chef has developed a brand and reputation for using local fresh and organic foods, then he is unlikely to be a fit for large, national providers of mass-produced food. So that chef, and chefs like him, is a separate market. These chefs are not the same market as perhaps the fast-food diner that doesn't exactly worry about buying local, fresh, organic produce.

In chapter 9, I discussed the landmark work of both Everett Rogers (*Diffusion of Innovations*) and Geoffrey Moore (*Crossing the Chasm*). As part of that, I offered illustrations with various elements of fit and expanded the dimension of product life cycle. A new and innovative technology is unlikely to be a good fit for people and organizations that are more conservative and averse to risk. I have often seen salespeople scrambling and searching for testimonials and case studies for unconvinced prospects who need positive affirmation for offerings that are new to the market. When marketing new and innovative offerings, define the target market as buyers who are looking for something new. If targeting a more conservative market, don't position the offering as new and innovative; position it as robust and proven. The primary consideration with fit, then, is defining and targeting the right market.

In some keynote speeches, I like to tell the fable of the floating Volvo to make this point. Now, let's say that Volvo, being the highly respected and dependable car manufacturer they are, has managed to create an antigravity technology, and they have incorporated it into their newest model. Their showrooms now feature at least one of these amazing floating cars. The cars have no wheels and no visible means of support. Needless to say, they cause quite a stir. Prospective buyers come in expecting to see the latest safe and solid variant of their favorite Volvo model, yet there before them is a floating Volvo. The sales reps take the buyers for test drives, and those buyers soon discover that the antigravity technology enables the car to accelerate, brake, turn, and cruise in the most amazing ways. Like buying journeys should be, the antigravity Volvo is frictionless. And wonder of wonders, the floating Volvo is no more expensive to run and maintain than their normal hybrid variant. Now what do people buy? Well, most opt for one of the four-wheeled, tried-and-true models they know and love. Simply put, the antigravity Volvo is just not a good fit for most Volvo buyers. They want to buy what they know. They want to buy what they trust. They don't want to buy a science experiment.

One of the morals of this story is that if you have discovered antigravity technology and you have the equivalent of a floating Volvo, perhaps it would be best to stick wheels and tires on it and not talk about the antigravity too much. Put another way, you are packaging and presenting your offering so that your target market sees it as a good "fit" for what they want and how they buy. Now, if it were Tesla . . . but that's a whole other story.

In summary, you can't overcome some aspects of fit, and as such, you need to define the target market to specifically exclude those buyers. In other cases, you might be able to change how you position, brand, promote, and sell the offering to overcome the specific buying concerns associated with fit.

9. CHANGE
The change, or at least the perception of change, that will occur as a result of adopting the new offering.

The last of the nine buying concerns—change—stalls so many Customer Buying Journeys, yet the prospect rarely shares this concern with the potential supplier, meaning that the supplier is largely unaware that change is the true cause of the friction. Despite what they may say, people generally don't like change. People live and work in a very busy world with many demands on their time, and they don't like moving away from old habits, set routines, and what they do daily. If the adoption of a new offering is going to change things, as almost invariably it will, then there is likely going to be friction in the buying journey. Most suppliers trivialize the change required to adopt their offering. And we often see a disconnect between suppliers, who simply focus on getting the order, and prospective customers, who are focused on the adoption and usage of the offering.

For an example of where change can get confusing, let's return to the example of a general practitioner ordering a particular medical test. Let's say she comes across a new test that is better for the patient and perhaps even cheaper, and let's say that she would order this test about once every few weeks. She decides to try the new test, so she talks to the office manager who orders the tests and says the office is going to switch to this different test. All well and good. But that office manager has always used a certain procedure to order tests of this type, and he now has to order the new test in a different way. However, the office manager goes ahead and orders it. Two weeks later, the GP has a patient who requires the same test and thus ticks the box for the office manager to order the test. You know what happens—the office manager goes back to the old test in the knowledge that this is what he has always done, it works, and he knows how to order it. Perhaps it was a very busy day, so he went back to the old habit, fully believing that the next time the doctor orders the test, he will try the new supplier. But guess what? Next time it is also a busy day, and on it goes. This as a real-life example of how the individual you would think is the buyer—the GP—makes the buying decision, but someone else who is involved doesn't change. It happens more than you might think.

We had another client who was marketing a range of ruggedized tablets used in a number of ways in warehouse locations. There was no doubt that these devices were at least as good as, if not superior to, the devices they were hoping to replace. However, the controls were on the side rather than on the front of the device. There were no operating differences, but it did mean that the clinical staff needed to change how they handled the device. It was as simple as changing from a phone that flips open to one that doesn't, but this one simple change was absolutely a buying concern.

With this client, we devised a Market Engagement Strategy in which they brought up the concern right away. They asked their prospective buyers if they thought they could manage the change in order to gain the cost savings and related benefits. They made the change a topic of conversation and offered help in the change management that would be required across the organization. By putting the issue proactively on the table and discussing it, it could then be successfully addressed.

When crafting the Market Engagement Strategy, you must consider any and all of the changes associated with adopting the offering. Then, as a part of that strategy, you have to develop a way of minimizing or managing the change for your prospective customer.

TAKEAWAYS

⇒ The most overlooked part of the revenue generation process is overcoming friction in the buying journey. Addressing and mitigating all buying concerns are key to a successful Market Engagement Strategy.

⇒ Many organizations are either blind to the buying concerns or trivialize their importance due to their own belief in the value their offering delivers.

⇒ The Market Engagement Strategy must consider how each buying concern can be addressed, avoided, or managed.

⇒ The Market Engagement Strategy should consider how to address buying concerns before they slow down or stop the Customer Buying Journey. This can sometimes seem counterintuitive.

⇒ Prospective customers across a market may not share some of their buying concerns with the supplier, but that doesn't mean that they aren't there and aren't real.

⇒ In today's world, buyers have many alternatives (including doing nothing), so even seemingly trivial buying concerns can divert attention from a buying journey.

CHAPTER 21

ENGAGING THE MARKET WITH ORION TECHNOLOGIES

T
O SPECIFICALLY ILLUSTRATE the actual application of Outside-In Revenue Generation, let's return to case study 1, where despite formidable competition, Orion Technologies successfully sold their services to DiaNascent. The development of their strategy can be illustrated by the five goals of the Market Engagement Strategy just covered in this section of the book. Here I present the key factors for success followed by how Orion's strategy was developed.

As noted, Orion's situation is more straightforward than many cases, as their market is well defined and their prospects will largely end up buying. Although less complex than many situations, it enables me to illustrate how the principles of Outside-In Revenue Generation can be translated into an effective Market Engagement Strategy. As I go through the five goals of creating a Market Engagement Strategy, the numbers in square brackets after each strategy refer to the summary diagram at the end of the chapter. In part 3 of the book, I then take this Market Engagement Strategy and use it to develop the CBJ Navigator for Orion.

MARKET ENGAGEMENT STRATEGY #1: HARMONIZING TO THE BUYING STYLE

The analysis shows that a prospect is likely to start in the bottom left (choice/product) quadrant of the 4Q Buying Style model, where they perceive that they know what they want and that they have a choice. However,

Orion's strategy is to shift this style in the early stages of the buying journey. First, Orion establishes credibility for their ability to successfully implement the Syncron software [1]. Building on that credibility, Orion then introduces the critical importance of end-user training and change management [2]. Orion then emphasizes the impact on the end users of changed workflow and the introduction of new technologies into their everyday operations. Orion uses a number of case studies of successful and less-than-successful implementations that illustrate the importance of end-user training and change management, and they might also introduce the prospect to other Syncron users who have experienced successful implementations. As a result of these discussions, Orion wants to move the prospect's thinking away from the belief that the organization has the in-house experience to manage this aspect of the implementation. Orion wants the prospect to start to see that they need Orion's knowledge and expertise of to be successful—in other words, to move from the bottom to the top of the 4Q model.

The second component of Orion's strategy is to position themselves as the only potential supplier with the expertise to ensure success in this area of end-user training and change management. They can achieve this through a number of approaches. First and foremost, Orion can seek to actively work with the prospect to [3] assess the extent and impact of the change of the new system on their end users. Although Orion could present all their capabilities to the prospect, there is no substitute for actually working with the prospect to demonstrate their expertise. They could, for example, conduct a survey of the end users and their current use of technology. In this manner, Orion would be clearly demonstrating their knowledge and abilities in the overall area of change management and end-user training. The result should be that the prospect shifts their thinking from the left to the right of the 4Q model.

Orion also considers how to handle prospects who do not shift their buying style. In the case of a prospect who fails to believe in the importance of end-user training and simply continues down the path of contesting various technology implementation companies against each other, Orion should simply disengage—it's not their market. This is always a tough challenge, but if the strategy is to differentiate and offer a premium offering, in the cases where a prospect fails to value that differentiation, then the only logical course of action is to withdraw.

MARKET ENGAGEMENT STRATEGY #2: TRIGGERING OR ENGAGING IN THE CUSTOMER BUYING JOURNEY

Orion's chosen strategy here is to engage prior to the trigger of the Customer Buying Journey and in some cases to actually trigger such a buying journey.

This buying journey has two very significant dependencies. The prospect must have decided to invest in Syncron's software, and they must believe they need a level of technical expertise to help in its implementation. Orion's strategy is to maintain a close working relationship with Syncron and its field teams. Their strategy is, in part, [4] to engage with potential users of Syncron's software prior to them even making the decision to go with Syncron. Here is a key component of their strategy. They know, and have proven to Syncron, that a major concern for their prospects is the successful implementation of the software. Prospects believe that implementation of this type of software is not trivial. With Orion's track record of success, the Syncron field selling team has no issues and even welcomes Orion talking to their prospects so that they can share success stories and help alleviate the anxiety that is in fact a *buying concern* in the Syncron buying journey.

At the very least, Orion's strategy is to engage with prospects during their evaluation of Syncron software and then, if the prospect has not already started thinking about implementation assistance, to engage in a discussion about their intentions.

MARKET ENGAGEMENT STRATEGY #3: ENSURING ADEQUATE MOTIVATION

Here Orion's strategy combines the elements of aligning to the *value drivers* and addressing the *key players*. Orion emphasizes that the key to successful implementation is end-user training and managing change in the end users' world. [5] Orion ensures not only that the prospect is thinking in terms of a successful technical implementation but that they fully recognize that the human side of the equation must be part of the overall scope of the project. Orion could share their unique and proven approach to ensuring that end users are onside and successful in using the new software. Orion also ensures [6] that prospects understand their "not to exceed" pricing proposals so that there are no surprises or hidden costs, ensuring that projects can be completed on time and on budget. At the same time, though, Orion realizes that they are rarely the cheapest, so a key component of their strategy is to ensure that the prospect is focused not simply on the price but on the ability to ensure a successful outcome. To achieve this element of the strategy, Orion shows how the investment in end-user training and change management (CM) correlates to success using a series of third-party articles highlighting that a lack of end-user training and CM is one of the highest contributing factors in failed software implementations.

MARKET ENGAGEMENT STRATEGY #4: STAYING ENGAGED AND ENSURING POSITIVE PROGRESS

Orion's strategy to stay engaged during the course of their prospect's Customer Buying Journey is to demonstrate their expertise in end-user training and CM aspects of the project as early as possible in the buying journey and then to continue to build on that theme. As they move the prospect across the 4Q model, they become a trusted resource to the prospect. The prospect should view Orion as having significant and relevant expertise in an area that will be critical to the overall success of their project. [7] Orion uses a number of tools and templates to work with the prospect across the stages of the buying journey. For example, they proactively work with them to look at the profiles of the end users, their current familiarity with technology, and their motivation for change. In this way, Orion not only stays engaged as a valuable resource to the prospect but also helps the prospect navigate their own buying journey. As a result of providing such expertise and guidance to the prospect, Orion can

- decrease the time the prospect may otherwise have dedicated to these activities
- increase the probability that the prospect will complete their buying journey and place an order with Orion
- increase the amount that the prospect may have otherwise invested in end-user training and CM

Note that the above three points align with the Sales and Marketing Imperatives and illustrate how this strategy not only keeps Orion engaged with their prospect but also ensures positive progress through the Customer Buying Journey.

MARKET ENGAGEMENT STRATEGY #5: OVERCOMING FRICTION

As I noted in the case study analysis, this particular buying journey has remarkably few buying concerns. The only one relevant to Orion is the issue of cost and budget. Orion's solution represents a higher cost due to its inclusion of comprehensive end-user training and CM components. This correlates to the "business" buying concern that shows up as the most significant source of potential friction across the buying journey. Because this is a component of Orion's Market Engagement Strategy, they will need to address it, especially with the key players for whom it may be of greater concern, specifically purchasing and finance. As Orion is planning to initiate or enter into the buying journey early, they can make it a key theme and even try to introduce the importance of end-user training and CM as early as step 1 of the buying journey as the prospect develops their Initial Scope for the project. To be assured of their ability to address this concern, Orion can seek to ensure that comprehensive end-user training and CM are viewed as "must haves" as opposed to a "nice to haves" prior to the prospect finalizing their approach at step 5 of the overall Customer Buying Journey. At this step of the Customer Buying Journey, Orion [8] provides a comprehensive implementation plan that illustrates how they will factor change management into the project and the details of the end-user training. This implementation plan will be the result of discussions throughout the buying journey with the prospect and will be totally customized to their situation. Success is marked by the customer taking this implementation plan as their final approach.

ALL LEADING TO . . . ORION'S MARKET ENGAGEMENT STRATEGY

Having explored each of the five goals of the Market Engagement Strategy, I will summarize the eight components of Orion's approach:

1. Establish, with the customer, the expertise we have in the successful implementation of the Syncron application.

2. Introduce the critical importance of the end-user training and change management.
3. Provide assistance in assessing end-user training and change management needs.
4. Work with Syncron to reassure their prospects about implementation success.
5. Ensure the focus is not just on technical implementation but on implementation success.
6. Position pricing as "not to exceed."
7. Continue to provide expertise for the success of implementation including templates and tools.
8. Provide a comprehensive implementation plan including change management and end-user training.

By reviewing these eight components of the overall Market Engagement Strategy, you should be able to see how Orion is seeking to positively impact the Customer Buying Journey for their market. Illustration 21.1 shows how each of these initiatives can be tied to a step of this buying journey. This schematic can be read in one of two ways. First, it illustrates exactly how

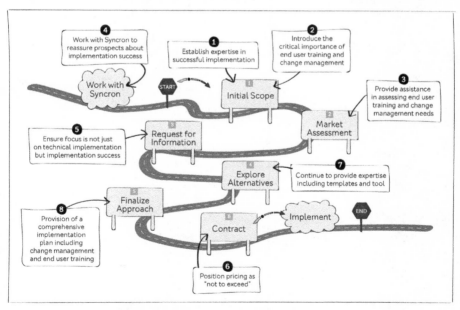

ILLUSTRATION 21.1. Orion's Market Engagement Strategy

each component of the strategy should impact the Customer Buying Journey. Alternatively, you can look at the Customer Buying Journey and see which component of the overall Market Engagement Strategy impacts it.

TAKEAWAYS

⟹ The Market Engagement Strategy defines how a business will manage a prospective buyer through each stage of their Customer Buying Journey.

⟹ The Market Engagement Strategy provides a consistent and predictable manner in which to create and keep customers.

PART 3
MANAGING THE CUSTOMER BUYING JOURNEY

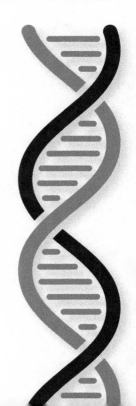

CHAPTER 22

TRANSLATING STRATEGY INTO APPLICATION

BEFORE I GET into the actual application of everything I've discussed up until now, let's look at where we've been, where we are, and where we want to be. Remember, as mentioned in chapter 1, our starting point is Peter Drucker's cornerstone principle that the livelihood of anyone in business depends on one thing: the ability to create a customer. It's not about the offering, whether it's the best or the newest or the cheapest; rather, it's about what you can do to create and keep a customer. Once you have understood and accepted that principle, it follows that all revenue generation activities must therefore focus fully on the process of customer creation and retention—usually the responsibility of the sales and marketing functions within an organization.

In chapter 2, you saw exactly what it takes to create a customer in today's world, and I shared my observation that we are now in the third generation of revenue generation. Thanks to the internet and its abundance of information, to globalization, to commoditization, and to general socio-economic trends, I posited that the customer buying process is now very different from what it was in the previous two generations of buying and selling. From the research my company has conducted over the past dozen years or so with hundreds of companies, I have no doubt that the Customer Buying Journey in today's business environment has changed dramatically. And most importantly, how customers now buy is more disconnected from how companies commonly sell than ever before. Customers are not waiting around for someone to sell to them, nor are they likely to buy whatever appears in front of them *regardless of the benefit they may gain by doing so.*

A customer is created only as a result of someone making a commitment to buy. Sales are not generated as a result of a sales process; sales are the result of a customer's buying process—what I have defined as the Customer Buying Journey. That isn't to say that certain sales and marketing activities will not impact that buying journey; indeed, they do and must. These actions are not wrong; they're just not usually enough. So I have offered a redefinition of the mission of sales and marketing: *to positively impact the entire Customer Buying Journey*—no more, no less. This, in turn, places the customer's actions and motivations firmly in the spotlight. To try to impact the buying journey without a thorough and clear understanding of *how customers buy . . . and why they don't* would be guesswork at best and incompetent folly at worst.

In chapter 3, we started decoding the Customer Buying Journey, the DNA of that process. I revealed the significance of this through our research, where we discovered that within a specific market, buyers behave in remarkably similar ways when embarking upon a buying journey for a particular offering. I even turned this around and offered that the very definition of a *market* should be "the collective set of buyers that approach their buying journeys in a similar way." Thus you can see that "car buyers" is not really a useful market definition, whereas "families that lead an active lifestyle, with 2–3 children from the ages of 4 to 15, who are looking to acquire a new SUV in the $35,000–$45,000 price range" is most definitely a market. So it follows that if you define a specific market by the parameters of the buyer and not just the offering, you must squarely base the focus of all revenue generation efforts allied to that offering on the thoughts, the desires, the motivations, and the activities of *the buyer*.

LET'S MAKE IT WORK

I'll reiterate some basic truths. My method redefines decades-old thinking about where customers come from and how prospects become customers. I am offering you a different way to look at sales and marketing by providing a clear map of how to develop a business strategy and then translate it into sales and marketing approaches and activities optimized around how customers really think and behave in their buying journeys. Here is what we know and what has to happen:

- The purpose of a company is to create a customer.
- Customers are created *only* if and when they buy.
- Customers only buy as a result of starting and successfully completing a buying journey, not as a result of a sales process.
- The sole function of sales and marketing is to positively impact the Customer Buying Journey.
- There are only four ways in which you, the supplier, can impact the Customer Buying Journey: *initiate, complete, expedite*, and *augment*.
- Our research has found that customers in particular markets, when faced with acquiring and adopting certain offerings, behave in remarkably similar ways. This is, in fact, how we define a market—otherwise, it is just a random bunch of possible buyers.
- Therefore, the success of any business entity hinges on how well it understands its market and its customers' buying journeys.
- All sales and marketing activities within that company must be structured around the target market's buying journey DNA.

When we decoded the Customer Buying Journey, we uncovered and defined the six DNA strands that determine how customers buy and why they don't for a particular market. To refresh, those six strands are as follows:

1. Triggers
2. Steps
3. Key players
4. Buying style
5. Value drivers
6. Buying concerns

You can now examine a target market's buying journey and the associated DNA in a logical and sequential manner as shown in illustration 22.1. What you see here are the steps of the buying journey and then the other strands of the DNA. Triggers are omitted simply for clarity. As a result of laying out the Customer Buying Journey in this fashion, you should be able to clearly see how that journey progresses, how different players become involved at the different stages, and how the buying style, *value drivers* and *buying concerns* change across the journey.

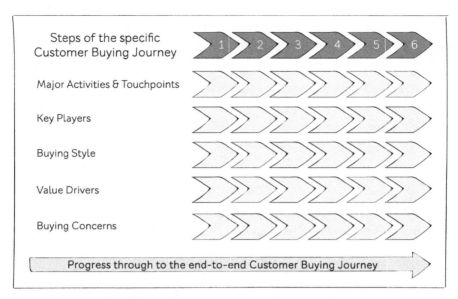

ILLUSTRATION 22.1. The DNA across a Customer Buying Journey

This leads to powerful insights in terms of requiring different activities, skills, roles, and positioning depending on where the customer is in their buying journey. This is where old selling approaches break down, because they neither acknowledge nor factor in that the customer is moving through a buying journey, and as they do so, things change.

In part 2, we saw how, armed with this in-depth knowledge of the Customer Buying Journey, an effective Market Engagement Strategy can be crafted. The Market Engagement Strategy's singular focus is to positively impact the buying journey and consists of five specific goals:

1. To harmonize your selling approach with how the market is buying or change how the market buys to how you want to sell
2. To initiate or engage in a Customer Buying Journey
3. To ensure the customer has adequate motivation to invest in the buying journey and ultimately in the acquisition and adoption of the offering
4. To ensure you remain engaged in the buying journey
5. To reduce friction across the Customer Buying Journey

Throughout the book, I have referred to the breakdown of Fallacy #1—the paradox that even when prospective customers are faced with an offering that they know will bring them value, there is no assurance that they will buy. The implications of this are far-reaching. I'm sure it will come as no surprise that I am not suggesting that it can be solved by simply changing the messaging, or talking about how great the offering is, or stressing the benefits that the customer will gain as a result of an acquisition. That's the simple stuff, and I'll even quantify it and suggest that it is less than 20 percent of the equation. The other 80 percent is the total immersion in the methodology and practices of Outside-In Revenue Generation, or how you move a prospective customer positively through the stages of the buying journey to the point of acquisition and adoption, *with the entire focus on the external reality of how customers actually buy*.

To get there, I must recommend what to many will seem extreme, but here it is. There should be no sales process. Forget about that approach from the 1960s and '70s of classifying leads, suspects and prospects, and pipelines. Get rid of any stylized wish list of imaginary steps that supposedly walk a customer through *qualification* to perhaps *solution definition*, to *proposal*, and then to *closing*.

The only thing that matters is where customers are in their buying journey.

You could go all the way through your sales process, submitting a proposal and being ready to close, but if the customer has not even started a buying journey, there won't be a sale. This is the root cause of why sales forecasting is so unreliable. It doesn't matter when *you* think you are going to close a sales opportunity, because the only thing that matters is when a *customer* is going to buy.

OUTSIDE-IN REVENUE GENERATION: THE MODEL

I will only focus on one process, and it won't be a superficial or generic buying journey and certainly not a sales process. It will be the specific Customer Buying Journey and its associated DNA for a specific target market acquiring a particular offering. I will give you a quick look at the overall approach here and delve into it with more detail in the subsequent chapters. Let's continue with the diagram in illustration 22.2, which illustrates the Outside-In Revenue Generation approach.

The *Steps of the specific Customer Buying Journey* create the foundation of the model. And we'll remind ourselves here of the mission of sales and marketing: to positively impact the Customer Buying Journey.

1. In the first layer up, we will define all the *sales and marketing activities* aimed at fulfilling that mission for each step of the buying journey, and I have two important points to make here:
   a. The suppliers should divest themselves of any internally based sales and marketing activities not directly related to that mission. Look to the Sales and Marketing Imperatives (chapter 15) and redirect any efforts not contributing to one or more of those into something more productive.
   b. The optimal sales and marketing activities are always dictated by where customers are in their buying journeys—a theme I will return to in future chapters.
2. The next layer represents the *information flow* between supplier and customer. All sales and marketing activities with a customer are about information: information the seller gets from the buyer and information the

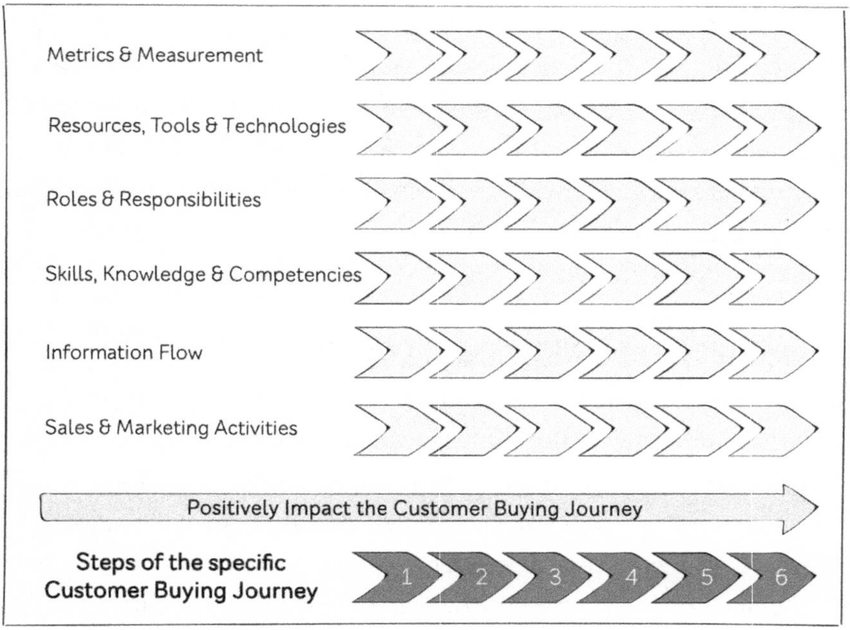

Metrics & Measurement

Resources, Tools & Technologies

Roles & Responsibilities

Skills, Knowledge & Competencies

Information Flow

Sales & Marketing Activities

Positively Impact the Customer Buying Journey

Steps of the specific Customer Buying Journey 1 2 3 4 5 6

ILLUSTRATION 22.2. Outside-In Revenue Generation layers

buyer gets from the seller. This information flow should be defined step by step in the overall Customer Buying Journey and not left to chance.

3. Moving up, we must define the appropriate *skills, knowledge, and competencies required by the organization,* again by each relevant step in the buying journey.

4. Next we define all customer-facing *roles and responsibilities* across the organization in order to align with the Customer Buying Journey.

5. These will then be closely aligned with the required *resources, tools, and technologies* to bring each Customer Buying Journey to fruition.

6. Finally, we can establish, analyze, and manage the *metrics and measurements* at each step across the buying journey, and we will see how these then become the vital signs of the health of a business.

Effective sales and marketing must be based on knowing where the customer is in their buying journey and then targeting the right activities to positively impact that buying journey in accordance to the Market Engagement Strategy.

The magic is to now join the two models (see illustration 22.3). This allows you to see how all of the revenue generation activities are aligned to the target

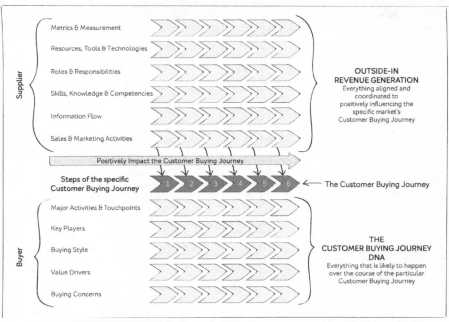

ILLUSTRATION 22.3. The Outside-In Revenue Generation model

market's buying journey and its associated DNA strands. We now have a model for implementing the Market Engagement Strategy—a model for an effective and precise manner in which to create a customer—from the Outside-In.

The next two chapters will address in detail that all-important first layer of the model: the sales and marketing activities—first with Outside-In Marketing and then with Outside-In Selling. In the following chapters, we will look at the remaining five layers of the model. But before moving on, let's compare how an organization might behave when adopting Outside-In Revenue Generation as opposed to the traditional, outdated G2 approach (illustration 22.4).

Overall, our focus must move away from the internal aspects of the offering, its alleged benefits, and the internal process of selling. We must refocus our efforts to directly impact the Customer Buying Journey, each element of which must be deliberately keyed to the specific steps of that journey. In short, our focus moves from imagining what the market and customers are doing (or wishing they would do) to much more objective considerations about what is actually happening across the particular Customer Buying Journey.

ILLUSTRATION 22.4. TRADITIONAL VERSUS OUTSIDE-IN REVENUE GENERATION

ASPECT	TRADITIONAL	OUTSIDE-IN REVENUE GENERATION
Focus	The features and benefits of the offering	Positively impacting the end-to-end Customer Buying Journey
Messaging	The features and benefits of the offering	Satisfying the customer's specific value drivers aligned to the key players and steps of the Customer Buying Journey Mitigating buying concerns
Organization	Roles defined by the internal structure	Aligning and coordinating roles to the Customer Buying Journey
Sales timing	Where I am in the sales process	Where the customer is in their buying journey
Sales approach	Following a traditional sales process	Managing and positively impacting the Customer Buying Journey
Sales activity	What comes next in the sales process	Synchronizing the optimal activity to where the customer is in the buying process
Forecast	When I can close the business	When the customer will buy

TAKEAWAYS

⇒ Sales are generated not as a result of a sales process but as a result of a customer successfully completing a buying journey.

⇒ The new role of sales and marketing is to manage and positively impact the Customer Buying Journey via the four Sales and Marketing Imperatives: *initiate, complete, expedite, and augment.*

⇒ As a buyer moves through the steps of their overall Customer Buying Journey, the optimal activities in which a supplier should engage change. In fact, the optimal activities in which a supplier should engage are determined by where the customer is in their buying journey.

⇒ The supplier should align and coordinate all the resources and activities that touch the buyer with the steps of the specific Customer Buying Journey.

⇒ When engaging in the market, the supplier must place the focus externally on the Customer Buying Journey and not on the internal aspects of their offering or sales process.

CHAPTER 23

OUTSIDE-IN MARKETING

THE BASIC FOUNDATION comprising that first layer of the Outside-In Revenue Generation model consists of all the activities that directly touch a prospective customer throughout their end-to-end buying journey. Examples of such activities include trade shows, websites, magazine articles, direct mail, advertising, or a meeting with representatives—likely salespeople—of the supplier. They include any and every instance in which either the supplier connects with the prospective buyer or the buyer connects in some way with a potential supplier. When the prospective customer expects or initiates such an exchange, I define these as touch points. These interactions fall into three categories:

- *Passive.* Nothing results from the exchange.
- *Reactive.* The prospective customer gets what they want, when they want it, but nothing has changed regarding their course of events.
- *Interruptive.* The prospective customer gets something of value to them, and in so doing, their likely course of events changes. Such an exchange may be positive for the potential supplier or negative. An example of a negative exchange is one that leaves the customer with the perspective that the supplier offers poor service or that their pricing is not competitive and thus discounts them from their search for a potential supplier. A positive exchange could be a strong reference from a similar company going through a similar situation.

Given that I have defined the mission of sales and marketing as positively impacting a particular Customer Buying Journey, it is clear that although we want to make sure that all customers get what they want how and when they want it, we really need to have interruptive interactions with them that will positively impact the buying journey. And while the salespeople will eventually and primarily instigate these initial contacts, it really is the supplier's marketing function that not only generates the actual information but in many cases regulates how and when that information is disseminated. So let's build on this notion by looking at what would typically be called marketing activities and how the concept of Outside-In Revenue Generation will impact them.

MARKETING FROM THE OUTSIDE-IN

It is my intent not to cover the waterfront of all marketing processes and activities but to offer a filter by which to view marketing actions in a different light. Based on a clear and deep understanding of the particular market's Customer Buying Journey DNA (as given in part 1) and then based in the crafted Market Engagement Strategy (part 2), we can undertake our marketing activities in a more precise way. Before going deeper, recall my four horsemen, the Sales and Marketing Imperatives: *initiate, complete, expedite* and *augment*.

I am often drawn into conversations where people believe that there must be other worthwhile results from marketing investments. No—these are it! A favorite topic in these conversations often is branding, because a lot of marketing is invested in developing a brand. But why is that? Surely to impact one or more of the four imperatives.

Maybe the strategy is that the brand will increase recall so that when a customer discovers a need, that particular brand will come to mind. The myriad signs, billboards, and hoardings plastered over all professional sporting venues are often based on that belief. But whatever the strategy and belief, the end result has to be to cause something to happen that otherwise would not, resulting in one or more of those four Sales and Marketing Imperatives being met.

Or perhaps the branding is to associate the supplier with a certain unassailable quality that could then increase the probability of acquisition and adoption (imperative 2): Toyota with dependability, Apple with innovation.

And it's not just the supplier setting the table, as you can find instances of customer-driven impetus in imperative 3—expedite. From the common pizza delivery promise of "30 minutes or it's free" to far more complex examples involving system installation and delivery bonuses/penalties. These are, in the case of pizza, obvious marketing directives, whereas in the corporate world, they can be much subtler and suggested. But they always have one goal in mind: distinguishing themselves from other suppliers by moving through the buying journey as quickly as possible.

And how about "Buy 2 and get one free"? It's easy to see the influence that would have on imperative 4. You get the idea. All these attempts at branding and promotion come down to positively impacting the Customer Buying Journey and thus one or more of the four Sales and Marketing Imperatives.

By referring to the DNA decoded for your specific target market, you will know exactly what is happening across the Customer Buying Journey. You will know exactly what will trigger that journey and what it depends on. You will know who gets involved when and what their key activities are. You will know the touch points and when they occur. You will also know each customer's buying style, what it is based on, and how it may evolve and change across the buying journey. You will also know the *value drivers* for each prospective customer and what their *buying concerns* are, and all the while you will be paying close attention to how these issues may evolve or change across the journey. The Market Engagement Strategy will then meet five distinct goals aimed at managing and positively impacting the target market's Customer Buying Journey.

THE FOUR Ps

Let's dig deep into Outside-In Marketing to gain an understanding of how the Customer Buying Journey DNA and its associated Market Engagement Strategy impact marketing by exploring those four classic marketing Ps—product, price, promotion, and place.

PRODUCT

The product, or the offering, can be a tangible "touch and feel" product or a less tangible item, such as service or advice. The product is everything buyers expect to get when they acquire and adopt the offering. This may also include warranty, service, support, and other augmentations that could extend to the user experience.

In the vast majority of cases I've seen, our clients have a well-defined product that will bring clear value to their target market(s). The challenge, which this book is all about, is understanding exactly how and why those target customers might buy that product and why they might not. By understanding a particular buying journey's DNA, it may become apparent that the product needs to be changed, usually expanded or contracted, to better synchronize with how the market will buy or why it may not. The two components of the Customer Buying Journey DNA that most impact the product are the buying style and the buying concerns.

How Buying Style Can Impact the Product

Part 1 laid out the four quadrants of buying style, what I call the 4Q model (illustration 23.1). In part 2, you saw how any brand or product must be optimized within one (and only one) of the four quadrants—either the quadrant that represents how the target market will approach their buying decision or the quadrant you believe you can move a particular market into. The quadrant you choose to operate in then dictates how the product and its associated marketing emphasis must appear to that target market. Let's look at each quadrant in turn and its associated market emphasis.

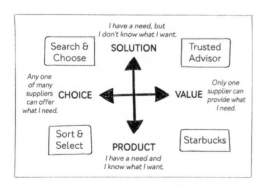

ILLUSTRATION 23.1. Complete 4Q model

Sort and Select

In this quadrant—the lower left—the customer perceives that they know exactly what product they want and that they have a choice of supplier. Operating in this quadrant calls for a product that meets the customer's needs—no more and no less—and this quadrant is also the natural habitat of commodity sales. The product must be a very good match to what the customer is looking for; indeed, the closer to the customer's exact specifications, the better. If the product requires modifications, customization, or configuration, the customer is unlikely to choose it unless the customer was expecting that and no other options existed. This quadrant is also home to the buying style we often call RFP Land. To satisfy the needs of the market—usually quite similar among buyers—the product must be readily available, easy to acquire, and easy to adopt. It may benefit you to have alternative types of product available so that you have at least one good match for what the customer is looking for. The concept here is to ensure that the target market can easily find, acquire, and utilize what they are looking for.

Search and Choose

In this quadrant—the upper left—the customer is looking for some level of help in defining what they need and believes they have choice in potential suppliers. In this quadrant, the offering must include the ability to assist the customer in defining their requirements and choosing what they need; it must become a solution. This could be something simple, such as an online configuration tool that, for example, helps potential buyers select the right camera for their needs. At the other end of the spectrum, it might be a consultant who helps determine the customer's needs and then makes a series of recommendations. In either case, the customer must see that the product comes with a level of credible expertise that will enable them to relatively quickly and easily arrive at the point where they can confidently acquire and adopt a solution that satisfies their wants. The product, in this case, needs to be easily accessible with a relatively straightforward process to understand, acquire, and adopt. Because the customer perceives that they have a choice, if it is difficult to gain access or complex to undertake, they will likely look for an alternative supplier.

Trusted Advisor

This is the top-right quadrant, where the customer is looking for assistance in determining exactly what they need and will tend to go to the same supplier due to their belief in that supplier's unique ability to deliver something of value to them. Here the total product being marketed must include profound knowledge and expertise in the relevant subject matter, proven market leadership, and the ability to engender whatever it is that the customer perceives as uniquely valuable to their needs. This could be a belief that the supplier's product expertise is unrivaled. It could be, and often is, an existing relationship, or it could be that the customer perceives that the supplier has a unique level of knowledge about the customer's organization, industry, or particular application that enables them to provide higher-quality recommendations. Whatever the case, marketing has to reinforce this belief. For example, if customers perceive you have exceptional expertise, then marketing has to reinforce that aspect of the brand through thought leadership, publications, awards, and possible speaking engagements—quite different from marketing a product in any other quadrant.

Starbucks

This is the bottom-right quadrant, where the customer not only knows exactly what product they want but will turn, time and time again, to the same supplier due to their perception of the unique value that supplier—and only that supplier—brings. Here the product's marketing must be all about the aspect of the brand the market perceives as unique and valuable. This could be all manner of brand attributes. The Starbucks experience, of course, is one. Or it could be service. Lexus has done an outstanding job in the United States of making their high level of customer service an integral part of their brand. This implies that all their marketing and all their customer interactions have to include this high level of customer service as an integral part of their product. Whatever the attribute is, it must be seen as unique to that one supplier.

A thought-provoking aspect of the 4Q model can be price. Price shopping is often, and correctly, associated with the bottom-left quadrant (Sort and Select), where the buyer shops based on price. However, you can build a brand so that the buyer perceives that you represent the best price. The difference between buyers in the bottom-left quadrant to those in the bottom right is that they no longer consider choice or do any comparison shopping. They simply head straight to their retailer of choice (maybe Costco or Walmart) safe in their belief that they will get the best prices. Again, in marketing these products, offering the best prices or everyday discounts has to be an integral part of the product being offered.

You can look across any number of markets and find examples of brands that have developed as offering the best price and have successfully switched a certain market to now buy in the bottom-right quadrant based on the belief that they are unique in their ability to offer low prices. It's not short-term strategy, but it can be a component of the overall brand strategy.

How Buying Concerns Can Impact the Product

BUYING CONCERNS

1. Process	6. Business
2. Priority	7. Implications
3. Individual	8. Fit
4. Organizational	9. Change
5. Alternatives	

In part 1, I discussed the nine buying concerns—areas that can cause friction in the overall Customer Buying Journey. And in part 2, you witnessed their importance in crafting an effective Market Engagement Strategy. A very effective way of overcoming a number of these concerns is by changing the scope of the offering. Once again, no simple solution exists, as each situation demands its own strategy. Remember Alliance Medical and how they changed their offering from just reprocessing equipment to partnering with a hospital to successfully embrace the whole reprocessing concept? By changing and expanding their offering, they were able to turn previous buying concerns into value drivers. After this adjustment, hospitals saw Alliance as a true solution provider with expertise in alleviating the headaches and challenges associated with implementing a reprocessing service of undeniable value.

The buying concerns that may be best addressed by a change in the scope for the product are the last three of the nine—implications, fit, and change. Let's look at each in turn and see how you may mitigate each by changing the scope of the offering, no matter if it is a tangible object or an intangible service.

Implications

When potential customers have buying concerns based on implications, they foresee issues with either the acquisition or successful adoption of the offering that could represent barriers or challenges, and these can slow down or even stop the buying journey. Recall the significant disconnect between the buyer, who is usually far more focused on the use and adoption of the offering (because the buyer doesn't attain the anticipated value until after successful adoption), and the supplier, which sees their work as complete with the receipt of the order and payment.

A number of important collateral implications can be associated with acquisition; among these could be the termination of a current supplier or the impact such a decision may have on other parts of the business. In case study 2, if CCHN had decided to go with the Digex surgical glove, then the loss of business to the current supplier could have resulted in upward pricing action on other goods and services that same supplier provided.

Implications associated with the successful adoption of a particular offering may focus on other acquisitions that will need to be made. People rarely get value out of buying bare-bones computers. They usually need to buy software applications to have anything more than a pricey paperweight. Companies might need to train users or change workflow. They might encounter housekeeping challenges, such as finding the space or changing physical workspaces. In many cases, suppliers trivialize the impact of these implications on the buying journey because they are blinded by their inherently strong belief in the value associated with their offering. They see how a customer will gain significant benefits, perhaps cost savings, as a result of adopting their offering. This is not to say that they are unaware that the customer might require training or might need to make other changes, but they see these as minor issues compared to the overall benefits of the acquisition. Conversely, the customer sees these implications as challenges they simply don't want or need in light of everything else going on in their world.

So the concept of changing the offering to mitigate these concerns becomes a key strategy. Should the offering include training, additional services, a different form of warranty or guarantee, or the provision of some level of expertise? Although a prospective customer may see many varied implications associated with a particular offering, you must determine how many of these you can mitigate by carefully changing the nature of the product.

Fit

Buying concerns associated with fit are those where the culture of the organization does not align with the nature of the offering. For example, a conservative organization that tends to be a follower in their industry is not likely to be looking for new or highly innovative products. This type of organization likely needs lots of proof that the product will work in their environment. They will need to feel secure in the knowledge that others just like them have successfully adopted the offering and realized the associated benefits. Therefore, if you are marketing such an offering, you can choose to do one of two things: you can target a market more likely to have visionary, risk-tolerant trendsetters, or you can change the nature of the product. In the latter case, you might downplay or even remove various aspects of the product to successfully offer it to a more conservative market.

Think back to the parable of the floating Volvo with the highly innovative antigravity technology (chapter 20). That would be a great product for trendsetters, those who love technology and are willing to try something different. But for the more conservative market, which incidentally is composed of a far greater percentage than the more risk-tolerant buyers, you might need to change the nature of the offering. You can stick tires on the product to make mainstream buyers more comfortable and then highlight fuel efficiency, low carbon emissions, and high resale value. The point is that you are changing aspects of the offering to allow it to be a better "fit" for a chosen market.

Change

This buying concern is present whenever you ask people to change something about what they do, how they do it, with whom they do it, when they do it, or in any other way that may suggest a change. It's not unlike implications, but it deals with the less-tangible aspects that may cause friction in the overall Customer Buying Journey. Once again, it is easy to underestimate how change can slow or stop a buying journey. For instance, I have seen several examples: a senior executive agrees to a new service, a manager makes a commitment to a new supplier, sometimes even new procedures are put in place. However, all too often people go on doing what they have always done because they don't want to change. Once again, you must be aware of these concerns and then determine how you could design the offering to cause—or at least imply—as little change as possible.

PRICE

The second *P* of marketing, price, includes not just the cost of initial acquisition but the total amount a buyer would have to invest for the overall and successful adoption of the product. I often see a disconnect between what the supplier and the customer view as the cost. The supplier is often focused on their price, whereas the customer is considering the total cost of everything they need to acquire to gain the successful adoption of the offering. This is very important to note, as it can often be a root cause of a buying concern a supplier can easily overlook. Here, however, I am going to largely focus on the price. Pricing is a very significant topic, and I could easily dedicate a book to it alone. However, that topic has been well explored by others, so I will focus attention on how aspects of pricing are impacted by the buying style and the buying concerns that have been decoded as strands of the market's Customer Buying Journey DNA.

How Buying Style Can Impact Price

On the left-hand side of the 4Q model are buyers that perceive they have a choice of suppliers. Therefore, if you are operating in these two quadrants, you must consider competitive pricing a primary issue. Competitive pricing pressure plays the most significant role in the bottom-left "Sort and Select" quadrant, where buyers know, or at least think they know, exactly what they want. Buyers often make decisions here based on price and price alone. Other factors, such as availability, warranty, options, and ease of acquisition, can play a part, but pricing must be very competitive.

In either of the top quadrants, where the customer is looking for assistance in determining a solution, pricing gets very interesting. In the top-left "Search and Choose" quadrant, customers believe they have a choice but are still looking for assistance in understanding their needs and recommendations as to what they need to acquire. Although the price must be competitive and match what the buyer sees as reasonable, the price need not be the cheapest, as is often the case in the bottom left. If buyers are engaged in a buying journey where they believe the assistance they have gained has been highly valuable, they will tend to buy even if the price is not the cheapest, but as I said, it must seem reasonable and comparatively competitive.

On the right-hand side of the 4Q model, customers will tend to buy, again and again, from one supplier or one particular brand based on some factors they value and see as unique to that supplier or brand. In particular, the top-right quadrant (Trusted Advisor) is where buyers will pay a premium for both offerings and advice. And generally speaking, price is rarely the number-one priority. Granted, the price has to match what buyers would deem reasonable, but these buyers have selected a supplier or brand over all others for a reason. What that reason is worth is often both intangible and difficult to assess but is dictated by the value that the buyers associate with the help they receive in determining their requirements. If this help is based on a deep and long relationship with the buyer and their organization, that assistance could be seen as not only unique but highly valuable and justify a far higher price for the offering. If you are targeting this quadrant of the market, the key is not to lead with pricing. If the advice and products are sound, the price will invariably take care of itself.

The bottom-right "Starbucks" quadrant is, perhaps, even more interesting from a pricing perspective. Here buyers not only know exactly what they want but also have a decided preference for a particular supplier or brand. Perhaps they have always bought Dell computers because they perceive that they are reliable, easy to configure and buy, and compatible with all their other computers. In that case, they may be happy to pay 10 percent more for a Dell than an equivalent computer from some other manufacturer—possibly 20 percent, but probably not much higher. Again, it comes down to what they perceive as reasonable. Interestingly enough, though, if Dell was to price at, say, 20 percent over the competitive equivalents, they might retain their existing customers but be unable to attract new buyers who have no allegiance to Dell and would thus be buying in the bottom-left (Sort and Select) quadrant in a more price-conscious way. If this were the case, perhaps a strategy of introductory benefits for first-time buyers would be appropriate.

Also note how price can be part of the brand strategy inasmuch as deliberately charging a higher price to illustrate the premium nature of the offering. It is difficult to build an image of prestige and premium in the minds of customers if your price is about the same as everyone else's. The logic therefore dictates that if you want a market brand that builds the market in the bottom-right (Starbucks) quadrant around prestige and luxury, you must demand a relatively higher price.

The illogical, or maybe logical, extreme of this is the phenomenon known as Veblen goods, named after Thorstein Veblen, the Norwegian American economist and sociologist who coined the term *conspicuous consumption*.[1] Veblen highlighted how certain buyers will buy expensive goods simply to illustrate how successful, or rich, or accomplished they are—in some ways, the more expensive the better. This is a stratospheric and sparsely populated land where a buyer can pay $38,000 for a Marc Jacobs handbag or $200,000 for a Patek Philippe watch. And you can't even argue that these expensive Veblen goods offer relatively greater functionality or utility over alternatives costing a fraction of the price. The handbag holds about the same as a McDonald's Happy Meal box, and the hours on the Patek are neither longer nor shorter than those on a Timex. However, the value these buyers are seeking is in the prestige associated with their ownership. They are bottom-right (Starbucks) buyers, where a high price is one of the most, if not the most, important attributes of the brand. And where would Rodeo Drive be without them?

How Value Drivers Can Impact Price

Much has been written on the difference between, and the relationship of, value and price, and there is no need to reiterate any of that existing body of work here. However, let's review a few Outside-In basics and how they may impact pricing.

Even though prospective customers might highly value a certain aspect of an offering, if they believe they have a choice of potential suppliers—buying on the left side of the 4Q model—then price will primarily drive their decision. On the other hand (and other side of 4Q), when buyers believe that only one supplier, brand, or offering can deliver what they value, then they will happily, or at least acceptingly, pay a premium price.

Also recall that the very same offering can be viewed differently by different markets. There are those buyers that may highly value certain attributes about a certain offering or brand, whereas others will fail to see or have no need for the value associated with that aspect. Because a market is defined as a set of buyers who buy in very similar ways, you must view such buyers as two different markets.

As an example, consider ACCord LLC, a company that provides accounting staff on contract. They always saw their market as companies that needed some quality advice and assistance, not as providing "temp" help for bookkeeping or administrative work. They invested in well-qualified accounting professionals trained and armed with the latest industry and regulatory information. Their market valued this type of knowledge and was happy to pay a premium over an everyday administrative bookkeeper on an hourly rate.

ACCord's problem started due to their success. People started to know and recommend them as a great resource for financial contracting. More and more people reached out to them with requests for proposals. They started to see that they were losing a lot of this business based on price and so started to lower their prices, which of course concurrently affected their margins. Their sales force found lots of opportunities, but many were predicated on lower prices. When looking closer into their Customer Buying Journey, we find that ACCord had unknowingly started to serve a different market. They were wandering over to the left side of the 4Q.

Their original market required and respected their knowledgeable and experienced staff. But another market simply wanted admin people who could work in accounting. This market did not value the qualifications of ACCord's staff, nor did they need such qualified people, and not surprisingly, this market was far more price sensitive. These new prospects were buying in that bottom-left "Sort and Select" quadrant believing they had choice. So what looked like more opportunity for ACCord to sell their services was actually compromising their brand. Interestingly, ACCord decided that this situation was an opportunity and developed a secondary group—an "ACCord-lite," as it were—that served this lower-priced market. And ACCord could get back to taking care of their more discerning (and better paying) clients on the right-hand side of the 4Q.

I have also found many companies that know what their market *should* value about their offering but lack a deep understanding of what their market, or indeed different markets, *actually do* value. Any pricing strategy must be built on what the target market truly values and have a very clear definition of who is in that market and who is not.

How Buying Concerns Can Impact Price

When it comes to buying concerns, there is a dichotomy. Some concerns can be totally eradicated by pricing action, while others cannot be. All too often, I see organizations using incentives like special pricing or discounts to get a buyer to commit to an acquisition. If the buying concern is financial, this might be a good strategy. Note that I say *might* and not *would*—it depends on a number of other factors. My focus here is that there are many buying concerns that slow down or stop the Customer Buying Journey that cannot be addressed through pricing. We have seen many examples where a prospective customer would not commit to an offering even if it were being given away for free. Whatever else pricing is, it is not a cure-all remedy for sorting out unrelated buying concerns. Once again, you must clearly understand a particular market's buying concerns for a specific offering, and only by understanding the detail behind those concerns can you develop an effective strategy.

PROMOTION

Promotion encompasses the overall approach to marketing communications. By adopting the Outside-In approach of keying everything to the Customer Buying Journey, you can take a much more precise and effective route to mapping out your communications strategy. Rather than take a scattershot, hit-and-miss marketing approach, a well-researched Market Engagement Strategy utilizing all the intelligence gained about the target market will be that much more effective in hitting the right players, at the right time, with the right message.

The foundation for this thinking is rooted in the simple observation that as the buyer moves through their specific buying journey, things happen.

Different players get involved. What they do changes. What they are looking for may change. Value drivers and buying concerns can change and flex within various steps of the overall Customer Buying Journey, similar to the way buying styles can change during the journey. Finally, and most importantly, you should be concerned not just with passive and reactive communication with the customer as they move through their buying journey but also with disruptive and relevant interaction. Indeed, your primary mission, and the redefinition of sales and marketing, is to think about how you can positively impact the Customer Buying Journey. The entire marketing communications approach should be about not only how you react to the customer's immediate whims and wishes but how you provide proactive interaction that will positively impact that buying journey. And the only way to achieve this is to take a far more precise approach based on a deep understanding of the specific market's buying journey.

Marketing Messaging

Marketing is in large part about communication to the target market and the messages we determine are appropriate for our customers. A great deal of time is usually dedicated to the topic. I have already underscored that communicating with the market about how great your offering is and its associated benefits may well be a component of what is required, but it is only the starting point. In today's world, a far more precise form of communication has to be designed to not only offer information about the offerings but impact the entire Customer Buying Journey. When considering effective market messaging in the world of Outside-In Marketing, you have to start, and base everything upon, the target market's Customer Buying Journey and the associated DNA. You have to consider how things change across the buying journey and then

- harmonize the messaging to the buying style and specifically the chosen quadrant of the 4Q model
- align your *value propositions* to the customer's value drivers
- target the right player at the right time in the right way across the Customer Buying Journey
- overcome the buying concerns across the Customer Buying Journey

The Market Engagement Strategy should set the direction for this work. It is now time to take it down to the very specific level of designing an effective and precise marketing communication plan.

Let's go back to the DNA diagram shared in the previous chapter, but now let's overlay some marketing messaging initiatives and note how they interact with other strands of the DNA. In illustration 23.2, four locations across the Customer Buying Journey have been highlighted for marketing messaging. Marketing message number 1 could very well be the provision of some information from the supplier targeted to the buyer that may trigger an actual buying journey. Perhaps it's a whitepaper about an urgent need for a specific market to respond to new legislation and the exposure and risk their customers may face if they do not change certain practices. No matter what it may be, it is carefully crafted by the supplier and delivered to the right player *to be disruptive* with a call to action of some kind that could trigger a Customer Buying Journey.

Looking further, marketing message number 2 is targeted to occur in the second step of this particular Customer Buying Journey. This initiative is perhaps also meant to be disruptive while reinforcing a certain value driver you know occurs at that step of the buying journey. In case study 1,

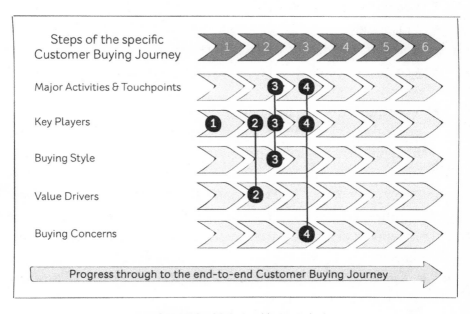

ILLUSTRATION 23.2. Outside-In Marketing

this might be the marketing element of Orion's that reinforced the value of training when considering the implementation of a new enterprise-wide software application. And again, it is targeted to reach the right player at the right time with the relevant message.

Marketing message number 3 is synchronized not just to the second step of the Customer Buying Journey but also to respond to a specific activity you know occurs at that point. It may be a touch point where a potential customer is searching for certain information. Whatever it is, you can see from the diagram that it is also aimed at reinforcing a certain buying style. It could even be aimed at changing the buying style.

Finally, marketing message number 4 occurs in step 4 of the Customer Buying Journey and is keyed to a specific activity you believe will happen at that time. However, this marketing communication is aimed at addressing one, or maybe more, of the buying concerns.

The one other dimension you need to consider is the delivery vehicle: how will you deliver the marketing communication to the target recipient? This varies by the nature of the marketing communication, but here are some examples:

- a whitepaper from the website
- a case study
- a presentation delivered by a salesperson
- a company overview delivered by a salesperson or available on the web
- a keynote address at an industry event
- an article placed in a magazine with reprints available for distribution from the web or by a salesperson

The examples outlined in illustration 23.2 are very simple ones. When we create these marketing communication plans with our clients, there may be twenty or more discrete marketing communication initiatives, and they will all be precisely aimed at a point in the overall Customer Buying Journey where we believe our client can positively influence the progress of their market's buying journey.

PLACE

The fourth and final marketing *P* is place. Originally, this referred to geographic location and fulfillment approach, but I am going to stretch this a little and move it into our G3 sales and marketing ideology by defining it as meeting customers where they are and taking them to where you would like them to be. When I refer to these as locations, they don't have to be geographic locations but are perhaps virtual locations—particular waypoints within the specific Customer Buying Journey. Once again, let's use some of the components of the buying journey DNA to explore this fourth *P* in greater detail.

How Triggers and Dependencies Can Impact Place

If the Market Engagement Strategy is "to trigger or engage in a Customer Buying Journey," then one of the most important components of marketing is to "be there"—to be in the right place at the right time in front of the right person with the right message that you know could trigger the buying journey.

Sometimes you might encounter an impulse buy, when a buying journey is triggered and the prospective buyer makes a commitment to acquire virtually moments later. That's great, but don't hold your breath, because you are far more likely to encounter a much more complex and lengthy buying journey. The trigger you are hoping to set might just result in a simple thought, where someone (hopefully the right person in the right market) is exposed to information that causes him to think that something may be worth exploring and that he might do something different, including buying, sometime in the future. I have talked about the difference between window-shopping, searching for new information, or being entertained versus actually triggering a Customer Buying Journey, and it is this triggering that you want to make happen.

Through your understanding of the Customer Buying Journey DNA, you want to create a disruptive marketing initiative with a high likelihood of connecting with the right player, at the right time, with the right information to trigger the buying journey.

You witnessed a missed example of this in case study 2, when the media article highlighting CCHN's poor infection numbers was not picked up by the Digex rep, or if it was, there was no immediate contact made with the hospital. It was the ER doctor who reminded his colleagues of the nanotech gloves and their anti-infection attributes.

Conversely, in case study 1, you saw how Orion Technologies differentiated themselves from the other short-listed suppliers by taking the lead on end-user training and the associated change management considerations. First, they made it their business to know that DiaNascent had indeed purchased a Syncron system, and they made contact early. And they knew from past experience and the DNA of their market that even when DiaNascent didn't initially bring up the topic of user training and change management, they could make it rise to the top. So Orion was there in the right place, at the right time, with what eventually proved to be the right answer.

How Key Activities and Touch Points Can Impact Place

To be in the right place at the right time, you need to address all the customer touch points to ensure that, at the very least, they are providing the right passive and reactive information to any prospective buyer. In today's world, this often means an online and social media presence. And let me highlight a very important point here:

Suppliers should structure their virtual presence to be able to recognize—by what people are searching for and accessing—where prospective customers are in their buying journey.

You should also strive to ensure that as many as possible of your touch points with a prospective customer are not simply passive or reactive. Instead, they must be disruptive—to have as their goal the ability to positively impact the Customer Buying Journey. As shown in illustration 23.2, you must ensure that you tie all marketing interactions with a prospective customer to where they are in their buying journey and have at least some element of a disruptive but relevant approach.

It's not just touch points you should be looking at, but all the key activities in which a customer is likely to engage throughout their buying journey. Once again, look at how you can be in the right place at the right time. What other marketing initiatives can you create to positively impact the

Customer Buying Journey by meeting the customer where they are or taking them to where you want them to be?

How Buying Style Can Impact Place

The 4Q model highlights another critical consideration when thinking about place. Specifically at the left-hand side of the 4Q model, the customer perceives they have a choice of supplier or brand. In today's G3 sales and marketing world, prospective customers are not going to wait for you. You need to be, once again, at the right place at the right time with the right message. You have to understand the market and the Customer Buying Journey in sufficient detail so you can predict where and how a buying journey may be triggered or, at the very least, be there when it is.

An example of being at the right place when a Customer Buying Journey may be triggered would be Orion Technologies in case study 1. First, Orion ensured their presence by making contact at the very outset of the DiaNascent buying journey. Because they sell implementation services for a major provider of software applications, the right place for them to be is when an organization is in the process of evaluating different approaches and different software providers. In this situation, such a customer is at a later stage in their software buying journey but is not yet in the buying journey for the associated implementation services. Orion can position their offering and either trigger the buying journey for implementation services or engage in it when it is triggered. They also get to set the stage for how the customer should evaluate services such as their own.

For Customer Buying Journeys that occur in the bottom-left quadrant, a prospective customer is likely to move quickly. The very name we have given this quadrant—Sort and Select—implies that the buyer will sort through their alternatives and then select the company they are going with. In order to effectively compete in this quadrant, you must be visible and easily contactable. You have to be at the place where and when the customer is searching.

In the top-left quadrant (Search and Choose), these buyers are looking for some level of assistance in making their decision of what to buy. This assistance could be anything from an online configuration tool to a series of consultative discussions with a subject-matter expert. Regardless of the type and nature of the assistance, once again it is critical that you meet the customer where they are. Your assistance must be readily accessible to the prospective customer at the time when they need it and at the place—geographic or virtual—where they are.

TAKEAWAYS

⇒ The supplier must consider their offering, product, or service from the buyer's perspective, starting with what the buyer is buying. The offering might need to change based on how customers buy and why they don't.

⇒ The 4Q Buying Style dictates what buyers are buying and how they want to buy it.

⇒ The offering must be packaged or presented in such a way as to overcome as many of the potential buying concerns as possible.

⇒ Although businesses focus on the price of an offering, buyers focus on their overall costs, which may include many items outside of the offering itself.

⇒ Where buyers are on the 4Q model dictates many pricing considerations.

⇒ With the DNA decoded and the buying journey mapped, marketing can become far more precise.

⇒ Marketing messages and initiatives must be targeted to specific individuals at different steps of their buying journey, harmonizing the buying style, accentuating the value, and/or mitigating specific buying concerns.

CHAPTER 24

OUTSIDE-IN SELLING

SO MUCH HAS been written about sales and selling that it may seem improbable that something new is worth investing time in. But this book and its central theme of focusing externally on how customers buy contributes both fresh and very necessary new thinking to the business of sales. This is a belief honed through a life's work in the upper echelons of sales and marketing and a belief that has now been thoroughly market proven as relevant, effective, and timely.

As I promised in the first chapter, this is not another sales process book but a book that redefines business, sales, and marketing. And if it has taken twenty-three chapters to get to where you are equipped to contemplate the new world of selling, it is for good reason: because this is not about introducing yet another selling methodology or a series of sales techniques; this is about looking at the function of sales and selling in a totally new light—from the perspective of how customers buy and why they don't.

In chapter 2, I described the three generations of customer creation and shared that each generation ended and the new one started as a result of discontinuous change brought about by more advanced forms of communication. Between G1 and G2, the telephone, radio, and TV opened up new buying approaches and channels changing how people buy. However, although there were significant advances in technology and communications, very little changed in the actual interactions between seller and buyer. The buyer still depended on the seller.

But G3's internet and broadband had a major impact on how people buy because unlike G1 and G2, not only has the technology changed, but the positional strength and leverage now enable the buyer. We are in a new world of buying that demands a new world of selling. Just as the shift from G1 to G2 buying witnessed the advent of the sales process, the shift from G2 to G3 is profoundly impacting sales and selling functions. The sales process no longer dictates what happens next; it is the Customer Buying Journey. G3 is here and the buyer is driving.

From this point, I will tackle the fundamental need of any business—defining the overall sales strategy—and also pause to reflect on why so many companies today fail to articulate, let alone implement, such a necessity. I will then introduce a simple yet very powerful approach to translating this sales strategy into a series of optimal selling activities synchronized to the buying journey: the Customer Buying Journey (CBJ) Navigator™. I will show you how you can use the CBJ Navigator to effectively manage, perhaps for the first time ever, all aspects of sales, including opportunity and pipeline management.

THE NEED TO REDEFINE SALES AND SELLING

I have not been shy in iterating my belief that the notion of a "sales process" is now less than useful. The only process that creates customers and yields revenue is the Customer Buying Journey. It is now the customer who determines what happens and when it happens. Sales must go well beyond simply positioning and explaining the offering and then proving its value to a prospective customer. Yes, these selling activities may generate *interest*—even sincere interest—but that falls woefully short of gaining the customer's *commitment* to buy. It is sad when I see companies investing in what they believe to be better ways of positioning their offerings, presenting sharper *value propositions*, or better proving the value or the return on investment (ROI) to prospective customers, yet the results consistently fail to meet expectations. In the vast majority of cases, these companies are solving the wrong problem. They are chasing the mirage of a belief that if the customer only understood the offering and appreciated its inherent value, they would buy. Hopefully I have shown this for the siren song that it is.

Sales and selling must go much deeper. Indeed, you must redefine sales as having a single purpose only—of positively impacting the Customer Buying Journey. You must enable, support, and manage a prospective customer through each stage of that customer's buying journey. Recall the five goals of the Market Engagement Strategy:

1. To harmonize your selling approach with how the market is buying or change how the market buys to how you want to sell.
2. To initiate or engage in a Customer Buying Journey.
3. To ensure the customer has adequate motivation to invest in the buying journey and ultimately in the acquisition and adoption of the offering.
4. To ensure you remain engaged in the buying journey.
5. To reduce friction across the Customer Buying Journey.

I've pointed out before that these sales objectives closely match strands of the Customer Buying Journey DNA. This serves to underscore one of the basic tenets of this book: the more you understand about your target market's buying journey, the more likely you are to be successful in creating customers and generating revenue. Without a deep, clear understanding of the target Customer Buying Journey, the more you are subject to luck for gaining business results. Sometimes companies find themselves in the right place at the right time and enjoy a particular market success. My own inclination, however, would be to know the game before rolling the dice.

SALES STRATEGY

Given Drucker's definition of the purpose of a business—to create a customer—what could be more important than defining and building a sales strategy? But go ask many executives to share their business's sales strategy, and I think you will quickly gain the impression that most organizations lack such a thing. You will usually hear about how they are organizing to go to market or which markets they are pursuing, but you rarely hear a statement that defines how they will achieve the sales goals laid out above. The reason, in my opinion, is quite simply a return to a syndrome I have referenced many times before: the all-conquering but myopic belief in the product. "Who needs a *strategy* for that?" they think. "Surely, we just need some good salespeople, armed with the right messaging and value propositions, and perhaps a dash of those persuasive G2 sales techniques, and we'll take the orders. Can't be that hard." I cry!

Now, to be fair, it is not always as blatant as that, and I don't want to malign organizations doing a good job here. But believe me, they are in the minority. Have a hard look at how most sales forces are trained. Look at what they are expected to do and how they are supported, managed, measured, and rewarded. Most sales organizations today still use G2 techniques focused on their own internal aspects of the offering with perhaps a sales process thrown in. Results sometimes will come, but they will be far more the result of incredibly hard work, tenacity, and luck.

This is why we have seen years of declining quota achievement and almost laughable forecast accuracy in sales forces. We see incredible waste where sales and other resources are heavily invested in opportunities where no one is actually buying. We see signs of unsynchronized selling where detailed proposals are being created and delivered to prospects who are nowhere near commitment. These are tough words, but I can assure you I see it regularly. This waste is all the result of highly individualistic selling activity where each salesperson is working, often earnestly and diligently, at what they think will win them the business. They stride valiantly toward what they believe and hope will be the close only to be challenged and disappointed, again and again, by surprises and events simply not unfolding as expected.

These salespeople are doing all they can with what they have been given to work with. And they do it day after day after day. Thanks to huge amounts of effort and some luck, every now and then they win. However, in most cases, the efficiency and efficacy of their work are discouraging at best and despairingly useless at worst. The good news is that there is a better way.

TRANSLATING THE MARKET ENGAGEMENT STRATEGY INTO A SALES STRATEGY

I have previously defined *strategy* as "a careful plan or method for achieving a particular goal." It is "important because the resources available to achieve these goals are usually limited. A strategy describes how the ends [goals] will be achieved by the available means [resources]."[1] In this case, the goal is to a create customer and the resources are the sales team. The sales strategy should provide the plan or method for best utilizing the sales resources to maximize the number of customers we create and, of course, the resultant revenue. This plan or method should create revenue in a predictable, scalable, and consistent fashion.

In part 2, I focused on crafting the Market Engagement Strategy based on decoding the six strands of the associated DNA and mapping the Customer Buying Journey. The Market Engagement Strategy provides the high-level approach for the sales strategy and usually addresses areas that are outside the domain of sales and selling. Such areas include the determination of the target market(s), the scope and pricing of the offering, and the development of an overall brand. The sales strategy takes this down one level to define how this is going to happen with an individual customer. As depicted in illustration 24.1, the sales strategy fits inside the Market Engagement Strategy and is concerned with how to optimally engage with a single prospective customer. By the time you get to developing your sales strategy, all the questions regarding what you are selling and how you are selling it have been answered by the Market Engagement Strategy.

In a nutshell, then, the sales strategy provides a clear path for sales activities that will result in a positive impact on the Customer Buying Journey by seeking to achieve the five Market Engagement Strategy goals stated above. As you study these goals, consider the fundamental role of any sales professional. In the workshops we run, we ask participants to document what

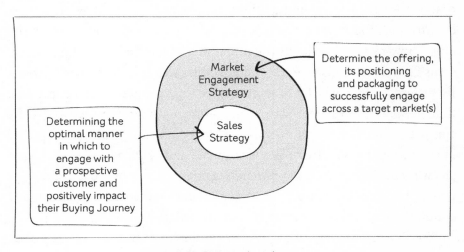

ILLUSTRATION 24.1. The sales strategy

they see as the primary role of the salesperson. We have probably asked this question of well over fifty thousand sales, marketing, and business professionals over the years. And we invariably gain relatively long lists of selling activities. These include, but are certainly not limited to, the following:

- developing relationships
- explaining our products
- taking orders
- providing a voice for our company
- understanding the customer's world
- negotiating
- generating revenue
- showing how our products meet the customer's needs

The list goes on, but as I hinted, these are sales activities or perhaps responsibilities. They are not, at least in my mind, the fundamental roles of a salesperson.

Now, having been around salespeople and indeed having called myself a salesperson for four decades, this question of the fundamental role of a salesperson is ironically ill defined. For me, though, it snapped into focus a number of years ago in Toronto when I lived next door to an accomplished television journalist. It so happened that she worked for one of the larger television stations, and as such, I could see her most evenings on the news reporting on major events happening across the city. Knowing nothing about the profession of journalism and reporting, I was fascinated to discover more about what she did. She shared with me how her day involved a lot of research, meeting people (often people who didn't really want to meet with her), pulling together narratives, creating compelling presentations, and always working against deadlines. At that point, I thought, "Oh, that sounds familiar," and I started to see that what she was describing had many parallels to the work day of those in my sales team. I hadn't noticed it before, and suddenly I saw that there were many common elements between reporting and sales.

This line of thinking led me to what has become an important and basic understanding of the primary role of the salesperson. Contrast that mission with the role of the journalist. The journalist's end product is the report she makes, the story she tells. She doesn't get involved, as things can quickly go wrong if the journalist enters the story or becomes the story. She stands, literally and figuratively, to the side of the event and tells the world what is happening. Not so for the salesperson. For him, the sole purpose of engaging in all these activities, from relationship building, through research, to proposing solutions, is to *change the course of events*. His primary role is to make something happen that otherwise would not have happened.

Sometimes when I share this point of view, a few people become uncomfortable with the idea that I am suggesting that salespeople manipulate the situation. Well, they do, and they should. I will, however, add that salespeople must do this for the benefit of the customer. After working with sales professionals, customers should be left with the belief that they are in a better position due to that interaction. The salesperson may have helped clarify thinking; opened up new possibilities; enabled them to do something quicker, faster, or cheaper; or introduced them to an idea that was previously not on the table. Whatever it may have been, the salesperson changed the course of events that resulted in a positive experience for the customer.

I occasionally thought that some of the salespeople I worked with over the years would have made far better reporters than sales professionals: there was lots of storytelling going on but little happening in the way of changing the course of events.

The goal of the sales strategy, then, is to positively change the course of events by impacting the Customer Buying Journey. I have also made the point that there are only four ways in which to do this—what I call the Sales Imperatives: initiate, complete, expedite, and augment. The sales strategy endeavors to meet those imperatives by pursuing the five Market Engagement Strategy goals.

By now, you will be very familiar with the idea that everything must be founded on the external Customer Buying Journey as opposed to an internal sales process. Indeed, this is the very heart of Outside-In Selling. As you look to develop your sales strategy, it will become very clear that the better you understand all that goes on in the Customer Buying Journey (CBJ), the better you can develop an effective sales strategy. The CBJ Navigator will show the way.

THE CBJ NAVIGATOR™

The CBJ Navigator is the device we have developed to document and render the sales strategy into a series of selling activities aligned to the Customer Buying Journey. The CBJ Navigator, or Navigator for short, offers a particularly powerful way in which to deploy the overall sales strategy and provides a consistent, effective, and highly prescriptive method with which to develop any and all sales opportunities. As you will see, the Navigator enables sales success. It provides an approach to measure and manage sales, a way in which to align and coordinate the resources of the organization to the task of creating a customer, and provides a common language and implementation plan for the sales strategy.

Like any navigational aid—from the stars and brass sextants to today's GPS—the CBJ Navigator sets out to answer three basic questions:

1. Where are we?
2. How are we doing?
3. Where do we go next?

Let's reflect on this for a moment. When you embark on any complex or unfamiliar journey where you might encounter certain variables—weather, daylight, tides—it is only common sense to have a map and something to tell you where you are on that map. I recall setting out on a yacht from Florida at night to reach the Bahamas by daybreak, a journey I undertook with a good friend and thankfully some good charts. After sailing for a few hours, those three questions became paramount.

To start with, you need to establish where you are. Without knowledge of your current location, you can't even begin to answer the other two questions. That's why those "You are here" icons on maps in buildings and parks are so incredibly important—especially if it is otherwise challenging to see any landmarks or determine your position with any level of certainty. Everything hinges on you knowing where you are. And remember, that map won't help much if you don't know your current position, so a positional device of some sort—a sextant, landmarks, or GPS—is also required.

Now, once you can state "I am here" with reasonable confidence, you can then move to the second question: How are we doing? Perhaps you haven't gone as far as you had hoped, or maybe you are off course to the west. This is incredibly useful information, as you can now see that you are not making the progress you had planned. Perhaps there are changing winds or stronger tides than you anticipated. Now you can use that information in future planning. It might mean that at your current rate of progress, you will not be able to make your destination with the supplies you have. Maybe a course correction is required, or maybe you need to rethink for the next leg of the journey. Whatever it may be, it is vital to understand how you are doing and to factor that knowledge into future decisions and actions.

This leads to the last question: Where do we go next? Do you stay with the original plan, or based on where you are and how you are doing, do you need to adjust, reprioritize, or do something altogether different?

The CBJ Navigator sets out to answer these three questions for any sales opportunity, at any time. Now let's look at how this device provides the information to answer these three questions and in so doing familiarize ourselves with the format and content of the CBJ Navigator.

WHERE ARE WE?

The only process that matters is the buying process, which I mapped as a series of steps that make up the Customer Buying Journey. Let's use case study 1 (chapters 10 and 11) as an example, where we mapped the Customer Buying Journey for software implementation services as the seven steps seen in illustration 24.2.

When you ask the question "Where are we?" you must answer it in reference to this process. A valid answer then might be "We're at the Explore Alternatives step." And before I move on, here is a weird but consistent anomaly I keep running into. From all the people we have worked with, there seems to be a tendency—one that I am at a complete loss to explain—to think one can be between steps. Well, just to set the record straight, there

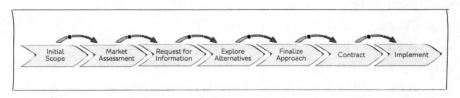

ILLUSTRATION 24.2. Orion's target market's buying journey

is no "between." A prospective buyer moves from the buying activities associated with one step directly to the activities associated with another. However, as I have noted before, customers might not move sequentially, and they will move at differing rates, but success depends on their positive progress through these steps in a sequential manner. If you see a customer jumping a step or two, you can be fairly certain they will, at some time, loop back once they realize they have missed some key activities.

Maybe you have already spotted the problem here: the customer rarely has this map of their buying journey. They don't have any charts. And even if they did know, they are initially quite unlikely to share with you that they are at, say, step 3 of their buying journey. But that's to be expected. You just need some objective way of determining, with a fairly high degree of confidence, where a customer is in their buying journey. Those familiar with maps and charts, or anyone who has done some basic GPS input, will recognize that we need *waypoints* here. A *waypoint* is defined as "an intermediate point on a route or line of travel," and because their main purpose is to tell us "where we are," waypoints are usually accompanied by very specific coordinates of latitude and longitude.[2] For our purposes, this is where I will introduce the concept of "exit criteria," which will be our coordinates.

Based on your understanding of the Customer Buying Journey and all that goes on within it, you would be able to define some observable and objective criteria to indicate that the customer has completed a step—in other words, the exit criteria for that step. For example, using case study 1, the exit criteria for step 4 (Explore Alternatives) would be when Sue Harris created a short list of potential providers and validated the budget, timeline, and resources. Thus you can be reasonably sure that if a customer has completed a shortlist, budget, timeline, and resources, you can tick the exit criteria for step 4, knowing then that they have moved on to step 5, Finalize Approach. In this way, you could then answer the question of "Where are we?" We're in step 5.

Using the same case study, you can complete this part of the strategy as shown in illustration 24.3. I have also added the key buying activities from chapter 5 to illustrate what the buyer is doing at each step.

You can see that the exit criteria are not necessarily the same as all the activities of a certain step, but they are usually a subset. They should all be observable and objective "stage gates" that a salesperson can reasonably

ILLUSTRATION 24.3. BUYING ACTIVITIES AND EXIT CRITERIA

STEP	BUYING ACTIVITIES	EXIT CRITERIA
1. Initial Scope	<ul><li>scope project</li><li>create an overall multiyear plan</li><li>appoint key players/determine roles</li><li>decision to assess third party providers</li></ul>	<ul><li>project defined and planned</li><li>key players assigned</li><li>determined to use an outside provider</li></ul>
2. Market Assessment	<ul><li>validate and document requirements</li><li>talk to colleagues and trusted sources</li><li>read case studies and trade magazine reviews</li><li>create a list of possible providers</li><li>initial research on potential providers</li></ul>	<ul><li>documented requirements</li><li>initial list of possible providers created</li></ul>
3. Request for Information (RFI)	<ul><li>cut starter list to list of providers to receive an RFI</li><li>liaise with Legal and Strategic Sourcing</li><li>create an RFI document</li><li>publish and send RFI to possible providers</li><li>meet with possible providers to understand their approaches and competencies</li></ul>	<ul><li>met with all providers</li><li>published the RFI</li></ul>
4. Explore Alternatives	<ul><li>create a short list of viable providers</li><li>validate the provider's approaches</li><li>assess different approaches</li><li>finalize approach, priorities, and requirements</li><li>validate/change budget/timelines/ resources</li></ul>	<ul><li>created a short list of potential providers</li><li>validated budget/ timeline/resources</li></ul>
5. Finalize Approach	<ul><li>conduct due diligence on short-listed providers</li><li>meet with possible providers to finalize their approach, plans, and proposals</li><li>check on references</li><li>finalize overall approach to the implementation project</li></ul>	<ul><li>final approaches received from potential providers</li><li>finalization of implementation approach</li></ul>

(continued)

ILLUSTRATION 24.3. (*continued*)

STEP	BUYING ACTIVITIES	EXIT CRITERIA
6. Contract	• meet with possible supplier(s) • clarify details/approaches • request final proposal/pricing • determine and assess alternative sourcing approaches • review terms and conditions • negotiate • legal review • complete contracts	• contract issued
7. Implement	• initiate project • hold project review meetings • report on progress • manage problems	• key players consider the project implemented

determine as complete or not. These exit criteria are waypoints that allow you to answer "Where are we?"

This is a far more objective way of measuring progress than simply asking a salesperson, "Hey, how's it going?" The response to such a question tends to be lengthy, perhaps interesting, but usually of little use. If you don't believe me, go try it. Also, note that you are answering only in terms of where the customer is in their buying journey, which is quite a contrast from thinking where you might be in a sales process.

HOW ARE WE DOING?

The second question does move the spotlight from buying to the selling. Once you have established where a customer is in their buying journey (including perhaps that they haven't even started one), you can then ask yourself how you are doing. This brings us to the selling activities we believe have to be completed at each step of the Customer Buying Journey.

Here is a very important fact: optimal selling activities are totally dependent on where the customer is in their buying journey—that is, the Customer Buying Journey dictates what a salesperson should do. To illustrate this point, here's a story.

Imagine you work for a company that sells a certain solution for automating workflow in a particular type of laboratory. Now, your sister happens to be intrigued by what you do and has a good working knowledge of your offering. She's at a networking event and meets an executive from an organization that has the type of lab that your offering is designed to help. She talks to the exec and mentions that you, her sibling, offer a solution to help with the workflow of precisely that kind of lab. The exec is genuinely interested, and they both agree it is a small world. More importantly, she learns from the exec that those at his company totally understand the benefits of automating workflow and believe that it's a direction they should be investing in. He is, however, almost sure that they have not talked to your company. Your sister calls you the next morning with the lead.

This is great for sure. But what do you do? The missing information is the "Where are we" in the buying journey. Has the client company just become aware of the benefits and have yet to explore anything? Have they been talking to a competitor? Have they determined their needs and are about to make a commitment to acquire a competing offering? Clearly, where they are in the buying journey dictates the optimal selling activity. In this simplistic example, you would want to call to discover exactly this information—and hopefully you wouldn't engage in any other selling activity until you had clearly validated where they were in the buying journey, because where the customer is in their buying journey dictates what the optimal selling activities should be.

Turning once again to case study 1, Orion Tech was able to win by getting DiaNascent to see that without an emphasis on end-user training and change management, their new software implementation was likely to be highly compromised. So as part of their defined sales strategy, Orion needs to make sure that as DiaNascent and companies like them are exploring alternatives, they come to see that effective end-user training and change management are major keys to success. And Orion was able to manipulate (not always a bad word) the scenario so that DiaNascent believed *they* had discovered this important need in their explorations. This is an ideal example of translating sales strategy into highly actionable selling activities. It is also a great example of synchronizing the selling to the buying. If DiaNascent had gotten past this step in their buying journey without believing that training and associated change management were key, it would have become significantly harder to change the course of events once budgets and approaches had been set.

In this fashion, then, we can list the optimal selling activities for each step—activities that are all synchronized to the buying and also translate the sales strategy into actions.

To remain synchronized between the selling and buying, some essentials must happen at each step. We call these selling activities the *GOs*. In other words, each activity needs to be complete before the customer goes to the next step. Remember, the customer doesn't wait around here for you—the customer moves forward through the steps of the buying journey. Gone is old sales process thinking that the salesperson is moving the customer through a process that will somehow yield a closed deal. *It is always the customer who is moving through the process*, and the question becomes, "Am I ready to GO to the next step as the customer moves forward?" In illustration 24.4, I have added the optimal selling activities and the sales GOs for case study 1.

As you review this, have a quick peek back to illustration 24.3, which lists the buying activities prior to the exit criteria. This will give you an idea of the flow through the Customer Buying Journey and show where, when, and why the optimal selling activities occur.

If you look at the four columns of the Navigator in illustration 24.4, you can now see how you can answer the first two questions. Where are we? Tick the exit criteria boxes and see what step the customer is at. How are we doing? Tick the Sales GOs we know to be complete.

Now you can see if you are synchronized—that is, all the GOs for each of the completed steps of the Customer Buying Journey are checked off. For instance, if the customer is at step 3, then all the GOs that align to step 1 and step 2 should be complete, and perhaps some at step 3. If you have a missing GO—let's say you we can't honestly say that you validated that you are seen as a viable provider—then that must be considered a red flag. It doesn't imply that the customer can't move forward; of course they can, because they set the pace. What it does imply is that considering where the customer is in their buying journey, you have failed in some way relevant to their strategy. Life goes on, and you might still win the day, but the red flag indicates that you are not where you would want to be.

ILLUSTRATION 24.4. ORION'S OPTIMAL SALES ACTIVITIES

STEP	EXIT CRITERIA	OPTIMAL SELLING ACTIVITIES	SALES GOS
1. Initial Scope	• project defined and planned • key players assigned • determined to use an outside provider	• work with Syncron to identify and gain introductions to new prospects • research the company and all key individuals • gain introductions to key players • introductory and discovery conversations	• met with key stakeholders • validated our understanding of their overall objective and plan • positioned the importance of end-user training and change management
2. Market Assessment	• documented requirements • initial list of possible providers created	• provide best practices • discuss end-user training approaches • assist in defining requirements especially in the area of end-user change management and training • assist in any funding analysis or business case analysis	• established Orion's credibility and capabilities • provided testimonials and case studies • validated that Orion is viewed as a potential supplier
3. Request for Information (RFI)	• met with all providers • published the RFI	• conduct meetings across the organization to validate our understanding of the background, project and priorities • review and clarify any assumptions • discover what concerns, risks and anxieties there may be • coordinate among key players to ensure common understanding and requirements	• met with all key players including Strategic Sourcing • validated that they see that end-user training will be critical to the successful implementation

(continued)

ILLUSTRATION 24.4. (*continued*)

STEP	EXIT CRITERIA	OPTIMAL SELLING ACTIVITIES	SALES GOS
4. Explore Alternatives	• created a short list of potential providers • validated budget/ timeline/ resources	• review our proposal and ensure it meets with their requirements • discuss their anxieties, concerns and the risks they see associated with the project • share our approach to implementation planning and quality assurance • discuss the importance of end-user training	• ensured that end-user training is built into the timeline/ budget and scope • responded to RFI
5. Finalize Approach	• final approaches received from potential providers • finalization of implementation approach	• discuss and review the details of our approach and especially the implementation plan for training • discuss how our approach may differ from other alternatives • discuss any remaining concerns and risks that they see with our approach • validate our information with all the key players across the organization	• provided access to testimonials • provided or assisted in the development of the implementation plan • met with and validated the approach with all key players
6. Contract	• contract issued	• meet with Strategic Sourcing to review all terms and conditions • ensure that they have all of our paperwork and we have all of theirs • review and resolve any final details • stay in contact with all key players • position our pricing as "not to exceed"	• all paperwork completed

(*continued*)

ILLUSTRATION 24.4. (*continued*)

STEP	EXIT CRITERIA	OPTIMAL SELLING ACTIVITIES	SALES GOS
7. Implement	• key players consider the project implemented	• introduce the key players to the implementation team • discuss progress with customer • ensure that the customer is willing to act as a reference for us	• services delivered as per contract • customer becomes a willing reference

WHERE DO WE GO NEXT?

In answering this question, suppliers naturally become very focused on sales activity—what are we going to *do* next? Here I will introduce the final element of the CBJ Navigator that defines all the key sales activities that translate the sales strategy into actions. First of all, reflect for a moment about what any selling activity is about. *Any selling activity is all about exchanging information or commitments.* The salesperson may be discovering something about her customers, or she may be providing some information to them. The salesperson could be asking for, or indeed making, a commitment. I call these the GETs and the GIVEs. The GETs are where the salesperson should be getting either information or commitments, and the GIVEs are the inverse, where someone on the selling team provides information or a commitment to the prospective customer. We can then define the GETs and the GIVEs for each step of the Customer Buying Journey. It's the GETs and the GIVEs that again translate the overall Market Engagement Strategy into the tactical selling activities required to meet the selling imperatives of positively impacting the Customer Buying Journey.

As you review the following example of a CBJ Navigator, I again remind you to keep in mind that this is a deliberately simple selling situation we have picked for illustrative purposes. However, I trust that it highlights these points:

- The exit criteria for each step should easily enable a salesperson to know where a prospective customer is in their buying journey.
- The sales activities are all synchronized with the steps of the Customer Buying Journey.

- The overall sales strategy is translated into a series of very straightforward selling activities.
- The selling activities are designed to manage and support the buying journey and in so doing achieve one or more of the four selling imperatives.
- The sales GOs are used to "interlock" the selling and the buying.

Again, using case study 1 as our example, illustration 24.5 shows what this may look like. Note that the Customer Buying Journey exit criteria have been moved to sit under the step name simply for space and clarity considerations.

In case study 1, an important component of Orion's Market Engagement Strategy was to differentiate themselves by stressing the importance of end-user training and change management and then offer an effective and innovative approach to achieving that goal. And as noted earlier, it was subtly conveyed. The strategy was not to simply present and talk about the training being offered; Orion endeavored to first discover DiaNascent's thinking about that user training and to then ensure that DiaNascent saw it as a critical success factor. At this point, Orion displayed their understanding of their market's DNA by bringing up relevant case studies and data from credible third parties to illustrate this often-overlooked component. This strategy was then translated into relevant and effective selling activities.

OUTSIDE-IN SELLING

In this chapter, I have focused on how you can take a comprehensive understanding of your particular target market's buying journey, develop a Market Engagement Strategy, and then translate that approach into a sales strategy producing a customer-focused selling approach. And I have further shown how these activities are defined and facilitated by the CBJ Navigator.

To see this in practice, reflect back on Orion Technologies. In chapter 11, I shared how the Customer Buying Journey for Orion's market can be mapped along with the associated six strands of the DNA. Chapter 21 then developed the Market Engagement Strategy for Orion, and I summarized the eight components of that strategy. If you now examine the CBJ Navigator given in illustration 24.5, you will see how each and every one of those

ILLUSTRATION 24.5. ORION'S CBJ NAVIGATOR™

BUYING JOURNEY STEP / EXIT CRITERIA	OPTIMAL SELLING ACTIVITIES	SALES / GETS	GIVES	GOS
1. Initial Scope • project defined and planned • key players assigned • determined to use an outside provider	• work with Syncron to identify and gain introductions to new prospects • research the Company and all key individuals • gain introductions to key players • introductory and discovery conversations	• access and introductions • business drivers and objectives • organization and key players • details of the overall approach to the project and to end-user training • scope and plan for the project	• introduction to our capabilities and credentials • overview of our project approach to ensure customer success • reasons to see the end-user training and change management as critical to the project	• met with key stakeholders • validated our understanding of their overall objective and plan • positioned the importance of end-user training and change management
2. Market Assessment • document requirements • initial list of possible providers created	• provide best practices • discuss end-user training approaches • assist in defining requirements, especially in the area of end-user change management and training • assist in any funding analysis or business case analysis	• validation of our understanding of their requirements • understanding of their approach and who's who • their feedback on approaches to end-user training • insight into their budgeting and project business model	• introductions to reference sites • assistance in assessing their end-user environment • reinforcement of our capabilities tied to their needs and environment	• established Orion's credibility and capabilities • provided testimonials and case studies • validated that Orion is viewed as a potential supplier

(continued)

ILLUSTRATION 24.5. (continued)

BUYING JOURNEY STEP		SALES		
EXIT CRITERIA	OPTIMAL SELLING ACTIVITIES	GETS	GIVES	GOS
3. Request for Information (RFI) • met with all providers • published the RFI	• conduct meetings across the organization to validate our understanding of the background, project and priorities • review and clarify any assumptions • discover what concerns, risks and anxieties there may be • coordinate among key players to ensure common understanding and requirements	• all constraints including key dates, budgets and resources • introductions and meetings with all key players including Strategic Sourcing • validation of their priorities and any concerns • clarity on any assumptions • copy of the RFI • their success criteria • confirm budgeting and approval process	• insight into the critical success factors for successful implementations • comprehensive response to their RFI • focused presentation on how we are equipped to meet their specific needs including the focus on the end-user training	• met with all key players including Strategic Sourcing • validated that they see that end-user training will be critical to the successful implementation
4. Explore Alternatives • created a short list of potential providers • validated budget/timeline/ resources	• review our proposal and ensure it meets with their requirements • discuss their anxieties, concerns and the risks they see associated with the project • share our approach to implementation planning and quality assurance • discuss the importance of end-user training	• agreement that our approach meets the needs • details of alternative approaches they may be considering • confirmation that our approach meets their business model and budget requirements	• confidence in our proposed approach • tools and templates to assist in finalizing the approach	• ensured that end-user training is built into the timeline/budget and scope • responded to RFI

(continued)

ILLUSTRATION 24.5. (*continued*)

| BUYING JOURNEY STEP | | SALES | | |
EXIT CRITERIA	OPTIMAL SELLING ACTIVITIES	GETS	GIVES	GOS
5. Finalize Approach • Final approaches received from potential providers • Finalization of implementation approach	• discuss and review the details of our approach and especially the implementation plan for training • discuss how our approach may differ from other alternatives • discuss any remaining concerns and risks that they see with our approach • validate our information with all the key players across the organization	• any and all remaining concerns and anxieties • validation and agreement on our proposed approach • any changes in requirements, priorities, time lines, key players, or constraints	• comprehensive implementation plan • full and complete responses to any concerns of anxieties • clarity around all pricing, terms, and conditions	• provided access to testimonials • provided or assisted in the development of the implementation plan • met with and validated the approach with all key players
6. Contract • contract issued	• meet with Strategic Sourcing to review all terms and conditions • ensure that they have all of our paperwork and we have all of theirs • review and resolve any final details • stay in contact with all key players • position our pricing as "not to exceed"	• any business concerns • confirmation of approval process	• details of pricing model • pricing assurance through the "not to exceed" pricing approach	• all paperwork completed
7. Implement • key players consider the project implemented	• introduce the key players to the implementation team • discuss progress with customer • ensure that the customer is willing to act as a reference for us	• testimonial, case study and/or reference customer	• introductions to the delivery team members	• services delivered as per contract • customer becomes a willing reference

eight strategy components is translated into specific sales activities. This is an example of the Outside-In Revenue Generation approach.

The very basis for this approach is the belief that in today's G3 business world, suppliers must look beyond their internal sales processes of presenting and proving the value of an offering; they must look to the external reality of how their customers really buy.

Let's look at two fundamentals of sales and sales management—namely, opportunity management and pipeline management—and to understand how they change as a result of working with the CBJ Navigator and Outside-In Selling.

OPPORTUNITY MANAGEMENT

Opportunity management is the process by which a salesperson, manager, or other interested party reviews a potential sales opportunity and determines its status and possible courses of action. This could be a formal and facilitated process, or it could be an informal elevator conversation in which a manager asks an often-unsuspecting salesperson what's happening with a particular opportunity.

As a salesperson, you quickly learn two things about these usually unstructured interrogations. First, they range from a few questions to the manager telling you what you should be doing. Second, if you are a good storyteller, you'll quickly see that a safe way around total transparency (which could be poor for your career's health) is to start into a long diatribe of what's happening, who said what to whom, and the brilliance you brought to each interaction with the customer. Joking aside, though, these conversations often do revolve around a lot of narration, and little business value is gained by either party.

Opportunity reviews with the CBJ Navigator can be achieved by simply asking the three questions: Where are we? How are we doing? Where are we going next? We often use an approach called the three Ss, and they correlate to those three questions. They are Step, Status, and Strategy (see illustration 24.6).

These three simple questions enable any sales opportunity to be reviewed and assessed, and an optimal plan of action can be agreed upon. Each of these questions should be answered simply by referring to the Navigator, in much the same way as a map or chart enables you to locate where you are, assess how you are doing, and determine where you should go next. And like that map, the Navigator provides a clear and unambiguous way to answer these three questions. Let's take a quick look at how this should work.

Step: Where Are We?

As always, you are interested in knowing about the *buying* process. You want to know where the customer is in their overall buying journey and if are they even in a buying journey. It's an easy question to answer—just look at the buying journey stage exit criteria and the answer should be both apparent and accurate.

Status: How Are We Doing?

To assess how you are doing, all you need to do is look at the GETs, the GIVEs, and especially the GOs on the Navigator. Ideally, you want to see the customer moving through their buying journey, hopefully with your help, and that you have completed all the sales activities outlined in your sales strategy associated with each particular step of the Customer Buying Journey. This implies that the selling is synchronized with the buying. If any activities are not complete or you are unsure of something—especially the GOs—then that is a red flag warning you of potential danger, that you might be missing something that will compromise your chances of being successful.

Now, what happens if you have some red flags? Well, it doesn't automatically mean that the buying or the selling comes to a stop. It means you

ILLUSTRATION 24.6. THREE QUESTIONS FOR OPPORTUNITY MANAGEMENT

QUESTION	3 Ss	HOW DO WE RESPOND?
Where are we?	Step	What step is the customer at in their buying journey?
How are we doing?	Status	What GETs, GIVEs, and especially GOs are complete in the current step and all those preceding it?
Where do we go next?	Strategy	What should the next selling actions be?

haven't achieved all you should have achieved at this point in the journey, and that's when the next question comes in.

Strategy: Where Do We Go Next?

If your situation is optimal—that is, the selling is synchronized with the buying and you and the buyer are traveling through the buying journey in lockstep—then you can simply turn to the Navigator and look at the optimal selling activities along with the GETs, GIVEs, and GOs for the current step of the buying journey, and they should show you exactly what you need to accomplish next.

However, what if you have those red flags and your selling is not synchronized to the buying? A classic example may be that the prospective customer has already started their buying journey by defining what they believe they need and are already assessing possible alternatives. Perhaps they have even connected with a few potential suppliers and have explored pricing to establish an overall budget. However, they then think they should formally approach a number of these potential suppliers, perhaps with a formal request for information (RFI) or request for proposal (RFP) or a less formal inquiry. As a potential supplier, this could be your first contact and knowledge about this opportunity. In the old days of the sales process, you might have thought you were at step 1.

The customer is at step 4 of their buying journey, which then implies that you are at step 4—you just haven't been in the game for steps 1, 2, and 3. So the first question, "Where are we?," can now be answered in step 4. To answer "How are we doing?" once again look at the Navigator to see where you stand with the GETs, GIVEs, and GOs for steps 1, 2, and 3. Typically you'll see a lot of red flags, missing information, and selling activities compared to where you would like to be. Now what? Well, for starters, at least you have an accurate view of where you are and how you are doing, which is far better than thinking that all is well. Now you have to decide your next step. Basically, you have three choices: *back up, catch up,* or *get out.*

Back Up

The customer has arrived at step 4 of their buying journey and you have not been previously involved with them. By this stage of their journey, the customer perceives they have a reasonably good idea of what they require, and they have worked out an overall budget. As you have not been involved with them during the earlier stages of their buying journey, there is a chance they may have missed something that you think could be important. Thinking back to case study 1, perhaps the prospective buyer is looking for a partner that can help them implement their software application but hasn't realized how important end-user training and change management are to their overall success. If this is the case, then you have the option to back them up in their buying journey. You could consult with them to get them to reassess their previous work. You could bring something new to the table—in this case, how important training and change management will be to their success—and cause them to go back in their buying journey to reconsider their assessments. In backing them up in their journey, you then have the opportunity to synchronize your selling to their buying and get back on the path of the Navigator. Of course, this strategy will only work if there is a valid reason—something new and pertinent you can bring to the equation that the customer views as significant enough to push them back in their overall process.

Catch Up

Let's say you find yourself in the same situation, where you, as a potential supplier, are not involved with the customer as they move through the first few stages of their buying journey. However, if it would be difficult to back the customer up, then the next approach is to catch up to where they are. Your selling approach would therefore be to complete the GETs, GIVEs, and GOs from the previous steps in the Navigator. This is not an easy job, so before you attempt it, I recommend you take a good, long look at the third option.

Get Out

The third option is to admit that it is too late in the game for you to make a difference and win the opportunity—even if you know you could help the potential customer and believe your offering is the best for their needs. In these situations, you must realize—with the help of the Navigator—that there are too many red flags, the customer is too far along into their buying journey, and too much has happened for you to now positively influence that buying journey. This is a situation where suppliers are brought in to simply respond to an RFP or perhaps help lower the price from the incumbent or chosen supplier. And as discouraging as bailing out can be, it is sometimes better to let go so you can better invest your time and resources in the opportunities you can win. To help in that decision, our research has also shown that the single biggest way in which to impact sales performance is usually to stop investing time into opportunities that are unlikely to close.

Opportunity management should be very straightforward and effective when you use the CBJ Navigator. It will ensure that you know where you are and that the selling is synchronized to the buying. It will put you in the best position to positively impact the Customer Buying Journey, and it will enable any salesperson to leverage the sales strategy of the organization to maximize results.

PIPELINE MANAGEMENT

Well, here it is: That trusty (rusty?) old funnel of a sales process pipeline (illustration 24.7)—the gateway to sales success, peer kudos, and commission riches. But all is not as it seems, so let's take a closer look. Pipeline management serves to develop, measure, and manage the development of a number of sales opportunities. And yes, managing the sales pipeline is an absolute foundation of successful business management, but it is also one of the most misunderstood processes across any organization. Reflecting what we often see in the overall sales process, pipeline management is often individualistic and highly subjective. Sadly, we also see countless hours invested into pipeline management and its subset of forecast management with little or no business benefit. It should be very simple. Pipeline management should be the process by which you can plan and manage the required sales, both pending and in development, across a given territory. That territory could be a single salesperson, a geographic territory, an industry vertical, or a business division. The pipeline plan should illustrate what is required at the various stages of that pipeline to create a desired result.

Let's start with the basics: illustration 24.7 shows an example of a seven-stage pipeline. In the old way of thinking, these stages would reflect the steps of a sales process or the different forecast probabilities associated

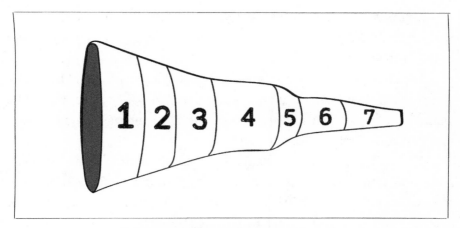

ILLUSTRATION 24.7. The traditional sales funnel

with a sales opportunity. But this led to much subjectivity and gaming of the system with little resultant value.

However, by defining the stages of the pipeline as the steps of the Customer Buying Journey, you finally have an objective and useful way in which to categorize sales opportunities. You can use the buying journey exit criteria, as defined in the CBJ Navigator, to create a common method for categorizing sales opportunities in the pipeline. Therefore you will know that all sales opportunities at the third stage of the pipeline are at that stage of the buying journey. Not only that, but you also know the optimal sales and marketing activities for those opportunities. Perhaps for the first time, you will have a common, useful, and consistent way to organize the pipeline and know what you should be doing for these opportunities to positively impact those buying journeys. You can also measure the flow through the pipeline and see what is happening, not in a subjective sales process, but in the Customer Buying Journey. You can see where things may be getting stuck or perhaps where opportunities fall out, and then you can adjust your overall approach to impact those hot spots. Perhaps you need additional tools from marketing or some skills development. Whatever it may be, you can make precise changes to impact overall performance and then continue to measure to ensure that your changes are indeed making a positive difference. In the next chapter, I will go into more detail about metrics and measurement, but before leaving the topic of pipeline management, let me illustrate how this can work with a simple example.

Imagine you are dealing with a simple four-step Customer Buying Journey (see illustration 24.8). The four steps may be gaining *awareness* of a problem that needs immediate attention followed by an *investigation* of possible solutions, *detailed planning* for how the solution would be implemented, and then finally making the *decision and awarding* a contract. This would be followed by a step for implementation, but let's focus on those first four steps for this illustration.

Now I will go into the mathematics of sales planning. First, let's estimate how long a typical customer may take to complete each of these stages. I want to emphasize that I am focusing on how long a customer will take, not how long would you like them to take or how long the sales step (if there was even such a thing) may be, but how long will the customer actually take. Of course, the exercise is that much more revealing if you have the actual data, but trust me, even if you don't, most salespeople will be accurate enough with their estimations. Note that I said *salespeople*, as we have seen a very interesting and almost invariable observation here. We have found the more senior the person in an organization, the shorter they think each of these steps will take. This is yet another example of Fallacy #1—that is, you are so in love with your offering that you can't fail to see how a customer wouldn't snap it up today. But I have seen time and time again that the salesperson, being closer to the action, has a much more realistic idea of what actually happens in the buying journey at that step. So for the sake of my example, I will estimate that the four stages shown here will take 5, 45, 20, and 15 business days, respectively. If you still have trouble with the concept of estimating these numbers, bracket them with a worse case and best case and see if there is any major difference between the two ends of the spectrum that you need to worry about.

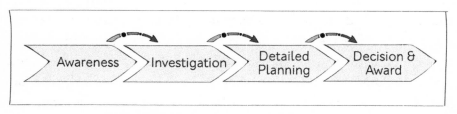

ILLUSTRATION 24.8. A simple Customer Buying Journey

With the times considered as accurately as possible, now I have to esti-mate one more aspect for this model to work: the percentage of customers who start a step that will successfully complete it and move on to the next step. For instance, let's look at stage 1 here and estimate that one in five of all the customers that gain awareness of this particular business problem will move on to stage 2 and actually investigate possible solutions. That ratio then gives me a 20 percent conversion percentage for stage 1, and I could then estimate perhaps 65 percent, 33 percent, and 65 percent for stages 2, 3, and 4. This is summarized in illustration 24.9.

You can now use these estimates to work out the total elapsed time of this particular Customer Buying Journey to be eighty-five business days and then how many discrete customer opportunities are required to yield one closed sale. Working the completion rates backward from the last stage, the logic goes that if 65 percent of all the customers at stage 4 actually com-plete that stage and commit to buying, you would therefore need approxi-mately 1.5 opportunities at stage 4 to gain one successful customer (i.e., 1.5 × 65 percent = 0.975), which is near enough to one for our planning pur-poses. You can continue to apply these ratios to see that you need thirty-six customers to start the buying journey at stage 1 to yield one customer that ends up making the contract award at stage 4 (see illustration 24.10).

You now have a useful model to conduct some basic business planning with. Let's say that you want to achieve a sales target of $300,000 over a certain period of time and the average order size is estimated to be $60,000. You can see you will need a total of five closed customers, which represents 180 (i.e., 36 × 5) customers to embark upon a buying journey to yield that $300,000. You can also see that it would take eighty-five days in which to do this.

ILLUSTRATION 24.9. EXAMPLE PIPELINE PLAN 1

BUYING JOURNEY STAGE	TOTAL TIME (BUSINESS DAYS)	CONVERSION RATE (5)
1. Awareness	5	20
2. Investigation	45	65
3. Detailed planning	20	33
4. Decision and award	15	65

Now, this calculation is often used to conduct what is called *pipeline planning exercises*, where that last column in illustration 24.10 is used to establish a classic sales funnel. This is where things start to go sideways in a hurry, and it explains why most sales pipeline plans are little more than useless and result in complete frustration for the salesperson and the organization. There are two problems with this simplistic approach to sales pipeline planning.

First, not all customers start their journey on the same day. Customers, as you have seen throughout this book, behave in far less accommodating ways than you may wish. If only you could get 180 customers to start their buying journey today! If they did, then you would indeed see, by these estimates, $300,000 of orders appear on the eighty-fifth day. This, of course, doesn't happen; customers are going to start their respective buying journeys over a period of time.

Second—and this is the mind bender—look at that pipeline plan and think about what it really should look like to yield one order. Interestingly, if you actually had just two customers at stage 4, you would get one order in a matter of fifteen days. Think about it: that would be all you need. By the same token, if you had five customers at stage 3, and no others, once again, in thirty-five days (the time for stage 3 and stage 4 combined), you would get one order.

Get it? The age-old concept of the sales funnel is based on incorrect thinking. You don't need all these opportunities *at any one time*. The numbers calculated here only reflect what has to pass through the pipeline in a time period. What you actually need, at any moment in time, is a "balanced" pipeline that will yield the business required for a certain period of time.

Let's say that in order to meet a revenue goal, you need twenty customers to contract with you over a period of time—say, one year or two hundred

ILLUSTRATION 24.10. EXAMPLE PIPELINE PLAN 2

BUYING JOURNEY STAGE	COMPLETION RATE (%)	NUMBER REQUIRED TO YIELD A SINGLE CUSTOMER
1. Awareness	20	35.86
2. Investigation	65	7.17
3. Detailed planning	33	4.66
4. Decision and award	65	1.54

sixty business days. You can then calculate how many sales opportunities you need at each stage of the pipeline to generate those twenty contracts. And if these estimations seem to be coming out of thin air, keep in mind that the algorithm to calculate these numbers is derived just from the fundamental estimates of the target time and conversion ratios. This only reiterates the importance of having a complete understanding of each market's Customer Buying Journey and basing all actions and calculations on that knowledge.

Now, look at the numbers in illustration 24.11—any surprises? Yes. For starters, it doesn't look like a funnel. Look at the number of opportunities required at any one time: it goes from fourteen at the first step of the Customer Buying Journey to twenty-five at step 2. This is hardly the traditional sales funnel, and it illustrates how fundamentally wrong this classical thinking is. What the pipeline plan demonstrates in illustration 24.11 is that we need to maintain a pipeline where we have fourteen opportunities at stage 1 at all times and that we should be expecting that one in five (20 percent) of those customers will successfully move on to the second stage of the buying journey within five days. If the pipeline is then managed and tracked and you meet these metrics, then all is good; you are indeed on track to yield those twenty customers. If, on the other hand, you find that real life does not track with this plan, you have two choices: either adjust what you are doing to get on track or change the plan to reflect what the activities are actually yielding.

This is the key: the two most important metrics to track in pipeline management are the *flow* of opportunities through the stages of the buying

ILLUSTRATION 24.11. EXAMPLE PIPELINE PLAN 3

PIPELINE STAGE	BUYING JOURNEY STEP	TARGET TIME (DAYS)	CONVERSION RATIO (%)	OPPORTUNITIES REQUIRED AT ANY ONE TIME
1	Awareness	5	20	14
2	Investigation	45	65	25
3	Detailed planning	20	33	7
4	Contract award	15	65	2
	Total	**85**		**20**

journey and the *conversion* ratios of opportunities from one stage to the next. This reflects that you are managing a dynamic opportunity pipeline. Outdated methods of simply trying to track a funnel are misleading and can result in frustration and futility. It is the movement of opportunities that need to be understood and managed, not simply the volume of the pipeline. And of course, it is the movement of opportunities through the Customer Buying Journey that you are focusing on here, not the movement through a hypothetical sales process.

We have facilitated this style of pipeline planning with countless organizations. People are often uncomfortable when they see the result, but it usually explains what is happening in their business and what they can be doing about it. If revenue goals have been projected based on some spreadsheet or overall desire to achieve a certain growth goal or market share, then they must be backed up by such a pipeline plan. This is the simple mathematics of creating a customer. You can't just imagine that revenue growth will happen as a result of hiring great salespeople. Customers still have to work their way through a buying journey, and business planning and management will always come down to a realistic and accurate pipeline plan.

TAKEAWAYS

⇒ Every business should have a defined sales strategy, a scalable way in which to consistently and predictably generate revenue.

⇒ The Market Engagement Strategy forms the basis of the sales strategy.

⇒ The optimal selling activity is always dictated by where the customer is in their buying journey.

⇒ The role of the salesperson is to make something happen that otherwise would not and in so doing positively impact the Customer Buying Journey.

⇒ The CBJ Navigator
  ○ translates the Market Engagement Strategy into actionable, manageable, and measurable selling activities.
  ○ synchronizes all sales activities to the specific Customer Buying Journey.

° determines with any sales opportunity where the customer is in their overall buying journey, the current status of the selling activity, and where the sales focus should be placed for success.

A PRACTICAL APPLICATION

Let me conclude this chapter with a practical application and the words of Rick Ferreira, former COO of Alliance Medical, which I have referenced earlier. We worked with Alliance and created an overall selling approach—their sales strategy—based on mapping their market's Customer Buying Journey and its associated DNA and then translated it into the CBJ Navigator. Essentially, this meant Alliance was giving its sales force a road map for success. Rick implemented that CBJ Navigator across his sales organization, and in a later interview, he shared, "It provides for repeatable, predictable, and scalable revenue growth. Whenever we add a salesperson, we give them the Navigator, and they then know what to expect." He went on to say, "Whenever we lose business, we can always—and I mean always—put our finger on the Navigator and see what we missed. And I am not exaggerating when I say that when we follow the Navigator, we win the business, not 95 percent of the time, but all the time."

Rick felt confident, and indeed his experience reinforced that when you follow the Navigator, you win. He became so convinced of this approach that he went to his sales force and committed to them that if they could show that they had followed the Navigator but did not win the business, he would still pay them the commission on the deal. In his opinion, if they followed the Navigator but lost, it was not their fault. This demonstrated to his salespeople that with the Navigator, they could expect the absolute best results possible and reinforced the notion that Alliance did not want their salespeople going off the path, no matter what. This was a total commitment to the approach. Stay the course, stay on strategy, and if you don't end up winning, you have still done what was asked of you and will be paid as if you had won. Rick felt secure in the knowledge that he would never have to pay a commission in such a case, and he never did. Results proved the strategy successful when the company was successfully acquired a few years later for many multiples of their revenue at the time.

You may not want to go as far as Rick, but I encourage you to reflect on his thinking. A very wide void exists between the thinking that proliferates in many organizations about salespeople going out there developing business in the way they see fit versus an organization that provides an overall sales strategy and approach to guide the salespeople through the maze of potential selling activities.

Sometimes I hear that this approach is too rigid, too scripted. That is not the case at all. I fail to see how an accurate road map takes away any productive freedom from professional salespeople. It doesn't script their calls; it doesn't even offer them the "how" of what it is they do. But it does offer them the "what" that they should do, and who wouldn't want to know that? Some say that it is too complex. But the Navigator usually comes down to only two sides of a standard piece of paper. No, these are the cries of the old guard, the folks that believe you should just let each salesperson go out there and do his or her own thing. That may work for a while in some situations, but it is certainly not what an effective and dependable sales strategy is built on.

The only way to enjoy sustained success in today's world is to positively impact the Customer Buying Journey by ensuring that all sales activities are synchronized to how the customer buys.

CHAPTER 25

THE OUTSIDE-IN REVENUE GENERATION SYSTEM

I N CHAPTER 22, I introduced Outside-In Revenue Generation, which showed how all the components that comprise an effective revenue generation system can be, and indeed should be, aligned to the specific market's Customer Buying Journey. At the foundation of the Outside-In Revenue Generation approach is the belief that *the customer's buying process is the only process that will generate revenue.* I have dedicated much of this book to sharing that process with you and how the role of sales and marketing is to positively impact it. I have also shown that how this is achieved changes with, and is totally dependent on, where the customer is in their overall buying journey.

As defined in chapter 22, Outside-In Revenue Generation is made up of six layers, starting with the sales and marketing activities that result in direct interaction with the customer. I will now look at the remaining five ascending layers:

2. Information flow
3. Skills, knowledge, and competencies
4. Roles and responsibilities
5. Resources, tools, and technologies
6. Metrics and measurement

It is essential to appreciate that these five elements are all delineated by the singular steps of the associated Customer Buying Journey. As the

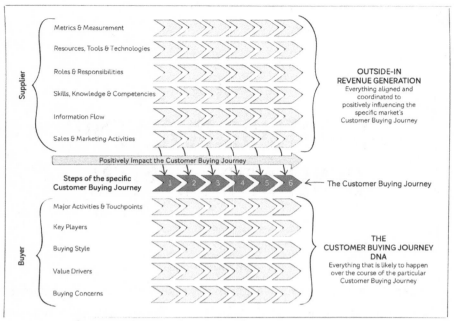

ILLUSTRATION 25.1. The Outside-In Revenue Generation model

customer moves through their buying journey, many things can and will change: what they want, what they believe, what they value, how they make their decisions, what their concerns are, and who is involved. The decoding of the associated DNA and mapping of the Customer Buying Journey provide the foundation that enables you to understand, predict, and manage this evolving process.

Let's look at each of these five elements in turn.

INFORMATION FLOW

Successfully moving a prospective customer through their buying journey is all about information. The customer will be looking for information about your offering, possibly the company, alternatives, pricing and availability, and then maybe configuration assistance and usage details. You may very well want to know about their priorities, background, budgets, organization, and so on. In fact, when you start to list all the information that most suppliers would like to know about their customers and what the customer would like to know and needs to know about the suppliers and their offerings, you can quickly see the complexity associated with any Customer

Buying Journey. In the pre-internet days, this information flow was apparent, as a lot of it was physical and happened between the salesperson and the prospective customer. Today, the salesperson is no longer the conduit through which all information flows. As I have shared before, the internet has changed all that. Nowadays the customer and the salesperson have a wealth of information available at the click of a mouse. Information can flow in a much more fluid and dynamic manner and also perhaps in an unmanaged and invisible way. To some extent, that's okay. But when it comes to managing the Customer Buying Journey, it may be best to think about these information flows in a more structured fashion.

So in order to successfully complete the buying journey, we recommend you make two lists: one for the information you need to know about the buyer and the other for the information the buyer needs to know about you. Once you have these two lists, the next job is to align the associated information with the appropriate step of the Customer Buying Journey. In this way, you end up with the information you would like to get from the customer and the information you think you should give to the customer for each step of the buying journey. From a sales perspective, these are the GETs and the GIVEs from chapter 24 in the CBJ Navigator™. There are likely to be additional information flows outside the direct responsibility of the salesperson. For instance, prior to even engaging with a customer, you might need to ensure that such a prospect can gain the right information from the company website for the early stages of their buying journey. This is more of a marketing activity than a sales activity, but nonetheless it remains a flow of information between the two parties. This is the type of information flow we want to manage and structure, at least to the greatest extent practical. For example, it would be highly beneficial to be able to know what step a prospective customer is at in their buying journey by the nature of the information they are looking for from the website.

It is also important to consider that information flows not just between yourself and the buyer but also within your organization. There could be a need for certain information about the specific opportunity to be communicated from sales to perhaps engineering, marketing, distribution, legal, the delivery organization, or management.

This element of the Outside-In Revenue Generation model should map out the essential information flows between the customer and the supplier, and within the supplier, for each step of the Customer Buying Journey.

SKILLS, KNOWLEDGE, AND COMPETENCIES

What makes a good salesperson? How I hate that question! Having worked with many, many salespeople around the globe selling an amazing array of different offerings, I can attest to the fact that there is no one-size-fits-all answer. It's like asking, "What makes a good bottle of wine?" It can depend on many things: the occasion, the budget, one's personal palate, the accompanying food. Once those things are determined, then perhaps you can start to zero in on what would be a good bottle of wine.

So in regard to salespeople, it's a hard question to answer. You probably won't be surprised to find out that I don't believe in generic tests or assessments that determine if someone will be good in sales because it depends on too many factors. For example, it depends on the actual situation—what is being sold and who it is being sold to. What does it takes to be successful in selling that particular offering to that particular market? Perhaps it sounds a bit simplistic, but the traditional tool bag of a few social engineering skills combined with encyclopedic product knowledge just doesn't cut it anymore; we need a more effective way in which to manage our sales resources.

With the help of the sales strategy and the CBJ Navigator, you can see exactly what is required, both overall and for each stage of the Customer Buying Journey. Outside-In Revenue Generation allows the optimal sales activities to be clearly defined. No longer are you dealing with vague mystical sales skills or attributes. The CBJ Navigator enables you to clearly define what you expect the salesperson to do and when he or she should do it. As such, you can define the specific skills, knowledge, and capabilities that are required, at each step of the buying journey, for the salesperson to be successful.

Another interesting and extremely powerful insight becomes clear when you go through this exercise. It often became evident that very different skill sets are associated with different steps of the journey. Perhaps you will find that the early-stage work of prospecting to find a target customer and triggering a buying journey is very different from the later-stage activities of managing implementation and expanding the opportunity. This then leads to the logical step of actually assigning different stages of the overall buying journey to different resources based on their different skills, knowledge, and competencies at different stages of the Customer Buying Journey.

ROLES AND RESPONSIBILITIES

When considering the roles and responsibilities, the first topic is to determine who in the organization "owns" each particular step of the Customer Buying Journey. You can use the same rules for any organizational design—that is, there can only be one step owner, and that step owner is accountable for ensuring the ultimate success of the work—or in our case, when we look at the CBJ Navigator, the completion of the GOs. This doesn't mean the step owner has to do all the work, but that person is ultimately accountable for ensuring that the work is completed in an appropriate and timely manner.

Roles and responsibilities follow from skills, knowledge, and competencies, all of which are based on the activities undertaken at each step of the buying journey. By understanding what has to be done and what it takes to accomplish it successfully, you can ensure that the appropriate resource owns that step.

For example, imagine a company that sells specialist electronic components—perhaps a memory or processor chip that will be embedded in larger electronic devices. This is often called a "design/win" sales approach, as it starts with the customer selecting what components they will use in their device. Then later, once the design is prototyped and developed, the buyer will issue volume orders for the component as they start manufacturing. The Customer Buying Journey may look something like what is described in illustration 25.2.

If you look at the optimal Outside-In Revenue Generation activities (as opposed to just the sales activities you were concerned with when we developed the CBJ Navigator) for this buying journey, you might see something like the second column of illustration 25.3. The third column illustrates the appropriate role, the owner of those activities.

You can see that the revenue generation activities actually start before the customer triggers their buying journey. Such activities as generating

ILLUSTRATION 25.2. AN EXAMPLE "DESIGN/WIN" CUSTOMER BUYING JOURNEY

CUSTOMER BUYING JOURNEY STEP	KEY BUYING ACTIVITIES
1. Commitment to a potential new product	Determine possible new products, perform business planning, assess viability, and determine which products to pursue
2. Initial design and determination of required components	Develop initial designs, assess alternative approaches, and determine what components will need to be sourced
3. Assessment and selection of sourced components	Assess what components are available and determine suitability
4. Development of prototypes	Develop prototypes, possibly testing alternative approaches
5. Final design and manufacturing planning	Finalize design and lock down on manufacturing approach, including sourcing external components
6. Volume production	Source components for volume manufacturing

ILLUSTRATION 25.3.
OPTIMAL ACTIVITIES ACROSS THE EXAMPLE DESIGN/WIN BUYING JOURNEY

CUSTOMER BUYING JOURNEY STEP	OPTIMAL OUTSIDE-IN REVENUE GENERATION ACTIVITIES	OWNER
	• generate awareness	• marketing
	• prospect for new clients	• inside sales
1. Commitment to a potential new product	• understand directions, priorities, and constraints	• account manager
		• account manager
	• determine requirements	• account manager
	• collaborate on possibilities	
2. Initial design and determination of required components	• recommend required components	• account manager
3. Assessment and selection of sourced components	• support technical evaluation	• technical engineer
	• finalize component requirements	• account manager
4. Development of prototypes	• support prototyping	• account manager
5. Final design and manufacturing planning	• collaborate on final design	• account manager
	• provide comprehensive plans for supporting volume production	• account manager
6. Volume production	• support ongoing demand	• technical support
	• leverage further opportunities	• account manager

awareness about your company and your offerings might occur at trade shows, in trade publications, and through content available on the website, which would generally be the domain of the marketing department. At the same time, you can see the need for an inside sales group to make outbound sales calls to generate interest and set up appointments for account managers to follow up on.

As a prospective customer triggers a new buying journey by exploring and committing to certain new products, you want the account manager to work closely with them to discover what directions and products they are pursuing and collaborate with them on possible approaches using your company's components. As the customer moves forward in their buying journey, their second step starts with a rigorous technical assessment of the various components. This typically involves a deep technical evaluation, and as such, you may choose to have a technical engineer take the lead in this step. However, as the customer starts to select the components they are going to utilize, you may want the account manager to head this up to ensure that all the commercial terms are understood and that the final selection is indeed favorable for your component. The account manager may then head up all activities required to support the prototype, final design, and selection. As the customer moves into manufacturing, you could choose to not have the account manager tied up in all the coordination and support issues of supplying high-volume components and instead assign a technical support role to these activities. However, the account manager would still be somewhat involved at this stage and would be responsible for leveraging the relationship to uncover new opportunities and potentially trigger new buying journeys with the customer.

In this example, I am keeping it simple by just focusing on the high-level activities and not going too deeply into the Market Engagement Strategy or full CBJ Navigator. However, the example serves to highlight some critical thinking:

- You can see how the role assigned to each step depends on the nature of the required activities and the skills, knowledge, and competencies needed to be successful. For example, it makes sense to use the technical engineer for the first part of the second step of the buying journey because that person will be working with equally knowledgeable engineers from the customer's organization. In this example, I have also optimized the time and cost equation by assigning the support of the ongoing demand to a technical support role rather than pulling the account manager away from the business development role.

- I defined a step that comes before the first step of the buying journey. This pre-buying journey step defines a role for marketing and inside sales.
- I have assigned two roles to step 2 of the buying journey, but each would have their own defined GETs, GIVEs, and GOs on the CBJ Navigator.

Once you have defined the primary roles—that is, who is accountable for the successful outcomes—you can then define the other roles that provide support. Using the above example, perhaps the technical engineer has a role in supporting the account manager in the fourth step of the buying journey in finalizing the design. Perhaps the legal department has a role in supporting the account manager at the second step of the journey to ensure that all the terms, conditions, and licensing agreements are understood, negotiated, and agreed to.

In this manner, you should end up with a clear owner for each of the optimal activities across the Customer Buying Journey that also include well-defined supporting responsibilities. When we have worked this through with our clients, we have sometimes seen the opportunity to redefine certain roles and in some cases even define totally new roles. As a result of using this approach, we invariably gain far greater clarity about who is supposed to be doing what and when. And not only that, but productivity increases as a result of having the right people doing the right things at the right time. The end result is a company that is fully coordinated, aligned, and optimized for their overall revenue generation activities.

RESOURCES, TOOLS, AND TECHNOLOGIES

With roles and responsibilities defined, we can then review what resources, tools, and technologies are required. We often find that resource allocation across our client organizations is far from optimal, often as a result of not previously having a robust model to determine what actions are actually required. We often see bottlenecks that can compromise the overall revenue generation equation. So, still using the example above, we should be answering questions such as the following:

- How many inside salespeople are required to generate enough leads for the account managers to follow up on?
- How many technical engineers are required to support the volume of opportunities at step 2 of the buying journey that we anticipate?
- How many technical support individuals would we need to support all the customers for this particular area of volume manufacturing?

Unfortunately, what we often see is a natural tendency, though entirely wrong, to invest in more salespeople at the expense of the supporting roles. This then leads to sales resources (often high priced) becoming defocused from their primary revenue generation activities as they are forced to pick up the support and coordination tasks necessary to maintain customer satisfaction. It is far better to have sales resources equipped with the relevant skills, knowledge, and capabilities focused on the primary revenue generation activities and then invest in other resources, equally well equipped, to manage the support activities.

It is only by mapping the Customer Buying Journey, developing the Market Engagement Strategy and the CBJ Navigator, and completing the previous four layers of the Outside-In Revenue Generation system that clarity can be brought to the equation of who does what, when, and how.

In a similar way to looking at each step of the buying journey and determining what resources are required, you can also determine what tools and technologies you will need. For each of these steps, you can review the revenue generation activities and who has to do what and then determine what tools and technologies will support and enable the successful accomplishment of these activities. As with each layer of the Outside-In Revenue Generation model, you look at these for each step of the buying journey.

Also, note that we are considering not just tools and technologies to support the sales team but also those that may be directed at the prospective customer. In today's world, many transactions between a supplier and a customer happen through technology, such as the ability for a customer to gain information about certain offerings straight from a website rather than going through a salesperson. But now this has extended well beyond the ability to simply gain information. We are now seeing how online configuration and selection tools are helping customers determine requirements and gain recommendations without having to talk to anyone. Think of Dell Computers, an early adopter of the online configuration matrix that allowed customers to both configure and order their own systems. Now we are seeing the adoption of artificial intelligence (AI) across online chat tools to support customers with inquiries and support. By understanding the particular Customer Buying Journey and developing the strategy to positively guide, support, manage, and impact it, companies can make careful investments in these tools and technologies.

METRICS AND MEASUREMENT

The final layer of the Outside-In Revenue Generation system is metrics and measurement. I've left this for last because there's little sense in discussing metrics and measurement until there is clarity about exactly what the system should be doing. You should now know exactly how your customers are going to buy, how you are going to engage with them, and who has to do what in order for this to happen. At this point, you can now think about the key metrics and how you can measure the performance of each Outside-In Revenue Generation system.

But why should you even be interested in metrics and measurement beyond revenue attainment versus the target?

W. Edwards Deming is often misquoted as saying, "If you can't measure it, you can't manage it," but without getting into the debate over exactly what management is and how data fit into the overall equation, I think we can safely say that the more factual and useful the information we have about something, the more informed a decision we can make. Unfortunately, it has been my experience that when it comes to sales and marketing, there is often a lack of factual and useful information. What we tend to see are too many individual war stories and hopeful opinions being related about certain market opportunities.

Let's start by defining what it is we are trying to achieve through our metrics and measurement.

1. If you have a certain revenue goal, the first step should be to develop a realistic and detailed plan for achieving that goal.
2. Once you have the plan in place, you can then execute per that plan.
3. By looking at how things are going compared to how you had planned they should go, you can learn what may be happening.
4. By learning more about what is happening, you can then adjust what you are doing to achieve the goal or conversely realize that you cannot make the goal.

This process can be summarized as the four-step process of Plan, Do, Learn, and Adjust.

Let me provide an example I often encounter that illustrates this process. I have a passion for flying, and I am fortunate enough to fly my own aircraft. Let's say that I am planning to fly from Sonoma to Las Vegas to meet with a client. Let's look at the four steps described above to explore metrics and measurement:

1. *Plan*. My goal is to fly from Sonoma to Las Vegas. Starting with the weather forecast, which indicates a strong southwesterly crosswind, I work out how long it will take, how much fuel I will need, and the exact direction in which I must initially fly. Based on these calculations and my own past experience, I plan that it will take me two hours, I will need forty-six gallons of fuel, and the initial compass direction is ESE, bearing 116°.
2. *Do*. I take off from Sonoma, set the direction as planned, and head for Las Vegas.
3. *Learn*. It would be beyond foolish to simply fly at that same heading for the predetermined two hours and expect to wind up at Las Vegas. Things never quite work out as forecasted and as planned, so about twenty minutes into my flight, I check where I am compared

to where I thought I would be. By comparing those two points, I can then learn what has happened. Perhaps that southwesterly crosswind is now more of a headwind, so I learn that my speed is slower. I calculate that it will now take me two hours, fifteen minutes to get to Las Vegas and that I will need an extra five gallons of fuel.

4. *Adjust.* Based on what I learned at my checkpoint, I can now revise what I am doing. Perhaps I have to fly a slightly different course to adjust for different winds. In the extreme, I may even realize that I can't get there with the fuel I have onboard, so I need to move to Plan B (and I always have a Plan B, I can assure you) and stop along the way to refuel.

This is the very same process you want to set up in managing the revenue generation process. You need to be able to plan what you need to do in order to achieve a specific revenue goal. You then need to monitor progress toward that goal before it's too late to do something about it. You need to learn what is impacting performance, either positively or negatively, and then make any necessary adjustments to refine the process and maximize results. This is what metrics and measurement are all about. They should allow you to establish the plan, continually monitor performance during the execution of the plan, and constantly learn and adjust to maximize results.

MEANINGFUL METRICS

I have added the prefix *meaningful* here because you want to focus only on the metrics that will provide the insight required to manage the revenue generation system. There are four of these metrics:

1. *Starts.* How many new sales opportunities are you identifying across a period of time?
2. *Conversion.* How many sales opportunities at each stage successfully move to the next stage of the Customer Buying Journey?
3. *Time.* How long does it take sales opportunities to move through each step of the Customer Buying Journey?
4. *Dollars.* What is the forecasted value of the sales opportunities at each stage of the Customer Buying Journey?

There are several points of interest with this set of four metrics. First, they deal with the dynamic of moving opportunities through the stages of the Customer Buying Journey. You can see how they focus on the number of new opportunities being generated and then how those opportunities develop and flow through the buying journey over time. This reinforces that you are concerned with a dynamic as opposed to a static process.

Second, you should have an established plan for this process that will generate the required revenue goal. For example, you should know how many new opportunities you need to secure over a period of time and then have a plan for how those opportunities should flow through the stages of the buying journey to yield the required revenue goal. Here is another example of Outside-In thinking: you are measuring the flow through a buying journey, not through a sales process. Gone are the days of asking how long it will take from a certain point in a sales process to get an order. You now focus on how long it will take a customer to move from, for example, determining the initial design to placing an order.

Third, you will have noticed that these four metrics align with the Sales Imperatives—the only four things you can do to positively impact the Customer Buying Journey. So you are aligning what you measure with what you can impact (see illustration 25.4). You may establish a plan and monitor these metrics for the entire business, or you can segment and then plan and monitor a particular territory, product, or industry.

I use the term *dollars* to relate to the expected dollar amount associated with a sales opportunity. At the early stages, it might be impossible or unwise to project the opportunity's worth. It is usually only after the customer has better defined their needs (and hopefully you have helped in

ILLUSTRATION 25.4. KEY METRICS ACROSS AN EXAMPLE BUYING JOURNEY

METRIC	SALES AND MARKETING IMPERATIVES
Starts	*Initiate.* Triggering a buying journey.
Conversion	*Complete.* Increasing the probability of completing the buying journey.
Time	*Expedite.* Decreasing the time through the buying journey.
Dollars	*Augment.* Increasing the size of the spending as a result of the buying journey.

that process) that a forecasted dollar value can be meaningfully placed on the opportunity.

It would be an oversight to not mention sales forecasting at this point. The sales forecast is obviously a subset of the total pipeline. Many, many hours are dedicated to forecasting across sales forces, and in far too many cases, this is simply time wasted. The topic is a dangerous one for me to bring up, as it could take many chapters to lay out the arguments for and against forecasting and the optimal manner in which to do so. However, let me make one point. In no way should you ever associate percentage probabilities with the stages of the sales pipeline, which in our case are the stages of the Customer Buying Journey. This widely used practice is nothing short of insanity. This practice is based on the very faulty logic that as a customer moves through their buying journey, the probability of them committing to buy your offering increases.

It could be argued that there is some correlation. Yes, as they move through their buying journey, it is indeed more likely that they will do something, and if your sales team has been doing their job of positively impacting that buying journey, then yes, that too could result in an increased probability of success. But I can share with you what *really* happens if you adopt this practice of associating a forecast probability: your sales force will game it so that they place each of their sales opportunities at the stage of the buying journey associated with the forecast probability they want to see for that opportunity. Bottom line: you lose all the integrity of the sales pipeline. You can no longer rely on a fundamental belief that all the sales opportunities at stage 3 are in fact at stage 3 of the Customer Buying Journey.

When considering the topic of metrics and measurement, there is not just the revenue generation side of the equation to consider but also the cost. We should again establish a plan for what we would expect to have to invest as a selling cost into each step, and then we can measure the actual to again learn and adjust. In this way, we can continually optimize resource deployment to ensure that we are managing the overall revenue generation process.

ANALYTICS: THE STORY BEHIND THE NUMBERS

Analysis of these metrics is key to managing and optimizing the revenue generation process. In my opinion, it doesn't matter if you are using the latest data mining tool or a spreadsheet or working your way through the numbers with nothing more than a pair of eyes. Analyzing what is happening compared to expectations and looking at trends over time will reveal the true story behind the numbers and provide the basis for performance improvement.

Obviously, this is a much easier task with a great software tool and associated dashboards. However, this is such a vital role in managing any revenue generation process that it must be undertaken regardless of the tools available. It's important to talk about the precision of the data. I often hear folks counter the argument for analyzing the revenue generation process with one or both of two arguments. They either perceive that (1) the data available to them, often through a customer relationship management (CRM) system, are not accurate enough to be useful, or (2) the overall process is so prone to variables that it is not useful to try to analyze it. I get it, but I have now analyzed enough data, even from questionable CRM systems and sales reps, to know that it *is* worth it and that invariably insight is hiding in the numbers. Now, if you were trying to split an atom here, you would need a great level of precision, but that is not the case. Herein lies the key: you don't need a huge level of precision. What you really want to do is be able to spot trends and anomalies, and that you can do even with data that are far from 100 percent accurate and looking at a process that has, by its very nature, many variables.

Here is a real-world example. We were working a number of years ago with a large software company that was selling training for their products. Standard procedure for any large software house, you might say, but our client was venturing into new territory (at the time) by providing the delivery of that training over the web. This was in the early days of people using the web for training that would have traditionally been delivered in the classroom. Had it not been for the sheer size and reputation of the software company, the idea of delivering such training over the web might well have faltered. Nevertheless, they persevered, and here is what we saw in the metrics over a nine-month period.

The product in illustration 25.5 is "Software Training via Internet Delivery." The top line represents the number of days an opportunity took to move through the stages of the buying journey, coming down from ninety-eight days to fifty-eight days over the nine-month period. The middle line

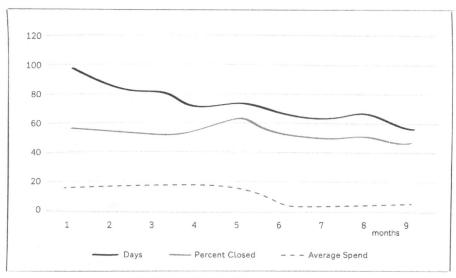

ILLUSTRATION 25.5. Web training metrics

represents the closing ratio of later-stage opportunities changing from 56 percent to a high of 62 percent in month five and then declining to 47 percent. The bottom line is the average spending, which shows a gradual decline from $15,000 to $6,000 over six months.

We could celebrate that the cycle time has significantly decreased, but the rest isn't all that good. So what's the story here? At the start of the period, this was a new offering, and it was taking prospective customers a longer time to evaluate it and make a decision. There were not many early adopters yet. Then, between month four and five of the analysis, two competitors appeared on the scene. This helped legitimize the approach and thus positively impact the length of the buying journey by making prospective customers more comfortable with the overall approach. However, it negatively impacted the conversion ratio and the spending as cheaper alternatives were brought to market.

By analyzing the metrics, you can gain insights like the one above about market and competitive pressures and trends. By comparing metrics across the organization, you can highlight best practices and performance issues. Perhaps the metrics of one team stand out from the averages, signaling something different and therefore an opportunity to learn and adjust. You might see areas where different tools or training can be used. Perhaps if the metrics reveal that a particular stage of the buying journey is elongating in time, you might need additional skills development or a different tool for the sales force to combat the trend.

Since we have developed this systematic approach to Outside-In Revenue Generation, I can argue with total certainty that it is never too much trouble to go through the process of designing exactly how to go to market. It takes but a few weeks to decode the DNA and map the target market's Customer Buying Journey, develop the Market Engagement Strategy, and implement the CBJ Navigator.

Outside-In Revenue Generation provides the organization with a focused approach to revenue generation—one that is predictable, scalable, and measurable—because it is based on how customers buy and why they don't.

HOW CUSTOMERS BUY . . . AND WHY THEY DON'T

THIS IS MY life's work. It is the culmination of everything I have done and learned over the past forty years or so. These are the lessons taken from my mistakes, my misperceptions, and my wanderings down wrong roads, rat holes, and tangents. But these are also the lessons learned from my application, my curiosity, and my self-insistence that I get to the bottom of the questions the title of this book implies. So let me be very clear about a few things.

If indeed the purpose of a company is to create a customer, then *How Customers Buy . . . and Why They Don't* should be required reading for anyone engaged in business. The overarching principle on which this book is founded is nothing less than a thorough and logical redefinition of sales and marketing. Drawing on my decades of experience and research, I hope I have essentially blown away any notions of better mousetraps winning the day, along with the time-worn sales processes abetting those endeavors. I trust I have clearly shown you that the very foundation on which most companies go to market is perilously outdated in today's business environment. No one buys anything because of a sales process; customers only buy because of their own buying process. So for all those whose livelihoods depend on successful revenue generation, the only rational course of action is to positively influence and effectively manage the end-to-end Customer Buying Journey.

I am confident in my belief that adherence to the oft-mentioned Fallacy #1 is at the heart of most revenue generation challenges today. Businesses too often try to solve the wrong problem, because time and time again, their customers actually do "get it": they understand the offering, and they truly believe in the value they would gain as a result of acquiring and adopting it, yet they hesitate and/or fail to buy. Why, then, do buyers not take advantage of an offering of undeniable quality supported by a seemingly guaranteed return on investment? The answer to this conundrum lies not in how suppliers sell but in deeply understanding exactly how customers buy and, more importantly, why they don't.

What I have formulated here is based on more than fifteen years of research at Market-Partners that includes looking at more than 1,200 organizations and conducting in-depth interviews with more than 2,000 individuals. Over this time, we have initiated and fine-tuned this methodology of mapping the end-to-end buying process—in effect decoding the DNA of the Customer Buying Journey. Using these methods, we went on to map hundreds of buying journeys for a wide variety of clients.

All this led to my second major finding: although customers don't always behave in what would seem to be a logical manner, they do behave in a predictable one. We found that organizations within a specific market, when faced with buying a particular offering, behave in remarkably similar ways. They share a common buying journey with a common buying DNA. This led to the revelations I have shared and detailed in this book.

In part 1, we introduced and illuminated the concept of Outside-In Revenue Generation. The six strands of the buying journey DNA were decoded, allowing us to fully map the Customer Buying Journey. We defined the nine *buying concerns*, any one of which can derail a purchase. I then outlined the deceptively simple and elegant 4Q Buying Style quadrant, which unlocks the intricacies of how buyers think. Two highly detailed case studies were then presented to illustrate how one company embraced a new approach to sales and marketing based on knowing how their customers buy and another company that did not.

In part 2, we took all that had been discussed and laid out the overall approach to engaging with a prospective customer within a certain market. This section rested on the major premise of changing the course of events, wherein I revealed that only four things—my Sales and Marketing Imperatives—can positively impact a market, those being initiate, complete, expedite, and augment. After close scrutiny of those four imperatives, I then turned to their practical application in the development of the Market Engagement Strategy and covered the five goals contained within.

In part 3, we translated the Market Engagement Strategy into actual sales and marketing activities by following the four imperatives and introducing the CBJ Navigator™. We then summarized the complete theory of Outside-In Revenue Generation and its application and relevance in today's world.

I hope I have delivered a persuasive argument that all those involved in revenue generation need to hear. And this argument is not just a theoretical wish list; it is well tested. The methodology this book espouses has now been used across forty-four countries in seventeen languages and has impacted more than eighty-five thousand sales professionals. Companies from start-ups to industry giants have put these approaches into practice, and the results speak consistently and profitably for themselves.

Here is, if not my promise, certainly my belief that armed with an understanding gleaned from *How Customers Buy . . . and Why They Don't*, a selling organization can move beyond the incessant fine-tuning of their product presentation to professionally managing the entire Customer Buying Journey within their given market.

This is not another new sales system, but just as importantly, neither is it a replacement for or repudiation of good sales skills and training. Rather, it is the logical evolution of whatever sales approach may exist by embodying a radical refocus on what really happens. As good as any sales approaches are, most do not go deep enough into the real-world process of how customers actually buy, because regardless of how great the *value proposition* may be, it is friction within the Customer Buying Journey that stops it from moving forward to acquisition and adoption.

To anyone concerned with business, I truly hope that *How Customers Buy . . . and Why They Don't* will not leave you unmoved. It could and should cause you to significantly change your sales and marketing focus and can undoubtedly impact how you sell. It has a clear and simple message, and I hope I have made a compelling argument that selling entities must look beyond their own internal view of how something is sold to the external reality of how customers actually buy.

Resources

ADDITIONAL RESOURCES ARE available to the reader to further expand on *How Customers Buy . . . and Why They Don't*. These resources enable readers to gain further information, contribute to the body of knowledge, and learn more about the practical application of Outside-In Revenue Generation.

Go to www.buyingjourneydna.com for

- Practical Application Guide
- Workbook
- Blogs
- Speaking Engagements
- News and Events
- Workshops, Training, and Consulting

Contact the author at mlewis@market-partners.com.

Notes

PROLOGUE

1 FYI, the original quote is "If a man . . . can make better chairs or knives, crucibles or church organs than anybody else, you will find a broad hard-beaten road to his house." The mousetrap bit was added after Emerson's death.

CHAPTER 1

1 Master salesman Arthur H. (Red) Motley (1900–1984) coined this legendary sales proverb while serving as one of the most highly regarded sales trainers of the 1940s and '50s.

2 From act 2 of Arthur Miller's *Death of a Salesman* (1949).

CHAPTER 2

1 Lori Wizdo, "Myth Busting 101: Insights into the B2B Buyer Journey," *Forrester Blogs*, May 25, 2015, https://go.forrester.com/blogs/15-05-25-myth _busting_101_insights_intothe_b2b_buyer_journey/.

CHAPTER 9

1 Everett M. Rogers, *Diffusion of Innovations* (London: Simon and Schuster, 2003).

2 Geoffrey A. Moore, *Crossing the Chasm: Marketing and Selling High-Tech Products to Mainstream Customers* (New York: Harper Business Essentials, 1991).

CHAPTER 12

1 The Centers for Disease Control and Prevention, *Antibiotic Resistance Threats in the United States, 2013*, https://www.cdc.gov/drugresistance/threat-report -2013/index.html.

2 Methicillin-resistant Staphylococcus aureus.

3 Middle East respiratory syndrome coronavirus.
4 A high-dependency unit (HDU) is a care level between the intensive care unit and a standard room or ward care.

CHAPTER 14

1 "Strategy," Merriam-Webster.com, https://www.merriam-webster.com/dictionary/strategy.

CHAPTER 21

1 Thorstein Veblen, *The Theory of the Leisure Class* (New York: Macmillan, 1899).

CHAPTER 23

1 "Strategy," BusinessDictionary.com, businessdictionary.com.
2 "Waypoint," Merriam-Webster.com, https://www.merriam-webster.com/dictionary/waypoint.